A SPRING-TIME SAUNTER.

Photo by *Greaves, Halifax.*

Yours truly
Whiteley Turner

A SPRING-TIME SAUNTER:

ROUND AND ABOUT
BRONTË LAND

BY

WHITELEY TURNER

(*THIRD EDITION*)

WITH
DRAWINGS BY A. COMFORT
AND OTHER ILLUSTRATIONS
(84 IN ALL)

THE AMETHYST PRESS
1984

Third Edition
First published by
THE HALIFAX COURIER LTD
1913

This Edition
Republished by
THE AMETHYST PRESS LTD
1984

ISBN 0 904203 09 2

Reprinted by
SMITH SETTLE
Otley, West Yorkshire

TO MY FRIEND
MR. W. E. DENISON.

MOUNT TABOR FROM SOUTH-EAST.
(*Drawn from Park Farm Barn-roof*).

PREFACE TO SUBSCRIBERS' AND SECOND EDITIONS.

WHEN I realized there must be a preface to this humble production of mine, I was nonplussed. How and what should I say? Until then my pen had flowed pretty freely. It dawned upon me, however, that whilst dealing with other villages in my "Saunter," I had said nothing of our own. So with a few remarks on this and other things which presented themselves to my mind, I flattered myself I might get through.

Perhaps not everyone who reads this book will be versed in the latitude and longitude of the home* of its author. Yet the knowledge is obviously essential. Therefore, friend, please turn to the map of England and in its largest County find Halifax, three miles west of which is a village 1,038 feet above the sea level, glorying in the Biblical name Tabor—Mount Tabor; it may not be indicated, but there it is, forming part of the universe. Its general appearance is the same as forty or fifty years ago, save for two or three dwellings demolished and a like number added. On the Halifax burgess roll the houses total 67.

The chief employment of the immediate neighbourhood (for the bread-winner) is stone-quarrying. Younger folk resort mostly to factories at Wainstalls, over a mile further westward. Aspirants to special trades must needs flee townwards. The only place of worship is of the Wesleyan denomination (Rhodes Street Circuit, Halifax), erected in 1820, abutting which is its Sunday School, built by subscription in 1835, and rebuilt and enlarged, as the tablet in the wall shows, in 1871.

Despite the village's isolation, trades are fairly well represented; only the tailor—the "ninth part of a man"—seems missing, and body, soul and mind would be well catered for. There is a brewery, an inn, stone merchants, farmers, general grocer, "fish and chips" (often "under

*See illustration on previous page. Note farthest building left of the road. The two end windows command the village and look away towards Haliax.

new management"), butcher, dressmaker, joiner, blacksmith, clogger & cobbler, post office, newsagent, penny bank, and public library—a branch provided by Halifax Corporation.

Subjected to every wind that blows, it is a matter of surprise how the solitary, youthly sycamore and the few straggling thorns in the village ever gained a footing. But it is healthy living. Invigorating breezes sweep across the moors, fanning colour into every cheek, and one sometimes feels grateful one's lot is cast in so salubrious a spot.

Less villages can boast some delightful phase in history ; the rearing of a statesman, an eloquent preacher, a great singer or person who has made a mark in the world. But no laurels can Tabor claim, that I can learn of, save a Mr. Thomas Briggs, who thirty years ago secured a position at York Cathedral as bass soloist. After fifteen years' service his voice failed, and at present (1912) he is verger there.

Our village *does* figure in history, but not to its credit, unfortunately. In *Annals of Yorkshire* is recorded one of the foulest of crimes, committed in cold blood in a house, years ago demolished, which stood at the bottom of Grey Jacobs Fold, at the Halifax end of the village. I cannot here narrate the deplorable story, but will give the date, July 4, 1843, and readers can turn to the volume themselves.

* * * * * *

Now let me unburden myself of thanks due to friends for help received in many ways.

First, I thank God for putting it into the hearts of so many friends to help me.

To my artist, Mr. Arthur Comfort, who has taken the utmost pains to produce drawings of high merit for my work.

To Mr. W. E. Denison, Halifax, I would especially tender warm thanks for revising and piloting my work to success ; and to Mrs. Denison, who, when time with me was exceedingly pressing, not only addressed some 600 circulars to old promised subscribers, but very generously volunteered to relieve me of the herculean task of placing in alphabetical order the present subscribers' names obtained through the *Halifax Courier*.

To my printer, Mr. Chas. H. Milnes, for the very kindly forbearance and courtesy he has shown me and for his willingness to assist me in every possible particular.

To Mr. Jonas Bradley, schoolmaster, Stanbury, for a ***mass*** of information, his permission to reproduce photos, and his untiring zeal in influencing many to enrol as subscribers.

To the 1,686 subscribers—representing 2,045 copies—whose names are published in this book; surely unique in number. It is certain but for you I should not have embarked on a voyage of publication of my "Saunter" in book form, for, as I stated in the *Halifax Courier* (in which the contributions first appeared) when the idea was suggested :

"Larger vessels may venture more,
But little boats should keep near shore."

Many of you, dear friends, at that time sent tributes which made me feel accused of obtaining merit by false pretences.

Then my thanks must be tendered to the *Halifax Courier*, Limited, for great generosity; to the Square Church P.S.A., Halifax, for an order of 110 copies for members; to Mr. John Grant, Publisher, Edinburgh, for consenting to my reproducing a very fine portrait of Charlotte Brontë from the Temple edition; to Mr. Joseph J. Green, Hastings, for granting leave to publish a photograph of a hand or work-bag in his possession, a precious relic showing the skill of Charlotte in needlework; to Mr. John Murgatroyd, J.P., Luddenden, for permission to sketch and introduce in these pages, Castle Carr; to Mr. F. Shuttleworth, Mr. J. H. Widdop, Mr. W. Edmondson, Haworth, Mr. J. J. Stead, Heckmondwike, Messrs. Westermans, Hebden Bridge, and the editor of the *Methodist Recorder* for permission to reproduce valuable photographs; to Haworth "Brontë Society," Mrs. Ratcliffe, Mrs. Argyle, and Miss Binns Haworth, for permission to reproduce sketches of Bronte relics; to the Vicar and Wardens of Haworth Church, for permission to publish the sketch, "Grimshaw's Pulpit"; to Mr. Wm. Aspinall* of our village, Mr. James Clarkson, Mr. T. W. Hanson, Supt. Brown (West Morley Division), Halifax; the Halifax Literary and Philosophical Society, Mr. T. Sutcliffe, Warley; Messrs. I. & I. Calvert, Wainstalls; Messrs. Kershaw and Ashworth, Hebden Bridge; Mr. J. H. Widdop, Haworth; the Rev. T. W. Story, Vicar of Haworth; and the Rev. W. H. Gunyon, Vicar of Oxenhope—all for much appreciated information.

To all surviving characters upon whom I called in my "Saunter,"

*Died December 13, 1911, in his 92nd year.

for interviews granted, information imparted, and permission to publish names.

* * * * * *

I feel it expedient to explain to readers having no prescience of my "Saunter," that some of the articles were published in the *Halifax Courier* (as before intimated) during the summer of 1905, under the title of "A Spring-time Saunter—with side-light glimpses." Twenty-five consecutive contributions had appeared when I was struck down with typhoid fever, and my life was despaired of. In spring, 1907, I again took up the pen, wrote a synopsis of preceding chapters, and resumed my narrative. When nearing completion (there were 51 contributions in all) someone suggested through the *Courier* that the "Saunter" should be published in book-form, and the idea "caught on," with the result that very soon some 600 promised subscribers (before mentioned) were enrolled.

Though the book has been long delayed, I have never given up the project, but have laboured strenuously, during spare moments, in my frail endeavour to extend the writings and produce a work which I hope will prove interesting and valuable to people living in, and visitors to, the neighbourhood coming within the scope of these pages. My motive throughout has been to infuse in the hearts of my readers a love for the country—to create ramblers—and to impart pleasure to those not permitted to enjoy in reality so long a "saunter." If I succeed in this, then I am repaid for my pains. I make no pretence to grandiose writing, and therefore claim indulgence in criticism. I have aimed to make my story, as it were, breathe the atmosphere of our heathy heights, and above all, true to life.

Three things readers must please remember :—

1. That you accompany me in imagination on my "Saunter;" thus I adopt the plural term "we" all along the line.
2. The year of grace—1905.
3. At certain points the height above the sea level is indicated by an arrow-head, or bench-mark, the character which is chiselled by the Ordnance Surveyors on buildings, walls, stone-posts, &c. : "⩚ 1,000," for instance, means 1,000 feet above the sea.

A word of apology for the presence of my photograph as frontispiece. It was neither my suggestion nor my desire that it should appear in the book ; indeed, a long time I emphatically affirmed it never would, to the deep regret of dear and sincere friends. Dogged persuasion, innumerable kind expressions and good wishes from subscribers at home and in foreign lands, however, eventually melted me to submission. Conscience argued that if the likeness would give pleasure to so vast a number of people, then I had no business to withhold it.

As I examine proofs and look on the pictures destined to grace the pages of my volume, I think of the dear faithful friend who, when I was originally engaged penning my "Saunter," said to me in all seriousness, "*Thee* goa on an' write a book, an' *aw'll* tell fooak aw us'd to laaike wi' tha." At the time, I remember, I ridiculed the idea, and intimated my fears of his having to cement friendship on other lines. Albeit, "dreams often come true," and my revered friend's vision is now a realization, to the astonishment of none more than

Yours, very humbly,

WHITELEY TURNER.

MOUNT TABOR, HALIFAX.

PREFACE TO THIRD EDITION.

It was with fear and trembling I complied with the requests for more copies of my humble work, encouraging as were the orders, for I seemed to hear in much clearer tones than when I first risked publication :—

> *" Larger vessels may venture more,*
> *But little boats should keep near shore."*

Nothwithstanding, I ignored this wise counsel and launched out on the deep. Subscribers considerably relieved tension of mind on my first voyage ; now I have to hope for equally favourable winds to bring me safe back again to port.

The very cordial reception of the Subscribers' and Second Editions of my " Saunter " evokes thanks I cannot express. Press opinions and readers' tributes were invaribly in happy vein. Critics have indeed been lenient. Only one disparaging note has reached my ears, and this did not come as a thunderbolt. My kindly critic was afraid I had unduly belittled my own village in singling out one individual only who had " made a mark in the world." I spoke of *laurels*. True, as I acknowledged, and was not unmindful of when I penned my preface, there have been others born of lowly estate in the neighbourhood who have risen in other spheres than those implied. To have travelled on lines my friend mapped out for me, I fear I should have found it difficult to pull up. He would, I believe, have had me give the history of the Appleyards, Calverts, Dewhirsts, Cleggs, and others who have soared in the *commercial* world. The last two families, by the way, formerly worshipped at our village Sanctuary, and it is pleasing and comforting to know that, in prosperity, they do not forget their native Bethel, but support it most liberally.

* * * * * *

Errors there were, due largely to subscribers urging publication ; in the present edition these are rectified. The volume has undergone revision, new matter and illustrations are added, the latter through the kind permission of Mr. F. Shuttleworth, Haworth, Mr. J. J. Stead, Heckmondwike, Mr. J. Rushworth, Balby, Doncaster, and Messrs. Hall & Siggers, Keighley.

* * * * * *

A feature which will be welcomed by many is the comprehensive list of district and county altitudes. Care has been exercised in the compilation, the lion's share of the work being done by my friend and collaborator Mr. W. E. Denison. Also, for the benefit of the Halifax public particularly, I have introduced Statistics of the Halifax Corporation reservoirs.

A special book-marker, containing the gist of observations by Press and readers, is presented with each copy of this Third Edition; and all possessing former editions may have this by applying personally to me, the *Halifax Courier* office, or forwarding a 1d. stamp. The *Courier* regards the book-marker as "a treasure in itself," which conclusion, surely, cannot be based on the photo thereon.

* * * * * *

Joy has bubbled over in my heart many times since my little work issued from the Press,—January 10th of the present year, 1913—knowing that in its production I laboured not in vain, but have accomplished, in a very satisfactory degree, that which I hoped to —created ramblers; for, to my knowledge great numbers, from smoky towns, have during the past summer, been "lured to the uplands" after perusal of the "Saunter" pages; and I have no little evidence from "those not permitted to enjoy in reality so long a 'saunter'"—some on beds of sickness and affliction—testifying to the pleasure received in reading the book. It is this which gives me unbounded delight, and compensates for my effort. My soul's petition is :—

> "If any little word of mine may make a life the brighter;
> If any little song of mine may make a heart the lighter,
> God help me speak the little word and take my little singing
> And drop it in some lonely vale to set the echoes ringing."

Again thanking all who have helped and encouraged me in any way, by word or deed,

I am, as before,

Yours, very humbly,

WHITELEY TURNER.

MOUNT TABOR, HALIFAX.

November, 1913.

CONTENTS.

LIST OF ILLUSTRATIONS.

A SPRING-TIME SAUNTER.

CHAPTER I.

WEATHER PROSPECTS—JOCKEY'S AND JENNY'S FORECASTS—VIEW FROM "TH' GUIDE STOOP"—STOODLEY PIKE—JOHN PRESTON—LUDDENDEN DEAN SPA—THOS. MIDGLEY—"OLD TOMMY O' TH' HEYS."

LIKE John Critchley Prince, we

> " Awake to new life with the coming of spring,
> When the lark is aloft with its fetterless wing ;
> When the thorns and the woodbine are bursting with buds,
> And the throstle is heard in the depth of the woods ;
> When the verdure grows bright, where the rivulets run,
> And the primrose and daisy look up to the sun ;
> When the iris of April expands o'er the plain,
> And a blessing comes down in the drops of the rain."

An adage we have somewhere seen quoted advises intending walking-tourists to abide at home till beneath one's foot can comfortably lie concealed ten bright-eyed daisies. When one's "understandings," however, demand a few sizes in excess of the average dimensions to yield fair comfort, then it is easy, ere spring is far advanced, to cover that number of the child's idolized flower. Basing action upon the authority of the adage, we saunter forth in exuberant spirits to make the acquaintance of a land we have long desired to see.

At the time of our departure May (1905) is fast ebbing. Through its twenty-eight days gone, little rain has descended on the extensive Halifax parish ; moreover, during that period, and indeed on many of April's reputed showery days, a biting north or north-east wind has swept these all too bleak and bare hills. The land in consequence is parched and dry. Almost everywhere in the ground we behold great spider-web-like cracks which seem to cry imploringly, "Give us to drink !" Corporations are beginning to feel the effect. Farmers and market-gardeners are experiencing a crisis ; they have

> " Ploughed the fields and scattered
> The good seed on the land,"

and now, we fear, are impatiently waiting for it to be "Fed and watered by God's Almighty hand," maybe forgetful of the Creator's promise that "while the earth remaineth, seed time and harvest, cold and heat, and summer and winter, and night and day shall not cease."

A few days ago the wind veered suddenly, and as we bid adieu to those at home, content to "tarry by the stuff," is blowing zephyr-like northwards; at times we might venture to predict rain were it not that in our discerning "the face of the sky" we have of late so often been at fault. Almost invariably we pin our faith in the verdict of the old lady and gentleman "keeping house" over the fanlight of our back door, for they are trusty weather presagers, and on this morning immediately we awoke we made to consult them. It pleased us to see Jenny positively refused to go inside, and that she stubbornly stuck to the position she took out on the verandah weeks and weeks ago. Force was of no avail: each time we brought it to bear she rebounded like a rubber ball, and Jockey, her docile partner, submitted complacently to the tossing.

Yea, 'tis an ideal morning for a tramp. The sun darts radiant beams between fleecy white clouds gliding across an azure sky; and fields around, despite the raw weather, reveal God's handiwork, whilst the heavens are being thrilled with the voice of the lark.

At "Th'Guide Stoop,*"—top of Luddenden Lane—(/\ 1060-4) only some 300 yards from home, we halt to admire the prospect in general but Luddenden Dean in particular, familiarity with which is unlikely ever to breed contempt. It is true that often:—

> "We look too high for things close by,
> And lose what Nature found us;
> For life hath here no charms so dear
> As friends and home around us."

Most prominent in the picture is Broad-fold Hall, in Midgley, the residence of Mr. John Murgatroyd, J.P., and the worsted works, Oats Royd Mills, built by the Murgatroyd family within the memory of some of the hands. Nearer, on the crest of a precipitous slope, is Booth village, a little to the right its imposing Congregational Chapel, and in the depths of the valley, 610 feet immediately below us, is Messrs. Jonathan Bracken & Sons Paper Mills, established in 1792. Less than a mile lower down the stream is the village of Luddenden—which takes its name from the brook Lud and the Dean—and about another mile still

*(Colloquialism for guide-post).

Stoodley Pike.

further down the valley is Luddenden Foot—the foot of the Lud—where the Lud joins the Calder. Beyond is Sowerby, crowned with its Crow Hill.

One striking object in the foreground is a round structure of masonry. This is an air-shaft, one of three in a 10¼ miles water-course from Widdop reservoir to Ramsden Wood—a sheet of water a few hundred yards east of Mount Tabor. Another of these shafts we see silhouetted on the western horizon. This is 476 ft. 5 ins. deep. Jutting above excavations about it, seen from certain points, it has the appearance of a chimney.

Six and a half miles across space south west, and seemingly grazing the sky, is Stoodley Pike, in Langfield, whose history is told over the doorway :—

"STOODLEY PIKE:
A PEACE MONUMENT,
ERECTED BY PUBLIC SUBSCRIPTION.

Commenced in 1814 to commemorate the surrender of Paris to the Allies, and finished after the battle of Waterloo when peace was established in 1815.

By a strange coincidence the Pike fell on the day the Russian Ambassador left London before the declaration of war with Russia in 1854, and was rebuilt when peace was restored in 1856.

Repaired and a lightning conductor fixed, 1889."

The original Pike was 37 yards, 2 feet, 4 inches high, was sugar-loaf shape upwards from a square base four or five yards deep. Inside was a staircase of one-hundred-and-fifty steps, at the top of which was a small room with a fireplace. Over the entrance was this inscription :—

"This monument was erected by public subscription to commemorate the peace, Anno Domini, 1814."

The present obelisk is 120 feet high—2 yards 8 inches taller than its predecessor—and was the design of Messrs. Watts & Walker, of Manchester. Mr. Lewis Crabtree was contractor. A sum of £812 was raised by two-hundred-and-three subscribers, and the re-building cost £750. The work done in 1889 cost £160. The Pike stands on an elevation 1,307 feet above sea level. The interior staircase has 39 steps. The *Halifax Courier*, June 3rd, 1854, thus describes it :

"It consists of a rusticated basement, flanked with buttresses, above which rises a balustrade and gallery 40 feet above the level of the ground ; this gallery is approached by a circular staircase in the interior of the structure, the whole surmounted by a square shaft diminishing upwards in an obelisk form."

John Preston.

A glimpse only at Luddenden Dean and instantly two noted characters appear in our mind's eye—Thomas Midgley, the veteran and eloquent Wesleyan local preacher, and John Preston, a preacher of another type. The latter was the first called hence. Poor, meek, smiling, honest John! The dale, somehow, has never seemed the same since he ceased to tread its woods and lanes. He often declared he would sometime "clap his wings and scage" across the valley and never return. Then he would express a wish to "dee sudden—as sudden as that," he would exclaim, bringing his hands together in sharp impact by way of illustration—"and on th' Catty Brig; an' if aw do," he would add, "just lift me ovver th' wall an' drop me into th' brook." This was not his lot, however, though, in truth, his end was tragic enough.

On Tuesday morning, Sept. 29, 1885, he was found by Thomas Midgley in an outhouse behind his dwelling, "ommost sparked," as one put it. He was removed to the Cat-i-th'-Well Inn (/\ 764-0), but too late; he had "clapped his wings" and his spirit had flown. At the inquest a verdict of "sudden death from natural causes, probably accelerated by cold and exposure," was returned. Mr. Midgley, in his evidence, said Preston had told him several times he came from Stanbury, near Haworth.

People marvelled that he had lived so long. For more than thirty years he dwelt in the valley, during which time he never slept in a bed, save a period when he was in the workhouse. Sometimes he "dossed" in the outhouse where he was found the morning he died; at other times, maybe, at Goose Nest, in his day an old low building with a beer license, and kept by "Daniel o' Tommy's o' th' Heys;" but usually, we believe, he "lodged" at Hutton, an Irish-looking shanty (only minus the thatching), set amid a green pasture sheltered by woodland, and to a part of which, it is interesting to chronicle, the Booth Independents trace their origin.

As the woman, thrice married, boasted and comforted herself she had buried her two former husbands "'andsomely, with 'am," so John was "put away—'andsomely," and a substantial tea was provided at the Cat-i'-th'-Well, at which a collection was made, which, together with funds already subscribed by neighbouring sympathisers, more than defrayed the funeral expenses. With the balance it was proposed to pay for hewing and lettering a stone voluntarily given by the master of Saltonstall quarry—Mr. Goodyear. But this was never carried out; indeed, after a time the stone mysteriously disappeared, and it ended in a small

head-stone being placed on the grave granted by the trustees of Luddenden Dean Wesleyan Chapel, where he had expressed a wish that his bones might rest. This may be seen on the western side of the sanctuary, and upon it the initials " J. P." None was ever more deserving of the title, " Justice of Peace." His funeral card states his age at 60, which may be a few years under the mark. On it also is this verse :—

" Now time with me has run its course,
A rough one I can tell ;
But now I leave you all behind,
And bid you all farewell."

We see " Old Preston "—as he was called, in later years—as if only last night, come pottering up the crooked staircase into the cobbler's chamber at Lower Saltonstall—his usual final call on his way to his " lodgings." How his face beamed as he cast wistful eyes on the American stove in the centre of the floor, and saw prospects of a warm supper of sliced potatoes, cockles, mussels, or whatever the " dry-fry " chanced to be the night he wandered in. Each evening we local youths were wont to meet here, not particularly " to tell or to hear some new thing," but more for companionship ; and the shoemaker—who was renowned far and near for quality of workmanship and a speciality in strong boots, and had always orders booked to last him the best part of a year—was prepared to work on as long as his company were prepared to stay, even far into the " wee sma' hours." A greengrocer lived conveniently near, and we rarely parted without joining in a " sissup " of the above description. The last time we tasted cockles was in that remote period ; we had our fill that night. When potatoes were in the menu, salt was in large request by John. His liking for salt was astounding ; he very nearly desired as much salt as substance, and it was seen, too, that he did not lack it.

John knew his Bible fairly well, and acted according to its instructions in two things particularly : he took no thought for to-morrow, and he ever regarded " sufficient unto the day is the evil thereof." Though he was never known to tackle any definite job, he was no beggar, wasn't John. To his credit be it said he was always prepared to give labour for bread. He would house a load of coal, pound a pail of sand (a former household essential now largely discarded), get a bundle of firewood —sticks or ling,—or gather bilberries, blackberries or mushrooms, whichever the season afforded, and expected no higher remunera-

JOHN PRESTON, NEAR "TH' CATTY BRIG."

tion than a pint of tea, a buttered tea-cake, and twopence. True, the coppers more often than not found their way to the Cat-i'-th' Well or "little Grace's" at the Rising Sun ; but he was always quiet, harmless as a dove, and molested no one. He would gather the children round him should he meet them coming from school, and catechise them, teach them their prayers, or prompt them in singing one of his favourite hymns. As testimony to his integrity of speech, we can say that never since we knew him did we hear anything approaching to blasphemy proceed from his lips ; and this is no light thing to his credit, remembering the company he often kept. Some may dispute that he was as mild as we depict him. These be they, however, who tried him sorely, and 'tis said "a worm will turn when trod on."

So far as we can learn, John was never seriously hit by Cupid's dart. Once, in his early associations with Luddenden Dean, he made overtures to one of the fair sex, but his offer, earnest enough, was spurned. He did not grow morose and sullen in consequence, nor did he do anything rash, as "Old Three Laps," who—but we cannot stay now to relate the story of that eccentric; we may introduce him later. Possibly the repulse Preston received had the effect of determining him henceforth to "shake a loose leg" and breathe the free air of heaven; possibly! Preston by "jigging" for hand-comb weavers only earned a few shillings weekly. The maiden of his choice waited long for another beau, but at last one, with brighter prospects and a commendable banking account, appeared, and after more than twenty years' courtship they tied the knot. But the bride's former suitor was oblivious of the union, since he had now been in his grave nearly five years.

Our friend John—aye, friend, for we and all who knew him had a kindly regard for him—had two elder brothers, also bachelors, not nearly so decent and respectable as he ; sheer wastrels they were, and of no fixed abode. A sister also there was, who married and for a time resided in the neighbourhood.

Preston had quite a fund of anecdotes, the scenes of which were invariably laid in Haworth parish, and chiefly in and about Stanbury.

Like one other, John was little of stature, standing not more than 5 feet 3 inches in his thick-shod clogs. How we became possessed of his likeness was in this wise. We—the cobbler's "sitters"—promised him three things if he would submit to being "photo'd" (he did not relish the idea) : a new cap—which he suggested wearing when "posing," but which we would not for a moment tolerate—a good dinner at the

completion of the operation, and last, but far the most important, 4 oz. of best Virginia tobacco. As we predicted, the latter cut short his hesitancy upon the point. Since he could not have permission to appear in his promised new cap, he elected to have its value in additional tobacco. O ! he loved a pipe.

So it came to pass that one fine summer morning the writer trudged off with him to Mr. T. Heap's in Sowerby, a matter of four or five miles. Folk looked askance at us, and some ventured to remark about our company, but we heeded neither gaze nor comment, and returned elated, having accomplished the desire of our hearts.

A little incident must here be recorded, since it confirms our statement that John was no impostor. At the studio the photographer, observing that his quaint-looking subject was a smoker, and that his pipe needed replenishing, tendered him his pouch and invited him to help himself. John quite politely accepted. When about to leave, Mr. Heap again held out his pouch and bade him charge his clay to the brim, but Preston courteously declined. " Noa, thank ya," said he, " aw nevver put o' good natur."

LUDDENDEN DEAN SPA.

John had more red letter days in his life than many of us ; he could always count on one a year. Each first Sunday in May he arose to the tuning of the feathered songsters, and wended his way down the woodland path beside the rippling brook to the Spa, distant from Hutton about three minutes, to watch people assembling from places miles round, some purely on pleasure, others to enjoy the early morning walk, and not a few to hear old Preston " preych " his annual " sermon." Wadsworth, Pecket Well, and Crimsworth, over the moor westward, contributed a large percentage of the rougher element, who showed no regard for the Sabbath, many being dressed in work-a-day clothes, shod in clogs, and each invariably carrying a straight, slender stem of holly, with the last shoots left by way of adornment, and these they incessantly switched against their corduroy trousers, making the cotton fluff fly. On their passage home, towards midnight, over a zigzagged, ugly and treacherous path, we will not dwell. It was astounding none ever met with serious accident by the way.

One who was most intimate with Preston, and best acquainted with his ways, says he was not always to the fore on these occasions ; he would sometimes repair to a secluded part of the wood commanding a view of the Spa, and when he considered the " congregation " sufficiently large,

and likely remarking on the absence of the "parson," he would come forth from his covert and idly stroll towards the spot, all eyes being centred on the "preacher planned," as he approached. But even now he needed persuasion to ascend the "pulpit"; for Preston, by nature, was somewhat shy. In his early "ministry" the people assembled on a flat place in the wood near the Spa, the "preacher" delivering his "message" from an eminence on the slope above. Since, however, the ground here was often swampy, the "congregation" decided to transfer their quarters to "th' New Brig," a little higher up the stream, and this Preston henceforth made serve as rostrum. It was generally known he would lead off with "O for a thousand tongues to sing." Then he prayed fervently, if irreverently, after which would probably follow "Rock of Ages," closing with "Jesu, Lover of my soul;" each hymn being sung more lustily than harmoniously. His discourse, which lasted twenty minutes or half-an-hour, could hardly be considered inspiring. He would introduce it by a few comments on the weather, pointing out the goodness of the Creator, be it sunshine or rain, then branch off into very discursive remarks, chiefly, however, on Biblical subjects. The "Amen" pronounced, two or three recognised "officials" "took up the offering," which usually amounted to a few shillings. On one occasion (in 1880) eight members of the Oats Royd Brass Band put in an appearance, bringing in their train "several hundred persons." When the collection was about to be taken one known particularly for his repartee exhorted those who had no money to borrow from their neighbour, adding "an' mind ya dooan't forget to pay back." This time the sum totalled 13s. 5½d., which eventually was made up to a sovereign—"all for Preston," it was announced. John never was so rich; he declared he "wodn't thank th' Queen to be his ont." It was a big haul, but it proved a bad catch for John. Childlike-hearted with little will power, he was tempted to imbibe too freely ere that Sabbath was ended, with the result that he was taken ill, and for days his life was despaired of. It was rumoured that his "deputy bankers" assisted him to squander half of the offering taken that morning at the Spa. The "congregation" got wind of it, and the succeeding year the collection dropped practically to nil. Once after this the Rev. Joseph Poynton, then Minister at Mixenden Congregational Chapel, preached at the Spa and took a collection on behalf of the Luddenden Dean Sunday School, at that time held in the body of the Chapel. On this occasion Mixenden Band turned up, and brought a large number of people.

HUTTON.

Later, the Salvation Army, who converted the old brick-kiln in New Road, Luddenden into "Barracks," and "stormed" the locality for a time, "held the fort" early each first Sunday in May, so that Preston—poor old chap!—had no alternative but to retire from the scene; "his services were no longer required." Truly, "the way of transgressors is hard."

Like many things of olden time, the Spa has lost its attractiveness, but the presence of the spring in the middle of the'stream, as it were, yet untouched by it in dry weather, may still be seen: its waters have scarcely a palatable flavour.

Only a few stragglers now turn up in the early hours, whereas in Preston's days at five o'clock the valley was quite animated with people; and they came and went Sunday through.

Thomas Midgley.

Thomas Midgley's end was more tragic than Preston's. Poor fellow! he was killed. It was on Sunday night, Nov. 21, 1897, and the last of a series of mission services was being held at Luddenden Dean Chapel. We ourselves were there, and had had a "good time." Mr. Midgley—recognised throughout the Circuit as the "Bishop of Luddenden Dean"—we remember, threw heart and soul into the service, as was characteristic of him, and especially so in the prayer meeting. At the close he engaged in conversation with Mr. W. H. Cockcroft, a brother layman from Hebden Bridge, who had conducted the service, and who, it transpired, had promised to see Mr. Midgley home if he would but wait until he had procured his hat and stick. While Mr. Cockroft was in the vestry, however, the old man walked out of the Chapel and down the yard, at the bottom of which, instead of keeping to the graveyard wall in making for home, he wandered across the road, absent-mindedly, it was thought, in his hilarious spirit, and fell into the field, a perpendicular drop of five feet. The night was exceedingly calm, and so densely dark that we could but distinguish a faint outline of a figure, which seconds ago was beside us. But we heard the thud, and we feared it was old Thomas. We called his name, but received no response; he did not even moan. We descended into the field, and striking a match found, alas, that our surmisings were only too true; it was the veteran layman in a state of unconsciousness. We placed him in a comfortable chair, and by the light of chapel oil-lamps bore him gently to his home (Victoria House), perhaps 170 yards away. It was a sorry procession.

We feared the accident might prove the beginning of the end. He soon regained consciousness, however, and showed signs of speedy recovery, he and we entertaining hopes of his being about again shortly. But the Master whom he served did not will it so. The following Wednesday he had a relapse, and passed away at seven o'clock the same night. Directly after, a fence was erected where Mr. Midgley fell—as was predicted there would be; but too late. One more case to the list of locking the stable door after the horse is gone.

THOMAS MIDGLEY.

The greatest epoch in Mr. Midgley's life, it is safe to say, was when on March, 27, 1892, he had the honour of preaching in City Road Chapel, London, founded by John Wesley, and a Mecca of his followers. Occupying the pulpit where Wesley had stood, naturally he felt on his mettle, and he chose his favourite text, " For I am not ashamed of the Gospel of

Christ; for it is the power of God unto salvation to everyone that believeth." It goes without saying he preached more eloquently than ever. He never tired of speaking of the event. He was assured that there he was fully appreciated; in his own country, he often said, "a prophet hath no honour," but a marble tablet erected in Luddenden Dean Chapel to his memory says otherwise, for on it we read:—

In affectionate remembrance of
THOMAS MIDGLEY,
of Luddenden Dean,
Born 4th March, 1814,
Died 24th November, 1897,
who for sixty-three years
served this circuit in the
capacities of local preacher
and leader, with great
efficiency and acceptance
and was very popular in
other churches in this district
This tablet was erected by friends in
the Hebden Bridge Circuit.
5th August, 1898.

A table-tombstone, right of the path leading into the Chapel, also records his death, and that of his wife Mary, who died April 3rd, 1887, in her 75th year; likewise their two sons, Matthew and Foster.

Mr. David Whiteley, in *Illustrious Local Preachers*, published 1891, gives a biographical sketch of Mr. Midgley.

"OLD TOMMY O' TH' HEYS."

Then there was another Luddenden Dean preacher, equally popular in his day. But we never knew him, since he passed to his reward well-nigh a decade before we made our debut on the world's stage. This was Thomas Greenwood, best known as "Old Tommy o' th' Heys." He was a tall, burly, navvy-looking man, unpolished in speech and manner and when he preached was "awfully noisy," says one who heard him "preych scoors o' times." His dress on the Sabbath varied little from that in which he did duty about the farm. He wore knee-breeches, grey stockings, and "gurt three-hoyl'd laced shoes." No starched collar stiffened his neck, but a thick muffler hung loosely from his throat. He rarely was seen in hat or cap, and he "'ad a heead es ruff es Soarby Moor," according to an octogenarian native who furnished this description All who knew him maintain that he never "laysh'd his hair," year in and year out, and that a poll at long intervals served as toilet

throughout his preaching career. One aged person we have interviewed concerning " Old Tommy " says he always reminded him of a farmer-acquaintance of his in Wadsworth, who " sheer'd 'is heead once a year," and that on rent day ; his locks were so matted that the " crop coom orf all in a piece, like a fleece o' wool."

Tommy's wife, Sarah (Sally, he called her), little as her husband was big, lived the Christian life she professed. Gossiping she abhorred, and she discountenanced backbiting. Her sympathy and help, however, could always be relied upon by a neighbour. Above all, she was extremely mild-tempered, which disposition sometimes was like oil on troubled waters ; for her dearly beloved was weakest in the directions in which she excelled. Notwithstanding, Tommy was a good man, and he made his presence felt wherever he preached. If not eloquent, he was earnest. His zeal and enthusiasm for the Word was intense. In praying, he raised his voice to a " fearful pitch." Manœuvring and capering in the pulpit was a characteristic, and boards needed to be sound and resisting, and lamp and gas-brackets out of arm's way, when he was in full sail. Once, at Luddenden Dean, he held the Bible in the air and brought it down with tremendous force on the desk, but a little too near the outer edge, with the result that it fell into the choir-stalls, where John Ratcliffe and John Feather (the former, choir-master 32 years, though " nooa singer 'isseln "—testimony of an old " Dayn Chorister ") were joint recipients of the Word. Tommy watched its descent, and then concernedly enquired of its victims, " 'as it 'urt yo ? " Seeing they and the congregation were convulsed with laughter, he added, " yo'll bi na war fer been 'it wi' th' Bible."

We have it on trustworthy authority that another time, at some other chapel, he stamped his foot through the pulpit floor crash into a pile of love-feast pots stored in a cupboard beneath. But he held forth, apparently unhurt and unmindful of the wreckage.

This calls to mind a story told us of Thomas Midgley by an eye-witness of the incident. It was at Fly Flat—a place in our day's programme—where he had delivered a load of provender, a line of business in which he did much turnover in connection with his primitive grocer's shop. It was noon, and a lot of rough quarrymen were about, so presumably he thought the time opportune to sow Gospel seed by the wayside. An upturned tub offered to serve as pulpit ; this he mounted, and began expounding in his original style, which in action was only excelled by his neighbour and brother layman " Old Tommy o' th' Heys." Presently

he warmed to his subject. "Every tub must stand on its own bottom," he said, and demonstrated his words by bringing down a stout No. 11 shoe on the temporary rostrum, which, alas, failed to withstand the shock. The preacher almost vanished out of sight! Happily, it was a case of "it mud ha' been war."

Of connected discourse our subject, "Old Tommy o' th' Heys," had none; "he just blundered at it." His lining out hymns was more amusing than divinely impressive. One old woman never forgets hearing him "shutter aght all in a piece"—every word, as delivered, being converted into the dale's vernacular:—

"Thou great mysterious God unknown,
Whose love hath gently led me on,
Even from my infant days,
My inmost soul expose to view,
And tell me if I ever knew
Thy justifying grace."

It fell to Tommy's lot at times to entertain travelling ministers. One occasion is sometimes narrated for the benefit of the Circuit (which in his day included Todmorden) and others. For dinner, Sally had prepared a bowl of porridge, which, after wimbling a hole in the centre, and pouring in an extra dose of treacle, set it before the minister, who quietly looked on.

"Nah then, hoss!" said Tommy, addressing the preacher in broad Yorkshire lingo, which, translated into readable English, means "Now then, commence!" But the parson, apparently not comprehending, sat motionless.

"Sally, put 'im some butter in." commanded the host, thinking his guest considered the dish hardly to his liking. And his good wife obeyed.

"Nah then, hoss!!" repeated Tommy. But the preacher took no heed.

"Sally, bring 'im some o' th' better milk." Sally did as bid, emptying a pint of new milk into the mess.

"Nah then, hoss!!!" urged Tommy, warmly, for he was getting impatient. Still the minister was deaf to his orders.

A light seemed now to dawn upon Sally, who remarked to her husband, "He's waitin' fer th' table ta be losed"—at which Tommy said grace, and the meal was proceeded with. Whether the parson relished the fare is not being handed down with the story.

Sally was renowned for her quality of porridge. One we have conversed with about "Old Tommy," and who worked for him as a

lad, "fer eightpunce i' th' day an' kept," avers "Sally's porridge wer' th' thickest aw ever 'ad ta band ; yo cud eyt 'em wi' a knife an' fork ; in fact, if yo gate a spooin into 'em—leead 'un, yo kno, ther wer nooa sooart else then—yo cudn't get it aght ageean baght cruck'nin' 't. Ay, Sally's porridge wer' like potted meyt fer stiff when they flopped aght o' th' pan," declares Tommy's "farmer's boy."

* * * * * *

The aged couple are buried at Luddenden Dean, and their memory is perpetuated in the following lines, inscribed on a table-tombstone left of the path, and in line with that of Thomas Midgley's:—

IN MEMORY OF
Thomas Greenwood, who de-
parted this Life August 30th
1856 aged 73 Years.

"Blessed *are* the dead which die
in the Lord, for they rest from
their labours, and their works
follow them."

ALSO of the above-said Sarah
Greenwood, who departed this
Life November 23rd 1860,
Aged 73 Years.

"Her soul hath o'ertaken her mate,
And caught him again in the sky,
Advanc'd to her happy estate,
And pleasure that never shall die."

CHAPTER II.

Luddenden Dean: Past and Present.

A stranger visiting Luddenden Dean wonders why the Methodists planted a chapel in such a remote and sparsely-populated place; we ourselves failed to see the wisdom of it till one day, seated by the fireside of an old and respected friend, a lifelong resident, we learnt something of the dale's history. We were reminded that when the sanctuary was built in 1828—prior to which, school and service was held in Catherine House barn, where the scholars were "up i' white," and still are on "Charity" day, first Sunday in June—"hand-loom weyvin' wor i' full swing;" and this, we were told, unmistakably justified the Methodists. Now our friend went on to make comparison of to-day and when he "wor a lad." He remembered when fresh farmer's butter was 1s. a pound, eggs 24 for a shilling in summer, and never less than 18 in winter, new milk 1½d. a quart, old milk ½d. a quart—"an' better old milk nor som' new is nah"—"net machinery skimmed"—said our friend, warmly; "an' this when rents wor nearly double whaat they are nah, an' provender a lot dearer," he added. He waxed indignant as he thought of present-day farmers asserting "farming didn't pay." He noticed, however, that when one commenced in that line he "stuck like a leech," or if he did let go, it was only to get a fresh and larger hold. "Didn't pay!" he exclaimed, "wi' butter one-an'-threppunce a pund i' summer an' one-an' six i' winter; eggs nevver abun thirteen for th' shilling i' summer an' dahn ta six an' less i' winter; new milk—et wodn't creeam if it stood a month—tuppunce-haup'ny a quaart, an' old milk—as blue as a whet-stun—a penny a quaart. If farmin' didn't pay nah, ha' then?" he asked us. But we could not argue the point, having no knowledge of the business; we only knew we had to pay the piper to the tune quoted.

Next we counted the present number of dwellings in the valley, and their inhabitants, taking in Hawksclough on Midgley side, and Upper Saltonstall on Warley side, and we found the dale more populous even

than we had thought. At our request he now conducted us on an imaginary tour round the valley fifty years back, visiting every farm-house and cottage, where we saw fathers and mothers "weyvin or kemmin" (weaving or combing), and children—some only four or five years old—busy winding spools. Many parents were introduced by a cognomen receding to the third and fourth generation, and often also designated by the place where born, had lived, or was then residing.*

By way of contrasting the valley's present desolation with its then humming activity, we took count of the name and numbers of each household, and here we append the list, indicating also where stood buildings since demolished.

PAST (50 years ago).			PRESENT (1905).	
Dwelling.	Tenant.	No. of Household	Dwelling.	No. of Household
Hawks Clough Farm	Wm. Ingham	12	Occupied	6
Cottage	Martha Ingham	8	Demolished	
Lower Mytholm Farm	Wm. Redman	3	Occupied	2
Upper Mytholm Farm	Richard Baldwin	10	,,	2
Cottage	Thos. Howarth	6	Unoccupied	
Clough Farm	Hannah Greenwood	3	Occupied	4
Cottage	Jonathan Midgley Wm. Foulds Timothy Howarth (Bachelors)	3	Unoccupied	
Hollin Top Farm	Jonathan Pickles	5	,,	
Pasture Farm	James Ratcliffe	12	,,	
Ferny Lee Farm	John Shackleton	4	Occupied	5
Cottage	"Joe o' Jim's"	2	Unoccupied	
Goose Nest Farm	Daniel Greenwood (Daniel o' Tommy o' th' Heys)	5	Demolished	
Catherine House Farm	Benjamin Tatham	6	Occupied	6
Arrowbutt Lee Farm	John Tatham	4	,,	2
Cottage	Wm. Foulds	1	Unoccupied	
Head House (one storey)	John Thomas	8	Demolished	
Castle Carr Farm	Squire Shoesmith	7	,,	
Cottage	John Greenwood	3	,,	
	("Old Jooanty")		,,	
Dean Head Farm	John Thomas	8	,,	
Cottage	Joseph Greenwood	1	,,	
Durham Farm	John Greenwood	1	Occupied	4
Fulshaw Farm	Peter Midgley	2	Unoccupied	
Deep Clough Farm	Wm. Wilkinson ("Old Sandy")	4	,,	
Folds Farm	Richard Whalley	8	,,	

*For sample see page 79.

Old Nook Farm	James Stansfield (" Red Jim ")	2	In ruins	
Cottage	Wm. Watson	9	,,	
Upperhouses (2)	Thomas Dewhirst	4	Demolished	
Stonebrig End Farm	Squire Mitchell	3	,,	
Low Farm	Geo. Greenwood	2	Occupied	2
Cottage	Wm. Sheard	8	Unoccupied	
Cottage	Henry Sutcliffe (" Th' war old Harry ")	2	,,	
Nunnery Farm	John Midgley (" John o' th' Lords ")	3	,,	
Hutton (one storey)	Henry Horsfield (" Th' better old Harry ")	7	In ruins	
Upper Height Farm	John Hodgson	3	Occupied	6
Lower Height Farm	Thos. Greenwood (" Tommy o' th' Heys ")	7	,,	4
Lower Heys Farm	John Sunderland	3	,,	1
Upper Heys Farm	Wm. Crossley	5	,,	5
Cottage	Robert Thomas	5	Unoccupied	
Lamb Hill (one storey)	James Nicholl	7	Demolished	
Upper Green Edge Farm	Thos. Murgatroyd	3	Occupied	7
Lower Green Edge Farm	James Calvert	6	,,	7
Cottages (2)	James Astin	7	Unoccupied	
Victoria Cottages	Henry Crabtree (" Little Harry ")	1	Demolished	
,, ,,	Henry Shaw	6	,,	
Throstle Bower Farm	Ambrose Patchett	3	Occupied	3
Throstle Bower	Wm. Brotherton	8	,,	2
,, ,,	Richard Brotherton	5	,,	4
Victoria House (Shop)	Thos. Midgley	3	,,	6
Owlet Hill Farm	John Horner	5	,,	7
Lower Hall Farm, U.S.*	Wm. Calvert	9	Unoccupied	
Old Oven House	John Lord (" Curly Jack ")	6	In ruin	
Upper Saltonstall (Shop)	Sarah (Sally) Calvert	2	Unoccupied	
Great House Farm, U.S.*	Abraham Patchett	4	Occupied	3
Cottage	John Horsfield	6	Unoccupied	
Lane Ends Farm, U.S.*	Wm. Hoyle	7	Occupied	1
Cottage	Wm. Fawthrop	3	Unoccupied	
			Castle Carr	2
			Low Lodge	3
			Height Lodge	2
	Total ...	280	Total ...	96

*U.S. denotes Upper Saltonstall.

Head House stood some eighty yards within the gate at Low Lodge, and on the right of the Castle Carr drive; a stout sycamore, whose branches trailed along the roof of the one-storey cottage, still lives and flourishes. The farm buildings and dwellings at Castle Carr—∧ 990-8—(so named when there was no castle at all) gave place to the present Castle (Halliwell Sutcliffe's Frender's Folly in *Man of the Moors*), which was begun in May, 1859, prior to which no trespass-board kept back the public from

CASTLE CARR (HALLIWELL SUTCLIFFE'S FRENDER'S FOLLY IN *Man of the Moors*).

enjoying the lovely scenery crowning the valley. Elderly Luddenden Dean scholars tell of wandering into Castle Carr woods (by way of aiding digestion of pastry dinners eaten round the stove in the Chapel), and there making the hillsides echo singing hymns.

Dean Head, buildings and land, were destroyed in the construction of the two reservoirs bearing that name.

Old Nook (locally referred to as "Tha'll Nuck"), south of Folds, still gives a general outline of its size and strength of walls.

Traces also remain of Upper Houses at Low, which stood beneath the group of sycamores—one the finest in the dale, we believe. Past here was formerly a public footpath ; the stile is now walled up and the steps forward are grass-grown. Mr. Samuel Murgatroyd, a working man, a little over seven years ago set out to test this right-of-way and, poor fellow ! he had to go to the wall. All honour to him, we say.

Stonebrig End Farm, occupied by Squire Mitchell, lay below Upper Houses, and nearer Low Bridge.

Hutton we are acquainted with ; our drawing shows only a remnant of the one-storey cottage.

Lamb Hill had a charming outlook in the field top, north-west and part of Upper Green Edge.

Victoria Cottages were spread to afford a site for Luddenden Dean Sunday School, built in 1878.

The cluster of farms and dwellings at Upper Saltonstall (apart from Old Oven House and a barn which since its erection has evidently been renovated), apparently remain as when built two or three centuries ago. Over the porch of Great House is this inscription :—

G. D. Built
this Houſe 1637.
B. P. Built this
Poarch, 1768.

"G.D." stands for Gilberte Deane, who, in the particulars of the rents of the graveship of Sowerby, presented at a court held at Wakefield, the 19th November, 1624, it is recorded paid 13s. 2d for seven messuages at High Saltonstall.

"The Deanes of Saltonstall were a distinguished family" said Mr. T. Sutcliffe, of Warley, in a paper to the Halifax Antiquarian Society a little while ago. He mentioned that according to the Halifax Parish Registers, Gilberte Deane was churchwarden for Warley in 1593, pointing out also that his son Richard attained eminence in the

theological world and became Bishop of Ossory, and his body lies buried in the Cathedral at Kilkenny, and that another son, Edmund, rose to distinction as a Bachelor and Doctor of Physic, and settled in York.

"B.P." stands for Benjamin Patchett, an eccentric layman who, says J. Horsfall Turner, "considered it his duty to tune pulpits to the key-note of what he deemed the true theology." In 1759 he had printed, at Halifax, a pamphlet, entitled "A Short Inquiry into the Proper Qualifications of Gospel Ministers, considered as the servants not of men, but of Jesus Christ, with some directions how we, who are hearers, may know whether the doctrines our ministers deliver from the pulpit are according to God's will and mind or not; and also how we are to attend on the Word preached in a profitable manner." As early as 1781 he was engaged in Sunday School work, and was one of the very earliest of voluntary teachers. Under Robert Raikes' method, Sabbath teachers were paid a small sum for their labour.

It is very probable this Benjamin Patchett was in a direct line from "Benjamin Padgett, of Coldedge," entered in the Haworth Church Burial Registers, January (no date), 1654.

Adjoining Great House is what is known as "th' Old Hall," stated to have been used by Roman Catholics in Queen Elizabeth's days, and by the Congregationalists of Booth from 1758 to 1761, when they built their first chapel. Later it is said to have been used, first as Wesleyan meeting-place, then as combing-shed.

Only one house was unoccupied when we made our imaginary tour of the valley; this was at Upper Houses. A building at Low, then known as "Wood House," and dubbed by the present artist-tenant "The Hermitage," had paneless windows and partial roof, and was stored with timber from the woods about Castle Carr. Old residents believe it was built for this purpose. It was converted into a dwelling and barn to substitute Stonebrig End, the land of which now forms part of the Castle Carr estate.

Bats at that time were common about Low, and they made Wood House their abode. "Old Tommy o' th' Heys'" "farmer's boy," born near to, tells of on summer evenings at dusk, watching the "articles wi' leather wings, fly in an' aght o' th' winder-oils." He is sure they could see and that "blind as a bat" applies to a cricketer's willow. The mammiferous animals disappeared when their quarters were disturbed, and not one has since been seen.

The first building to "depart" within the memory of the oldest

native was a one-storey cottage, named Summer Booth, which stood between Folds and Deep Clough. A story goes that one winter the cot was buried in snow save for a few inches of the chimney. This attracted a sheep, which, it is said, fell down the flue, and was accorded a hearty reception.

Betty Rothery's School.

CHAPTER III.

BETTY AND SAMMY ROTHERY'S SCHOOLS—SLODE FARM—COLD EDGE BOTTOM: STORM RECALLED—OLD SAMPSON.

"Th' Guide-Stoop," where we now stand, is a delusion. Seventy years ago, though, one stood sentinel and guided travellers, until, as a feat of strength, it was torn from its bed by one Robert Titterington and pitched across the road, where it remained till broken up and utilized as boulder. Mr. William Aspinall, a native now (1905) 85, an authority on local events, remembers the incident well.

As we saunter on, the clang of the old-time factory bell—the only one we know still in vogue—at Messrs. Bracken's comes rolling up, summoning the hands to another week's toil.

What memories flash across the mind as we look down on the higgledy-piggledy group of buildings. We see ourselves as children—what a long time ago! yet seemingly but yesterday—early each Saturday hurrying to the mills—then only a few tumble-down buildings—where we scratched the rubbish-heap, replenished that morning, for buttons severed from old rags, as industrious as a hen searching for food for her brood.

* * * * * *

There is a world of significance to many of native origin and past their prime in the end cottage of the three on our left. Sandy Fore is associated with their earliest recollections, since they remember sitting, as infants, for the motherly tuition of Betty Rothery. Surviving girl pupils especially recall the pains she took with homely lessons such as sewing and knitting. Aye, the instruction Betty imparted had a practical basis. And how precise and orderly she was in everything! If her pupils were knitting say, when on the point of dismissal, and the order went forth to "get to your seams and fold," woe to any caught folding between the seams. It meant the imposition of a difficult scriptural task which had to be done before liberty was granted. Those living entrusted to Betty's charge well remember, too, the dining accom-

Sammy Rothery's School.

modation at noon; how they sat on two narrow forms set parallel to each other, a third doing duty as table for the brown meos-pots of steaming tea or coffee. What an array of currant cakes, "presarve" cakes, "pasties," etc! The open triangular plot of ground near (now a poultry run) was an excellent play-ground during "all-aght" time. To announce "all in," neither whistle nor bell was used. Betty stood on the step in the doorway and waved her arm overhead. The act worked like magic upon the children, some of whom had perhaps raced to the old and higher road two hundred yards away. Boys who misbehaved were bundled into the coal cellar until they promised amendment. One we know relates how once he made his exit by the grate, but on his return to school he was "thrust into an inner prison," from which it was impossible to escape.

Betty died Dec. 21, 1881, aged 75 years, and is interred in the new cemetery at Mixenden, just over the hill.

Then there was the seminary of Sammy Rothery at Kell (now an offshoot of Luddenden Church), whose scholars were mostly graduates from his Aunt Betty's. Could the walls of that "upper room" beside Appleyards' old mill-dam speak, they might tell of incidents humorous and tragic; of "many a conflict, many a tear." O! what ecstacy on discovering old "Lijah o' th' Stooans'" donkey roving at will! The temptation was irresistible and often ended in scholars being truant. Those Turpin impersonations afforded unbounded delight; but over the sequel we will draw the veil. Many things more pleasing to recall befel those who sat at Sammy's feet, for he was indeed kind, lenient and considerate. After enjoying the late Joseph Crossley's benevolence some years, meanwhile preaching the Gospel, the respected schoolmaster entered into rest May 26, 1902, in his 83rd year. He was interred in the old ground at Mixenden beside his wife Bridget, who predeceased him just over three years. A plain horizontal stone, on the western side of the Chapel, marks the place.

* * * * * *

Again we wend along and keep to the main road at the crossing—Cross Roads—(/\ 1019-5), where again we mourn the lack of a "guide-stoop," (un)speakable boons to strangers. Further on we note the white-washed house at Slode, and observe over its porch these characters:—

I S F
1662

Wainstalls, from West.

At Shibden Hall is a copy of Ovenden Court Rolls, which says that when Daniel Holdsworth died in 1660, his lands at Slode passed to his sister Sarah, wife of Jacob Farrar. The first and last letters, then, are the initials of Jacob Farrar, and S stands for his wife's christian name. It has been humorously suggested that the S may have been placed so conspicuously in the centre to remind Jacob, every time he approached, that house and lands had come to him through his wife. Perhaps this explains why the S was cut significantly larger; certainly there seems an air of ruling authority about it. This manner of coupling the names of man and wife, however, was common in earlier days, a fact exemplified on many Elizabethan homesteads.

Slode was formerly a licensed house called "Ash Tree." Its life as such, however, ebbed out August 24, 1887, and the two trees in the adjacent yard, which presumably suggested the name for the beer-shop, seem doomed to premature death, despite their vigorous efforts to "defy age and time." "The Rising Sun," near to, "set" Oct. 10, 1895.

* * * * * *

On June 30, 1886, there passed away, aged 66, a respected resident, Aaron Robertshaw, boot and shoe maker—a character in his way, one of the old type, and a scholar of no mean gifts. He was the first person buried in the consecrated ground of the United Methodist Free Church, now on our left, and built, we observe, in 1857. A plain stone perpetuates the memory of the cobbler and his wife Betty, a good, quiet, inoffensive woman, who died May 8, 1900, at the age of 80.

To follow the telegraph wires we should pass Wainstalls Council School—where Mr. A. S. White has been headmaster since its erection in 1877—then Slack village, "Kell Schooil," and over the moor to Height Lodge, which consists of two embrasured structures connected by a Norman arch spanning the entrance to Castle Carr estate. But we keep to the paved road leading past the New Delight Inn until beyond the next building—New Holme (⋀ 1054-7)—past which we take the narrower road to the left.

Cold Edge Bottom. Storm Recalled.

Across the two meadows rising on our right is Cold Edge Bottom, two farms in close proximity to each other—the scene of the most disastrous thunderstorm within the memory of the oldest inhabitant. It was Whit-Tuesday, June 3, 1873, and shortly after nine o'clock at

HEIGHT LODGE.

night when the storm broke out. In the early morning the day promised to be ideal for the Whitsun festivities, instead of which it soon turned exceedingly boisterous and cold. Joshua Hoyle, who rented both farms and lived at the north one, was from home negotiating for another farm for his son James, who was 23, married, and lived at Lumb, which place we are approaching. James was officiating in his father's stead, and had just ceased milking one of four cows—the one in a stall nearest the back door—and was travelling a few yards to pour the milk into a larger can when, closely succeeding a terrific peal, a vivid flash darted through the mistal, and knocked him senseless. His forehead came in contact with the pavement and he sustained a fracture above the left eye, from which blood flowed freely. After some minutes he recovered consciousness, but could not rise. It was then evident he had received other serious injuries. His left side, it was found, was paralyzed, and he was shockingly burnt from feet to shoulders. His trousers (woollen cord) were slit from top to bottom, his boots cut into narrow shreds, and almost wrenched off his feet. A silver hunter watch that he carried was irreparably damaged, the glass, to use Mr. Hoyle's own words, being " melted like sugar." He was attended by Dr. T. Crowther, of Luddenden, and for some time his life was despaired of. Happily, however, he recovered, and to-day is hale and hearty and working as then, at the quarry. The cow he had milked, though killed, had no visible mark of injury, and the other cows were unharmed. Another young man named Samuel Tatham was in the mistal, and had one hand on the neck of the cow that was killed. He also was struck senseless, and when he came round found himself in the middle of the mistal floor, several yards from where he stood when lightning struck the place. Beyond a shock he was little the worse. The building was very little damaged. A foal, six weeks old, which was out in the field, was knocked against the wall and received injuries which much reduced its value. Mr. Hoyle, who did a large amount of stone leading, had other horses out to grass, and the drivers the following morning had difficulty in stabling them, so affrighted were they.

The lightning also wrought havoc in the adjacent farm-house—the one with frontage towards us. Here resided Timothy Binns, his wife, and an adopted daughter. The lightning entered partly by the chimney and partly through the roof, pierced a partitioned wall, and passed out by the windows, cleaving the framework, and shattering every pane. A bedroom door was wrenched off and splintered, solder was melted off a

SAMPSON'S HUT.

pair of scales, a brush was split into fragments, and a lantern and numerous articles were smashed. Mrs. Binns in her fright sought refuge in a dark place at the top of the cellar steps. She was no sooner here, safe as she thought, than a flash of lightning glanced down the wall and knocked off a huge cake of lime, terrifying her. She, however, was left unscathed. Their daughter in the house had her hair singed. The building was perceptibly shaken, and called for immediate repair.

Presently we shall pass on our left a clump of very old cottages, a small farm appropriately named Stones, with which even yet we associate Elijah Aspinall, though he died 25 years ago—May 30, 1880—in his 79th year. Two of the cottages are in ruins. When the storm occurred the lower cottage was occupied by one Jno. Binns. Here a party of young men sought shelter. One, James Balmforth, was struck by lightning, rendered temporarily insensible and was unable to walk home till the following day, though living only a short distance away. The newspapers reported it was thought his brain was affected, but this was not so ; to-day, like Mr. Hoyle, he follows his employment.

Old Sampson.

At the top of Cold Edge hill yonder is Sampson's Hut. Doorless, windowless, and soon 'twill be roofless. Chimney it never had, but of windows there were originally three—north, west and south. Persons of Sampson's acquaintance and who remember the cabin being built, say glass was never inserted ; that the windows were always walled up, as now, and that it was ever dark within, save from light obtained when the door was opened. The introduction of glass would have meant assessment and rates, one reminds us, which the builder, owner and prospective tenant, Sampson, undoubtedly fully considered.

It seems incredible, but time was when those four square, dry walls—the one facing west seemingly constructed for all time—formed the "home, sweet home" (?) of a human being. A surname Sampson had and a nickname, but we will know him only as Sampson. Another hut of somewhat similar design he purposed erecting a little lower down, arguing "it 'd be a bit warmer i' winter"; but this he never completed, and to-day the ruins remain.

Sampson, a bachelor through force of circumstances—though encouraged by a Mixenden dame—was no hermit or lazy lout, as his choice of life might imply, but a plodder in his way. In his younger days he was commendably thrifty, trading in fleeces he bought first-hand

from moorland farmers, often burdening himself with several stones' weight across trackless moors. Jealous of his success the spirit of Joseph's brethren made life at home intolerable. Refusing to comply with their demands to share his gains, he was denied the room to house his purchases, and this ended in his severing himself from the homestead, and altering his career. Such is Sampson's early biography as repeated to us by a relative he confided in, and who, at his death, followed him to his grave.

With the money saved in those days Sampson bought the field wherein he put both his "summer seat" and "winter residence"—appellations bestowed by neighbours upon his whole and one partially erected dwelling, many of whose stones he wheeled from Fly Flat quarries, more than two miles away; not a few which he picked up in the road were dropped from passing carts. He owned a smaller triangular plot higher up the road side. This he purchased for an old song from Commissioners when the Enclosure Act was passed. This plot he fenced with sods and stones, sowed with corn and then shaped a riddle. Said he, in his drawling way: "If ther' com's nooan, ther'll com' som', an' if ther' com's som', ther'll com' nooan." Interpreted, Sampson's first "nooan" has reference to the birds of the air, and the latter "nooan" to the prospective harvest.

Farm labourer, waller, drainer, trencher, and comber by turn, he worked as mind dictated, craving "little here below" by way of comfort, much less luxury. He had no furniture, we are told, save one cranky, backless chair, and a box to guard his treasures. A sheet of rough felt swung near the slates kept rain and snow from falling on his bed, which had supports ingeniously contrived out of loom stocks. He rarely had a fire, and when he had it was made gipsy fashion, between stones laid on the earthen floor—which measures some 14 feet by 11 feet 6 inches—the smoke passing out by the doorway; and this, we observe, the architect had discreetly put in the south wall. A septuagenarian friend of ours once asked him how he managed to dry his clothes after a soaking.

"O-o-o, aw just put 'em 'tween th' blankets (in truth, sacks) when aw goa ta bed, an' the're nice an' dry when aw get op i' th' mornin'," drawled Sampson.

He had a secret way of fastening his door, and when "at home," there was "no admittance." Sometimes, though, curious ones stole a march upon him, and they had the alternative of sitting on stones set on end or of taking up quarters on the edge of the bed. One of the few

he admitted to his abode once intimated that the wind came through crevices in the wall ; Sampson pointed to holes on the opposite side through which stars were visible, and slowly retorted : " Ther's a way aght theer for it, sithee ! "

Returning one night to his shelter—it was little else, scarcely that—he found the door broken open. His will, deeds, and valuables, which strangers would never suspect he possessed, were missing. The robber, a youth, whose morals in after life we could not conscientiously hold up as an example, was tracked and brought to justice, and Sampson received back his property.

Eccentric as we may imagine Sampson, he was a man of many parts, and intellectually above the average. He could read as few were able to in his day, write a flourishing hand, and sing a song in fine rural style. His favourite ditty was " The Spider and the Fly," which he gave best, we learn, when primed with Beverley's XXX, back at Cross Roads yonder ; for Sampson was not an abstainer when the beverage was cheap.

" Will you step into my parlour,"
Said the spider to the fly,
" 'Tis the prettiest little parlour
That ever you did spy."

ran Sampson's little sonnet, the sequel of which is obvious.

Chapels, too, received visits from Sampson, but not at services. Mount Pleasant and Luddenden Dean could rely on his patronage at each tea-party ; but his visits did not necessarily mean support. To children at these functions Sampson was the centre of attraction. Usually there were three " sittings down " (nowadays two are counted a success), and Sampson sat through them all. It is said, though tradition is sometimes based on weak foundation, that he once accounted for nine cups of tea, which, if true, was inconsistent with one prescription he gave, that " dry corn made th' strongest 'orses." He had a set of white teeth—all his own—" like those of a Scotch cur," says one who knew him. Sampson's storage must on the occasions mentioned have been taxed to the utmost. But then he lived in " hungry Cold Edge." In 1870 he would be 64 years of age, therefore he could not have been one of five young men who set out from Cold Edge for a lark on the night of Nov. 14 of that year, as chronicled in the *Halifax Courier* the following Saturday ; besides, the expenses involved in a spree at once frees Sampson of the stigma.

Briefly, they first called at an inn on Midgley side, and regaled themselves with five-and-a-half pounds of steak, five penny cakes and sundry pots of beer. And their appetites were unappeased. At the end of the feast a neighbourly butcher dropped in, and ascertaining what they had devoured, undertook to satisfy them for sixpence each. A bargain was struck. The butcher produced a piece of beef weighing eighteen-and-a-half pounds, and from this twelve pounds of steak were cooked and disposed of by the gourmands. Added to this were two loaves, and a fish, eaten raw, swilled down by several quarts of beer. The butcher looked on and marvelled. The reporter of the incident drops the curtain before the gluttonous band at this stage and concerns himself about the butcher's profits on the transaction. "Worse than beasts," was a justifiable heading to the paragraph. That there are still a few good trenchers in Cold Edge we do not dispute, but not organically constructed like the above.

To revert to Sampson. Notwithstanding miserly traits, we have it on authority that he was honest as the day, and generously disposed towards those in his good graces. Pots of tea and meals made for him when working away he would insist on paying for, and that unstintingly. This calls to mind yet another story, vouched for by an eye-witness, revealing Sampson's mode of living. Sometimes when going combing to some farm-house or cottage he would take dinner with him; about a handful of flour. At noon he made this into dough with water, added salt, and flattened it with his hands into a cake. He would then request the loan of a frying pan, and in oil used in the combing process would cook the cake on the "comb-pot-plate" till nicely brown. To see Sampson relish his "dumb-boy," as he called this mid-day meal, might rouse the envy of some sickly mortals.

Though the public may not know it, they are chiefly indebted to Sampson for a right of cart-road from Haigh Cote to Withins Gap ("Withins" on the Halifax Burgess Roll), the large and newish barn we see to the north, standing out so clearly against the hill. The case of Kitchen *v.* Tattersall was heard at the West Riding Assizes, August 15, 1874.

A certain witness was called for the defence who proved so illiterate that Justice Denman observed that "If this was the class of defendant's witnesses they were 'worse than useless,'" and he suggested that the system he had seen pursued under similar circumstances in Scotland be adopted, that somebody who had power of investigation and some

knowledge of the law, should go to the spot and have everybody before him who professed to know anything about the case, making all inquiries he could. To this both parties agreed. On the November 19 following, all "who professed to know anything about the case" were got together, and Sampson was one. Through the kindness of Mr. James Clarkson, of Halifax (who succeeded to the former practice of Norris, Foster and England, solicitors for the plaintiff), we are able to quote Sampson's evidence. He said he lived at Cold Edge Bottom, that he was 68, and was born at Haigh Cote. He could not remember how long he lived there; his grandfather occupied a cottage at Haigh Cote. Samuel Scholfield† was his schoolmaster. There was no other road to Haigh Cote for horses and carts. He used to go to Withins Gap when he was nine or ten. His uncle then owned and occupied Withins Gap. The same house was occupied by Kitchen. He remembered Jonas Foster* living at Haigh Cote; he lived there before his uncle left Withins Gap. The road was past Withins Gap when his uncle lived there, and when J.

†Prior to issuing the first edition of this work the author made diligent enquiries respecting Samuel Scholfield, with the view to gleaning something of his life and character, but none remembered or ever heard of him living at Cold Edge. Since then he has learnt that Sampson's schoolmaster was a card-maker and cotton spinner at Spring Mill for seven or eight years, from about 1815. Besides this he was a farmer, and owned a stone quarry at Southowram. On certain evenings he held school at his farm-house at Spring Mill, and taught young men of Cold Edge. He was a tall, strong, vigorous man, and somewhat eccentric. When he had amassed a fortune he changed his name from Scholfield to Schorfield, his object being to disassociate himself from poorer relatives. Once he sent to the mint for a "sack" of farthings with which to pay his hands. He had thirteen children, six sons and seven daughters. Two of the sons entered the army, one serving with the East India Company, the other with the Oxford Blues. Another son, Henry, was a cardmaker in Halifax, and built premises in Back Rhodes Street, which to-day are occupied by his descendants in another industry. Sampson's schoolmaster is buried in Coley church-yard, where, on a box-tomb south of the church, is inscribed :—

IN **Memory** OF
Samuel Schorfield late of *Southowram*,
card-maker, who departed this *Life*, April
22nd, 1825, in the 61ft Year of his *Age*.

"Our Lives hang by a fingle Thread,
Which foon is sever'd and we are dead;
Then Reader boaft not of thy might,
Since Death may feize thee ere 'tis night.
But learn on Heaven to fix a fteady Eye,
And fo to live that thou may'ft dare to die."

ALSO of William, Son of the above,
Who departed this *Life* at Bombay in
the East Indies, Jany. 1st, 1829, in the
34th *Year* of his *Age*,

ALSO *Sarah*, Wife of *Samuel*
Schorfield, who departed this *Life*
October 6th, 1837, *Aged* 71 *Years*.

"In Life respected, in Death lamented."

In a line of graves, counting four from the road west of the church, a horizontal stone records the death of four of Samuel Schorfield's children—two sons and two daughters. These died between 1790 and 1818, and bear the name of Scholfield.

The author of this volume is indebted to Mr. C. E. and Mr. J. Schorfield (grandchildren of Samuel) for this information. The former is now (1913) 76 years old; he has been on the Rhodes Street Wesleyan local preachers' plan since 1854. Mr. John is a retired schoolmaster.

*Jonas Foster was the owner of Haigh Cote at the time of the dispute, was 87, and lived in Halifax.

Foster lived there. He remembered his uncle selling Withins Gap to Thomas Kitchen of Saltonstall, about 1818 or 1817 ; he went to America after he sold it. Withins Gap was occupied by J. Holgate and Thomas Wade in two parts. He had been a cart driver, and had gone up and down the road past Withins Gap with horse and cart. He remembered a wall being built : there was only a wall on one side.

Cross-examined : He remembered about 1820, John Holgate occupied one part and Wade the other. Wade's son lived at one time at Haigh Cote ; the son had no horse and cart, but employed them when he required them. When John Holgate occupied part of Haigh Cote and Withins Gap he went up and down the road in question with horse and cart.

Re-examined : He went along it when he did not occupy it. Wade's son's name was Thomas Wade, and he occupied Haigh Cote ; he was married and lived in the house.

Kitchen lost the day, and paid dearly for his hostility, for the proceedings, we are told, cost some £1,600, and involved the selling of three farms. Though the road disputed was not (nor is now) any real public benefit, it was of infinite value to Tattersalls, living at Haigh Cote, since it meant the saving of two miles at least.

* * * * * *

Yes, Sampson was " a man of many parts," but it is doubtful if he ever played a role so important as the one just cited. Who was the richer when he changed his earthly tabernacle for another sphere (Sunday, April 16, 1876) is not our concern, so we saunter on.

CHAPTER IV.

ROBIN HOOD'S PENNY-STONE—SIR RICHARD SALTONSTALL—WHITE ROCK —A CHILD'S DROWNING—"OLD EBEN'S SCHOOL"—COLD EDGE DAMS—BROTHERS DROWNED.

ON our left is Upper Slack farm, a beer-shop until 1870 when, on grounds of ill repute, we learn, the owner refused to further re-let it as such. Attached to the adjoining cottage is a one-storey building, where at that time Mary Brearley baked oat bread. Though it is only an hour since we ate a hearty breakfast, we believe we could relish a cake of Mary's, freshly cooked from the "baxstun," with a layer of treacle between. We have much faith in oats and syrup: they tend to longevity. Mary lived till she was 82, and she and her husband John are neighbours in death to Sammy Rothery, an upright stone marking their resting place.

A little further is a disused quarry; it is marked on our map as the "site of Robin Hood's Penny-stone." Our dictionary defines "penny-stone" as "a flat, circular stone; a substitute for an iron quoit." The Rev. John Watson, referring to this "penny-stone" in his *History and Antiquities of the Parish of Halifax*, published in 1775, says :—

"Soon after I had left the moor, on the right of the road leading to the village of Luddenden, I saw what is generally called Robin Hood's Penny-stone, for the country people here attribute everything of the marvellous kind to Robin Hood, as in Cornwall they do to King Arthur. Thus, for instance, he is said to have used this stone to pitch with at a mark for amusement; and to have thrown the standing stone in Sowerby off an adjoining hill with a spade as he was digging; but I confess that some of the common people will smile when they relate these stories; they are not quite so credulous now as their grandfathers were. This last-mentioned remain is a stone of several tons weight, laid upon a massy piece of rock, with a large pebble of a different colour between them, which is wedged so fast that it is very plain it was put there by human art or strength. I could not learn whether this would ever rock or not (meeting with but one person to converse with), but if it did, probably it was poised on this pebble, and might sometime or other have been thrown off its centre."

The same historian also says :—

"On Saltonstall moor is also a large heap of stones, which, at a distance (for I had not the opportunity of viewing them nearer) looked like a carnedde, rising to a considerable height, and which might possibly be the sepulchre of some considerable person, for human bodies have been actually found under such heaps."

ROBIN HOOD'S PENNY-STONE.
(*From a drawing in Watson's "History of Halifax."*)

Possibly Mr. Watson stood at "Robin Hood's Penny-stone" here and saw what we can see less than a mile away up the moor in a westerly direction, viz: a heap of loose stones which, however, does not rise to any "considerable height." Yet it is the only heap of stones we know of on Saltonstall Moor. It is characterized on our map as a trigonometrical station, and is called "Sleepy Lowe."

* * * * * *

Though at no great altitude the prospect is admirable, if not exquisite. Up in the fields on our right is Moorfield House, till recent years the home of the Calvert's, ivy-clad, and commanding Wainstalls, Kell, Castle Carr road, and Saltonstall moor.

SIR RICHARD SALTONSTALL.

Crouched at the foot of the moor is Lower Saltonstall—a group of dwellings and barns huddled together, reminding one of Runswick and

similar hamlets on the east coas' Saltonstall, we read, was the ancestral home* of Gilbert Saltonstall, father of Sir Richard Saltonstall, Lord Mayor of London, 1597-8. And here at Lower Saltonstall was born, in humble circumstances, the Rev. James Crossley, who, ordained in 1763 (the year death claimed the Rev. William Grimshaw, who, with the Rev. Geo. Whitfield, was largely influential in bringing about the conversion of Crossley), officiated as first Pastor and leader at Booth Congregational Chapel.

In South Ockenden Church is a stately Elizabethan monument of marble, to the memory of Sir Richard Saltonstall, Knight, and his wife. This, erected in 1601, bears the following inscription :—

"Here lieth the earthly part of Sir Richard Saltonstall, Knight, whose age was blest with this honour to be Lo. Maior of the Citie of London; his dayes did like bright and puer incense shine in Holy Labos to God, his Prince, and his countrie. Hee was joynt Lord of this Towne, and Patron of this Church. When hee dyed the glass of his life rann out foll to that of Fower score years, of which number he spent fifty in the chast and holy lawes of marriage with his deere beloved wife Susanna, the only daughter of Thomas Poyntz, of North Ockenden, Essex, Esquire. The Blessings which God in ample measure heapt uppon him were made foll with the happiness of XVI children—VII sonnes and IX daughters of all whome God spared IIII sonnes and VII daughters to do honour to their father's funerall. Yorkshire challengeth his birth and this place his buriall. The poore of both shedd tears for this loss, because the poore of both tasted comfort by his life. He dyed the year of Redemption 1601, and now dwells where hee shall never dye. In remembrance of whom Ladie Susanna Saltonstall, his wife, erected his monument."

Sir Richard in his will, dated 1597, among other provisions, bequeathes :—

"To Samuel Saltonstall and every one of my sons-in-law £3 6s. 8d. each, for a gold ring. . . . . To thirty poor men who shall attend my body at my funeral, forty gowns at the price of 10s. a yard. . . . . Out of my goods and chattels, £100 to buy a yearly rent to be distributed among the poor of Halifax, and this the church-wardens of Halifax distribute same in ready money or penny loaves four times a year in the said Parish Church in remembrance of me, the said Richard Saltonstall."

"It is to the honour of Sir Richard that he did not forget his native parish, though, to the discredit of his family, the poor whom he designed to benefit never enjoyed the fruits of his care," said Mr. Sutcliffe, of Warley, in his paper to the Halifax Antiquarian Society (previously mentioned).

These are Saltonstall's sunny features; it has also, according to tradition, a shadowy one. When the plague of 1631 (recorded in the Halifax and Heptonstall Parish Registers) visited Erringden, Heptonstall

*The arrow left of the illustration points to farm-house built on the site of Sir Richard Saltonstall's ancestral home; the arrow top of the photograph points to White Rock.

Lower Saltonstall and White Rock.

LUMB MILL.

and Ovenden, and carried off in some cases whole households, nearly all of whom were "buried near their own dwellings," Saltonstall, so tradition says, was laid under the scourge, and all the inhabitants died except one, and he, it is said, dug his own grave, expecting soon to follow. Though there is no proof of the pestilence visiting Saltonstall, to-day a meadow with a footpath running through is known as the "grave field."

White Rock.

On the moorland slope above Saltonstall we see a snowy patch, a landmark a long way southward. The first Sunday in May (Luddenden Dean Spa) twenty-three years ago, residents were astonished on seeing a white object among the bilberry bushes. Scores (the writer included) flocked to ascertain its nature. What a sell! Nothing but a clump of rocks newly white-washed! It was never discovered who did it. What is more, though the rocks ever since have periodically received a fresh coat, no one has been caught with brush and pail. Still we surmise, and we think we could track the artist to his lair.

On the sky-line, to the left of the air-shaft we noted at "Guide Stoop," we see the flag-pole of the Calder Valley Rifle Club. Now we take an imaginary jump over Midgley Crow Hill (1,251 feet), and alight apparently near the foot of Stoodley Pike. To the right of Sowerby Crow Hill (1,257 feet), away back, the sun shows up the road leading to Blackstone Edge, the higher route to Littleborough. The Crow Hills of Sowerby and Midgley are strikingly impressive, akin in shape and almost in height. Nowhere better than here, to our knowledge, are they together so well outlined; each to us is suggestive of a monster hot-cross bun.

* * * * * *

We jog on Some thrity-two years back Messrs. Hollinrake and Clegg forsook the little factory here at Lumb, driven by water-power and employing less than a score of hands, and removed to Sun Works, Halifax, later establishing the large worsted business in Miall Street, in that town. Square Mill, two storeys high and twenty-two windows long, a meadow length above, boasted not much larger area than this, its neighbour, when Robert Crossley, brother of the Halifax philanthropists, was in business there, between sixty and seventy years ago.

Child Drowning.

A step from the highway, yet in the road, is a small loose plank, let into a socket level with the ground. Here is a sluice connected with a conduit conveying water under the road and field into the little dam we see some sixty yards away. Each time we pass, which is once a week, we are reminded of a fatal accident which occurred just over thirty years ago.

On Friday afternoon, Jan. 8, 1875, two wagons, laden with stones for an engine-bed at Square Mill, broke the cover of the conduit, but the drivers, according to their story, were ignorant of it, and drove on. Shortly after, two little brothers, the sons of William Aspinall (not related to William Aspinall, our village veteran), ran in home close by, and requested of their mother (Sarah Ann Aspinall) a piece of bread. Then out they went again to play. A few minutes only had elapsed before the eldest, Job (about seven) returned to say his brother Riley (nearly five) had fallen through a hole into the water. The mother hastened to the spot, and was just in time to see her darling's tiny hands clinging to the broken cover. Before she could reach him, alas, he lost hold and disappeared. There was no other opening in the conduit where the mother might have hope of rescuing her boy, so it was assumed he would be carried by the current into the dam. The water was turned and the dam let off, but the child could not be found. He must have caught fast in the conduit thought the neighbours, and a young man, Hy. Cockroft, volunteered to crawl up the drain. About midway he discovered a cover broken in two, standing V-like across the channel, and here the little fellow was trapped. Three-quarters-of-an-hour before he was bright as a sunbeam and happy as a " sand boy " ; now he was a corpse. At the inquest it was supposed the wagon wheels must have broken the stone covering or had crushed it so badly that when the boy went on it, it gave way beneath him.

Old Eben's School.

A few old people remember, though not with pleasantest recollections, attending " Old Eben's " school, in the pretty one-storey house called Rose Cottage, on our left. Just now it is attractive because of its neat garden. At the back is a walled-in doorway, then the entrance to the school ; similarly darkened is the little window which let in the afternoon sun. Even prior to Ebenezer Cockcroft—to accord " Old

Eben " his full christened name—building this, scholars tell of being taught (?) by him in a " low biggin, oppen to th' thack an' five stooreys long," on land now occupied by Bridge Terrace, in close proximity to " th' Kell Schooil." This, of course, was before Sammy Rothery's days. " Old Eben " died July 1, 1867, in his 77th year, and was interred at Mount Zion, Ovenden.

Cold Edge Dams.

Moorfield House, Moorcock Inn (Moor Side) and Moorbottom Farm are evidences that we are bordering on the moor itself. Behind the inn is a profusion of marsh-marigolds, which, held back by drought and intense cold, are now in very pomp. We stay and admire the show, and meanwhile wonder if farmers appreciate the golden carpet ; we trow not : they may approve of marry(ing) gold.

Forward, the road is rougher as it skirts the moor up to, and beyond Spring Mill (locally known as " th' Ovver Miln "), small in size and with power on a par with that at Lumb. This road we really ought to adhere to, but to get the full benefit of the invigorating air we strike a well-worn path leading over the embankments of Cold Edge Dams, originally known as Saltonstall Moor Reservoirs. At the foot of the first we read the notice :—

" These grounds are private, and unless visitors refrain from doing damage to the heather and reservoir embankments, they will be closed, and trespassers will be prosecuted."

What a pity the authorities should have cause to post such warnings.

One sharp spur and we have mounted the embankment, where we squat and inhale the exhilarating breeze. Looking back, one-and-three-quarters miles away is the village from which we started, and our home* from which during western gales we have watched the water wash over the place where we sit, while the spray, like smoke floating over the black heath, has been driven an amazing distance ; at first glance a stranger might fancy the moor was smouldering.

Beyond the western end of the embankment, and some two hundred and fifty yards south, in the heart of the moor, is a hollow, about 24 feet in circumference, and 4 feet deep, the work of ages. It is difficult to locate. In years past, many, we have heard, were wont to rise at three or four in the morning, and with an interesting book would wend their way to this delightful spot. With legs dangling o'er the cavity they

*See the Wainstalls illustration on page 29, and note the tallest of buildings on the right horizon. Mount Tabor lies immediately beyond, three miles further back, and 563 feet lower is Halifax Town Hall.

"OLD EBEN'S" SCHOOL.

would long sit watching the springs first juggling the white sand at the bottom of the shallow pool, then mingling and flowing across the bleak waste to serve farms at Upper Saltonstall, a mile or so away. The public are now forbidden to visit either springs or moor.

Steering northward we stroll on, crossing the dry channel for the overflow from Leadbeater Dam—named, we believe, after its contractor—and very shortly we have scaled the embankment of Haigh Cote Dam, where it is essential to make our caps secure lest they should take "a ride on the ocean wave."

By the kind research of Messrs. Calvert, we ascertain that the aggregate storage of the three reservoirs now seen (setting aside the small lodge down on our right) is 22,682,281 gallons; Haigh Cote, 11,089,049; Leadbeater, 7,646,413; Blackfield, 3,946,819. The latter is by far the oldest, dating back over a century. The first reference to it, we are told, is in 1806, when the three owners of mills at Spring, Lumb, and Wainstalls formed a company and constructed Haigh Cote Dam, which was enlarged in 1831. Other owners on the stream threw in their lot with the company, and in 1835 Leadbeater was added. Into this is poured daily from the Halifax Corporation Reservoir at Fly Flat 1,440,000 gallons of water, which is conducted along the moor about two miles, one half the distance underground and the remainder in open channel, which needs much attention during winter, that the water may have free course. "'Tis an ill wind which blows nobody good." Frozen-out quarrymen and others dependent upon the weather find relief in the work and it is welcomed, though unenviable and harassing. Prior to the construction of Fly Flat, the mills, in seasons of extreme drought, such as we are at present experiencing, were subject to long spells of idleness.

Brothers Drowned.

Haigh Cote Dam, which depends solely upon its gathering from the moor, is being held in reserve. And what a beautiful sheet of water! The ripples race over the place where nearly seventy years ago occurred a most lamentable incident.

The hearts of John Greenwood and family, the occupiers of Slade, whither our steps are tending, were intensely saddened. Two of that family circle on Friday, June 16, 1837, ere the evening shadows kissed their native hills, were borne home on farmers' ladders, lifeless. Three of the brothers, Joseph, William and Thomas—the latter eighteen and youngest of

D

Cold Edge Dams, from North-east. Midgley Crow Hill in Background.

the three—in company with a young man, John Parker, had during the forenoon been peat-getting. It was a scorching day, one of the kind when children ran about without clogs and stockings. James Horsfall, hale and hearty at 81, recalls how he (then 13) and his father were returning from Calvert's mills at Wainstalls with cart laden with wool, after having delivered a load of tops combed at their own home at Oxenhope. When about the centre of Fill Belly—a short length of fenceless and exposed road over which we shall presently pass—they met these four young men, fresh from the peat pit, to quote Mr. Horsfall, "plump burned orf, wi' neck-bund thrown oppen, shirt abun th' middle an' bare-fooit an' bare-leg, an' befoor neet word coom ta Haworth Parish (no telephone communication in those days) et two on 'em had getten drahnded." When Mr. Horsfall met them they were going to the dams to bathe. Nothing serious befel them until they were about to leave the water. Three of them had reached the bank when Joseph excitedly shouted "E, gow, ahr Tom's drahndin'" and hastened to his aid. To his consternation he found the boggy bottom would not sustain him; still he pressed on, and eventually the brothers clasped hands. For a short time they struggled together, when it was seen both were sinking. William, a youth of frail physique, waded in to attempt a rescue. Shortness of stature, however, handicapped him, but not until hope of saving them was gone did he abandon his painful task, and then he had the utmost difficulty to reach shore. Samuel Widdop (Ebenezer Cockcroft's brother-in-law), a youth over six feet, who afterwards served his Queen and country twenty-five years, being Lifeguardsman, succeeded in fetching out the bodies. Four days following this distressing event Queen Victoria ascended to the Throne, and the nation rejoiced, but at Slade people sat in misery, overwhelmed by this sorrow.

* * * * * *

We trudge on with the breeze at our backs, and making sails of our garments, it urges us forward. Lines of flapping clothes remind us it is Monday morning; they betoken thrifty housewives who have been very early astir. As we proceed we hear the wild, yet musical note of the ring-ouzel, and the drumming of the snipe as it skims the ruffled waters, and alighting on a breaker, seems to be incessantly imploring intruders begone. We feel a sense of indebtedness to the Dam Company for the privilege as we step from the embankment tapering to the level of the moor and land on public road again. Gently we lift aside the

rickety iron gate at the bend near Haigh Cote farm and take a velvet-like path, little wider than a rabbit track, beside a moorland rivulet meandering beneath shadowy tussocks of reviving ling, impaired tufts of bent grass, and decayed overhanging rushes. The hum of the world is being left behind. Nothing breaks the silence save the whisk of the heather and the rill babbling in its rocky bed. Excited by our presence, a pair of grouse start up and cross our path, bidding us "ga-back, ga-back, ga-back." We heed not their command, however, so go-on, go-on, go-on.

Woe to any quadruped which attempts to secure the alluring bait beneath the "Samson Traps" we observe lying in wait for victims.

Crossing the stream by a rural bridge, we step lightly o'er the springy, dry turf, discarding the deeply sunk stepping stones we could not so well afford to ignore in less droughty times. We stay a moment to quench thirst at a spring immediately at our feet, and, producing a pocket horn drink heartily; we have tasted it before and know its merits, icy-cold even on summer's hottest day. And what a thick stream! While we linger it seems to say:—

"Men may come and men may go,
But I go on for ever."

CHAPTER V.

VIEW FROM SLADE—VETERAN GAMEKEEPER—DR. FAWCETT—WARLEY MOOR ROCKING STONE—POACHING EPISODES—DISPUTED FOOTPATH.

GIVEN an ideal day, what a panorama is obtained from Slade (1350 ft.). Hills roll away southwards some twenty-five miles. To the right of Sowerby Church—a most prominent land-mark some six miles away—backed by the Booth Dean Moors, lies the picturesque Ryburne valley. In the rear, beyond Meltham, rising some 1,900 feet and o'er-topping the pointed summit of West Nab, is Holme Moss, the dividing line of Yorkshire and Derbyshire. With the aid of a glass Tinker's monument, near Hepworth, and Cook's study, beyond Holmfirth, some eighteen miles away, are discernible. Yea, how very charmingly situated is the one-storey farm confronting us. Many remember it as a licensed house, opened probably in view of accommodating workmen employed constructing Fly Flat Reservoir. In January, 1865, the place was registered "Reservoir Inn." Five years afterwards the late Sir Henry Edwards, Bart., leased it for seven years and relinquished the license. Subsequently he purchased it from Dr. Sunderland, of Halifax, tacking it on to the Castle Carr estate. Over the doorway are the initials "J.H.S.," and date "1828," but the original dwelling at the rear dates from a more remote period. An adjacent barn is dated 1831.

VETERAN GAMEKEEPER.

Out of regard for the occupants and by way of a rest, we will turn aside for a chat with the veteran gamekeeper; providing he is not out on the moor. In response to our rat-tat on the wide-open door, two voices unite in bidding us "come in." We are invited to a seat beside the ingle, and to "sit a tooathry minutes an' get a pipe o' bacco."

"We seed yo' comin' up th' lotment, an' wonder'd wheer yo' might be makin' for sooa sooin on i' th' mornin'," remarks our octogenarian

SLADE.

friend, as he proceeds to measure his tall yet spare figure, reaching from the mantel-piece a spill with which to light his pipe.

We briefly describe our programme, then manifest concern for the welfare of the old keeper, who reluctantly confesses he has not been very well of late, and adds "Yo' kno' old 'ns dunnot rutch up like young 'ns."

Few indeed are spared to celebrate their golden wedding. Our friend William Watson (of Old Nook, in Luddenden Dean list) honoured his on December 28, 1890, and we make allusion to the event, and also delicately mention the vacant chair on the hearth.

"Aye, aw lost her sin' that doo," says Mr. Watson with a perceptible tremor, "tho' shoo wer' spared to mi nearly ten yeear longer—till July, 1899. Another six month an' we should a 'ad ahr diamond weddin'."

We ourselves were invited to our friends' golden wedding, but through a heavy snow which fell during the evening, were unable to attend. Many guests from a distance, Mr. Watson tells us, had to remain overnight. "Aye, aw lost her sin' that doo," repeats the old man.

By way of diverting his thoughts, and for our own edification we beg to be excused remarking upon items hanging on the walls—almost invariably a true index to character and taste.

Stuffed and arranged in life-like attitudes, in cases, are a sparrow hawk, partridge, owl, woodcock and snipe. Here is seen a brace of grouse surrounded by chicks only a few days old, and grouped as if picking amongst the heather. Here is a case of "varment" of the polecat and weasel species, including a fine specimen of the foumart, which the trusty keeper prides himself in having captured close on fifty years ago, upon ground since acquired for the reservoir at Fly. In company with these are teals and petrels which fell to his practised hand when that basin was being first filled.

Dr. Fawcett.

Our line of thought is somewhat abruptly turned. On the white-washed wall hangs a small mezzotint engraving of "Dr. John Fawcett, D.D., æt 75," the once famous Baptist preacher of Ewood Hall. It depicts the Doctor in his study, reclining far back in an easy-chair, in clerical jacket and vest, which seem inclined to pinch. Round his neck is a white muffler (no detestable starch), over which hang two distinct chins. A solitary curl from beneath the round velvet cap, which he always wore when preaching, looks down, as it were, on a plump, clean-

shaven face. On a rack in the picture are two volumes of the "Devotional Family Bible," his greatest work, begun in 1807 and finished in four years, when he was in his 72nd year. In recognition of this a university in the United States conferred upon him the degree of Doctor of Divinity. The kindly and devoted spirit of this gentleman was the subject of the tribute of a correspondent to *Yorkshire Notes and Queries* a short while ago. The writer mentioned that in 1772 Mr. Fawcett made a nine-weeks' stay in London, preaching fifty-eight times.

He was then pressed to take Dr. Gill's place and decided to do so. "If he had been actuated by worldly considerations or personal ambitions," continued the writer, "he would probably have been lost to the West Riding. His farewell sermon had been preached to a congregation which extended into the graveyard; his household goods had been packed, and he was on the point of leaving when the sorrow of his people, and his own feelings, so moved him that he resolved to stay. The wagons were joyfully unpacked by his people, and the incident was pathetically commemorated by the beautiful hymn 'Blest be the tie that binds,' which he composed as the joint expression of their feelings."

Mr. Fawcett and his son conducted at Ewood Hall a school which must have been one of the largest private seminaries in the North of England; in 1811 the inmates (exclusive of servants) totalled 85.

And this is the portrait of the man who, on July 31, 1765, was ordained Pastor of Wainsgate Baptist Chapel, near Hebden Bridge, and for half a century was contented with the salary of £40 per annum.

Mr. Watson tells us his father worked for that "gentleman"—pointing to the engraving—as a cowman for forty years, and in the latter part, by way of promotion, it was chiefly his duty to keep tidy the lawn, and to trundle his infirm master upon it in a chair on wheels.

An amusing incident our entertainer repeats we listen to with peculiar interest. His father and others were engaged to exhume the remains of Dr. Fawcett and his wife from Machpelah, Hebden Bridge, and remove them to Wainsgate. To avoid the curiosity of the neighbourhood, the gruesome task was carried out in the dead of night. One body at a time was taken up and conveyed away. As the men neared the graveyard with the last corpse, day was just dawning. Suddenly they halted. In the twilight they beheld a moving figure amongst the tombstones which filled them with awe. Each wondered whether, since his departure the trumpet had sounded and the dead were being raised.

After all it was only an old woman who, having got wind of the affair, had come to witness the second interment, and had sat on a tombstone patiently waiting the scene. A tablet-tomb, fenced with railings, denotes the place where they are laid; from it we once copied:—

Within this Vault
are deposited the Remains of
John Fawcett, D.D., of Ewood Hall,
late Pastor of the Baptist Chapel
at Hebden Bridge,
who died July 25th, 1817,
aged 77 years.

* * * * * *

In introducing the Fawcetts in the conversation we have struck a vein which appeals much to Mr. Watson, who, we glean, was ushered into the world Jan. 21, 1818, six months after the death of Mr. Fawcett. He speaks of the time when he was employed as farm-hand at Ewood Hall by "that gentleman's" son; beginning work there when a boy, and receiving 6d. per day and food. He lived with his parents in a tumble-down place called "Thyme" (long since demolished), which stood in a field below Ewood Hall. "We lack'd nowt as far es owt t' eyt went," Mr. Watson assures us, "we'd five meals i' th' day: porridge mornin' an' neet, an' a basin o' skimm'd milk to 'em, an' es mich avver breead es yo liked; an' it *wor* avver breead wer that. Ther's nooan sich nah—ommost a quarter of an inch thick, an' when yo' steeped it i' milk it swelled aght twice th' thickness; yo' kno' ther were nooa adultrashun then. We grew all es own mayl. Then we'd allus a for'-nooin drinkin', an' supper; plenty o' mayt an' tates; fer we'd ooashuns o' puttates an' never nooan to buy."

All grain produced on the estate was milled at the corn factory then existing at Brearley, which calls to Mr. Watson's mind an incident there which had a tragic side. If he remembers rightly, the then miller, depressed by financial trouble, brought his life to an abrupt end. It transpired, when too late, that he had been the victim of systematic roguery. Certain individuals were suspected and traps were laid. "Aw wer' an eye-witness to a part o' that affair," declares our friend. "Aw saw a constable, arm'd wi' a sieve, enter th' 'aases o' them et suspishun 'ad fall'n on, an'—

"Excuse us," we interrupt, "why the sieve?"

"Dooant yo' see," our friend explains with a twinkling eye, "that wer' to separate thro' th' mayl all th' little bits o' paper at it wer' mixed

wi', sooas ta make double sure o' catching th' reight thief. It turn'd aght ther wer' four ov 'em ; aw saw 'em all 'ancuff'd together an' ta'en ta th' lock-op; aw'm just th' same es aw con see 'em nah, tho' aw wer' nobbut i' mi teens."

"Nooa ! yo' guessed wrang ; they worn't transpooarted for life, tho' aw believe i' former times mony one es fun ther way to th' gallows for takkin' stuff o' less valla."*

* Since this was written we find Mr. Watson's story perfectly correct. The trial, at the West Riding Summer Sessions, Bradford, July 2, 1834, revealed an ingenious capture. We will quote the trial :—

Mr. Baines, for the prosecutor, said Mr. Murgatroyd, " as well as other millers in the neighbourhood of Halifax, had been suffering from robberies in their mills, and in consequence of their not being able to identify the articles in which they dealt, the offenders were rarely brought to justice. Several millers, therefore, had lately adopted a plan of watching their premises, and on the night when this robbery was committed, Mr. Murgatroyd had stationed himself in his mill a few yards from the place where the flour was kept, and close to a broken window, which enabled him, as it was a clear night, to see distinctly what occurred. One of his men was in another part, also on the watch. About one in the morning Mr. Murgatroyd observed John and William Mitchell and Abraham Akroyd approach where the flour was deposited, carrying bundles like empty sacks. They passed within a few yards of him, so that he could distinguish them ; and as he had known the three for years (they had resided in the neighbourhood), he could not be mistaken. William Mitchell was lifted to the landing of the door by the other two ; he unlocked the door and went in. He presently came out with a light, and told the others " there was something for them," or words to that effect, on which Akroyd was also lifted up by John outside, and, in company with William, entered the building. After remaining a quarter-hour they returned with a sack nearly full, and this they passed to John ; the door was locked, and the party went into a field a short distance from the mill. They soon returned, and Akroyd and Mitchell entered as before, leaving John outside ; in a quarter-hour they brought out three sacks, partly filled, and these they carried away, Akroyd going in one direction, and the two Mitchells in another. They passed by Horsfall, who, recognising them, attempted to seize them, but they got away, leaving one sack behind. To detect the receiver of the stolen property, Mr. Murgatroyd adopted," said Mr. Baines, " the following ingenious plan. On the evening of May 5, before he began to watch, in the presence of Horsfall, he mixed with the flour a quantity of circular bits of paper, punched, and bearing a mark to which he could swear. It happened that on May 8 (two days after the robbery), Christopher Cheeseborough, the inspector under the Worsted Committee, having occasion to search Riley's premises for embezzled materials, found flour mixed with meal in an old chest in his house. He asked Riley where he had obtained it, and got the answer, " off Mr. Murgatroyd," from whom he had at times bought flour, etc., and who, he said, had sold this to him in 1833. Mr. Murgatroyd was sent for and having passed some of the mixed thirds and meal through a sieve, found several of the bits of paper, which enabled him to swear that the flour was part of that stolen from him on the 6th. Under the circumstances (concluded Mr. Baines) there could be no doubt of the prisoner's guilt."

The prisoners said they were not on Mr. Murgatroyd's premises that night. They called two witnesses—one of whom, it was stated, had previously been convicted of felony.

The Mitchells and Akroyd were transported for seven years, and Riley, for receiving the stolen flour, received like punishment.

The chairman expressed his sense of the tact and prudence Mr. Murgatroyd displayed in detecting the robbery, and added: "If others would only look after their property as well, and provide means for the discovery of offenders, there would be a considerable diminution of crime."

There is in the possession of Mr. J. Sutcliffe-Thomas and Mr. J. T. Sutcliffe, at Mayroyd, Hebden Bridge, a silver cup, subscribed for by a grateful public, which bears this inscription:

"This cup was presented to Mr. Champion Murgatroyd, Brearley Mill, on the first day of January, 1835, as a testimony of gratitude for his successful exertions in bringing to justice several persons who were found guilty of committing depredations on the public, and transported for the same."

* * * * *

Poaching Episodes.

The black-oak clock ticks on; the hands of its brass dial are fast approaching nine. For more than an hour we have been listening to stirring events, and a theme we are most anxious to introduce has not been touched upon. So in eager anticipation we decide to spend a few minutes more with our friend.

"If yo' stop whol aw finish all th' tales aw could tell yo' o' th' experiences aw've 'ad wi' pouchers, yo'll never get to Haworth Parish to-day, net ta mention wheer yo've set aght for," declares Mr. Watson in reply to our request for a few episodes in his fifty years' gamekeeping. His churchwarden is replenished from an old brass tobacco box lying on a slab in the corner. Lit by a splinter, blue wreaths ascend as he throws himself into his high-backed chair and re-crosses his tightly-breeched legs with the agility of youth.

To illustrate first that a gamekeeper's lot is not of the happiest, we are cited the Marsden Moor tragedy of September 9, 1903, and of one at Sherburn, near Scarborough, Nov. 25, 1904. The first experience which flashes across his mind is an exciting race he and a fellow-keeper had early one morning in the shooting season. Men were prowling the moors; keepers were suspicious and gave chase. Only one out of the gang, however, was run down. He was in sheep's clothing. Another, whom the pursuers could positively swear to, they traced to a lonely farm, where was found the farmer busily milking. He, asked had he seen or heard anything unusual about the premises, replied in the negative. However, with his permission, a search was made, with the result that a two-barrelled gun—which the farmer could not account for—was found. Further exploration failed to "put up" the "hare" from his "seat;" nevertheless, the suspected man was summoned, and

mulcted in a fine. Afterwards the poacher admitted having been deeply buried in the hay in the barn, " an' 'e booath 'eeard an' felt 'em lompin' ower 'im." When the keeper had left he came out, and dislodging a slate in the roof, climbed through and made good his escape unperceived.

Another time, Mr. Watson tells us, he was taking a daily round when, as was often the case, he discovered snares in the ling. He went home to await nightfall, suspecting that the poacher would return in darkness to learn the result. Night was far advanced when the keeper went again to the snares. A hollow quite near afforded convenient cover. He sat hour after hour, divested of boots, and eagerly scanning the dark surface of the heath. He must keep absolutely still and silent: he dare not even indulge in his favourite pipe. " Patience is a virtue, and hath her reward." Towards dawn, when some haze hung over the moor, he saw a figure advancing stealthily. It was the man he had expected. The poacher was stooping to examine the snares, when a slight sound behind him caused him to hesitate. Then, as he seemed to sniff danger, he made off, with the bootless keeper in hot pursuit. It is not easy to say who would have been victorious had the race continued; the poacher fell and broke his ankle. The game was up. The keeper assisted the man home, and to bed; later, he answered the summons by going to Court on crutches.

Mr. Watson and family were before their peat fire one night in the autumn of 1864 when a chubby but thinly-clad girl entered, and appealing to Mrs. Watson, said: " If yo' pleeas mi mother whants ta kno' if yo'll bi sa gooid es ta 'em 'er this 'ankerchy wi' yo'r masheen ?"

The late hour and the nature of the errand roused their suspicions. Being asked if her father was at home, with unsuspecting child-like simplicity she answered " Eea ! "

The experienced gamekeeper was convinced the whole thing was a ruse to ascertain if he was indoors. The child's father was known to be a notorious poacher. Mr. Watson proved equal to the occasion. His plans were at once drawn and acted upon. In the presence of the child he feigned weariness and said he would retire, feeling " fairly done up." Divesting himself of coat, waistcoat and boots, and procuring a light, he bade the household and the little one " gooid neet," and went up the stairs seemingly drowsy. Shortly after, the child left with her handkerchief; but the sound of her clogs had barely died away before the keeper bounded downstairs, very much awake. Boots

were quickly re-laced, leggings adjusted, overcoat put on, and in a few moments he was lost in the outer darkness. Drizzling rain fell, but nothing would have stopped the keeper going to inspect snares. One, he found, had done its work effectively; a grouse lay strangled amongst the ling. The keeper squatted near, and curled himself up like a hedgehog to await developments. And not a minute too soon, for his trained ears now detected a slow approaching tread. He dared scarcely breathe, so exceedingly calm was the night. A few paces only now lay between the keeper and the oncoming figure. The lifeless bird was on the point of being unfettered when Mr. Watson, then quick and nimble, pounced upon the poacher, who by the subtle handkerchief trick meant to hoodwink him. For this offence the magistrate (Col. Edwards, the owner of the moors, retired from the bench during the hearing of the case) committed him to prison for six months, and said that when the sentence had expired he would be asked to find sureties, himself in £20, and two bonds of £10 each, or one of £20, to keep from poaching for two years. If the sureties were not forthcoming, he would be kept in prison a year longer. Two previous convictions for poaching were recorded against him, in 1858 and 1859, for which he served terms of three months respectively.

An episode of a still more sensational character was yet to be told.

It was during the early sixties, one fine September morning, when Mr. Watson, a fellow-keeper named John Greenwood (mentioned in our Luddenden Dean list), better known as "Old Jooanty," and a young gentleman were out sniping on Midgley Moor. They noticed what appeared from Bare Clough Head to be a company of ling gatherers making towards them from White Hill. As they drew nearer, however, the three discovered their business was not quite so innocent. They numbered twenty-eight or thirty; more than half of them had firearms, and the rest shouldered either muck-rake, hay-fork, besom, or cudgel. To intensify matters the gang had blackened faces and peculiar clothing. The young gentleman, whom Mr. Watson considered his charge, was advised to "make tracks" off the moor to some place of safety lest mischief befel him, which advice was speedily acted upon. Of the two left to do battle with the enemy, Mr. Watson confesses Greenwood was the most fearless. To be faithful to duty there was no alternative but to face the foe. A preliminary salute from a number of the enemy's muzzle-loaders cut the air, rousing "Old Jooanty's" ire. He drew near to the Philistines;

his colleague following gingerly some distance in the rear. Still the rebels advanced, and their voices could now be heard.

"Yer thi," said Jooanty, "dus ta 'eear whaat they say? Some on 'em 's callin' aght to us; an' ses if we com' another yard they'll let fly at us."

"Hi! an' they meean it too," replied the other, feeling that for the time being these people were masters of the situation, and that to face such odds was the essence of folly. "Jooanty" scouted the idea of retreat, and advanced until an echoing bang! bang!! bang!!! and shot whistled overhead. This brought him to an abrupt stop. Even "Jooanty's" spirit was quelled, and the two now thought it prudent to retire. What to do next was discussed in ambush. It was approaching noon and time was precious. They could not afford to return home on the Warley side of the stream owing to the distance. Ultimately they agreed to round on the "black niggers" and hunt up reinforcements on Crimsworth hill-side.

The factory bells were summoning hands back to work after dinner when the keepers again scaled the moorland leading to the site of battle. With them were fourteen recruits—all they could muster—armed after the fashion of the enemy. On they marched in the hope that their appearance would strike terror into the villains. At sight of the oncoming force the enemy arose and deployed for combat.

"Jooanty," warrior-like, led his men on, the while signalling the foe to desist. They retorted by levelling guns, indicating that nothing would induce them to surrender, nor suspend hostilities. Shots were exchanged at long range, and it was soon plain that "Jooanty" and his little squad were powerless to cope with these desperadoes and that had they continued blood would have been shed. Hence Mr. Watson advised a withdrawal.

"We wer' glad an' fein ta skedaddle, en sharply too," he tells us. It was at this juncture, he thinks, that his coat-laps were riddled with pellets. Others in the flight received slight bruises, but no one was seriously injured. From now throughout the day the lawless regiment had full liberty, and at night, to the mortification of the keepers in covert looking on, marched over High Brown Knowl, thence across Cock Hill, disappearing Lancashire way, whence Mr. Watson believed they came.

The affair blew over, nothing whatsoever coming of it. Our venerable friend adds:—

"Ther's nooan sich carryin's on nah; wi liv' i' mooar peeaceable

times, tho' mind yo'! wi've nah an' then a toffish custumer er two ta deeal wi' yet; but nowt like es ther' wor i' them days."

* * * * * *

Time wags and the old keeper's assertion, "If yo' stop whol aw finish all th' tales aw could tell yo', yo'll never get ta Haworth Parish ta-day," rings in our ears.

Disputed Footpath.

No doubt he could entertain us for hours; he could tell of moorland fires with which he has had to battle—some caused by accident, others maliciously ignited; of twice journeying up to London, the last time in 1898, when he spent eleven days waiting to give evidence in the Castle Carr right-of-way case (referred to in our "glimpse" at Luddenden Dean). It came off on March 30 of that year, after having hung in the balance since October, 1896, and the decision roused the indignation of some to no small degree. Judge Kekewich took great interest in Mr. Watson's stately figure and homely speech.

It was contended by the defence that the disputed footpath was substituted by one leading past Slade to Height Lodge (wherein are two typical rural bridges), which, to one whose business requires haste, is irritating. Beforetime it stretched in a moderately straight line from Low to Nab-Water—a point in our line of saunter.

We prepare to journey further. Pipes are re-lit and the keeper insists on going "a-gate' ards" with us "op th' moor, as far as th' Fill Belly." The day continues in splendour, giving promise of many more such, and our friend, ere he leaves us, buoys us up by saying there is no likelihood of a break-down just yet. Forsooth, we never were so much concerned about the weather.

A fine type of his calling is Mr. Watson, we soliloquise, after taking leave of him; a "grand old man." We have known him long, and we never saw a frown on his brow.

Warley Moor Rocking Stone.

Standing sentinel-like over Dean Head, westward yonder, is Warley Moor Rocking stone (1350 ft.). Our friend Mr. Watson,* returning home, is unable to give us any information respecting it, but his namesake, the Halifax historian, can. He says:—

*Wm. Watson died July 28, 1906.

Rural Bridges between Slade and Height Lodge.

"On a common, called Saltonstall-moor, is what the country people call the Rocking-stone. The height of this on the west side (which is the highest) is, as I remember, about three yards and a half. It is a large piece of rock, one end of which rests on several stones, between two of which is a pebble of a different grit, seemingly put there for support, and so placed that it could not possibly be taken out without breaking or removing the rocks, so that in all probability they had been laid together by art. It ought to be observed that the stone in question, from the form and position of it, could never be a rocking-stone, though it is always distinguished by that name. The true rocking-stone appeared to me to lie at a small distance from it, thrown off its centre. The other part of this stone is laid upon a kind of pedestal, broad at the bottom, but narrow in the middle; and round this pedestal is a passage, which, from every appearance, seems to have been formed by art, but for what purpose: that is the question."

For answer, Mr. Watson turns to Borlase, who, he says,

"Gives us an account of something of this sort, called in Cornwall and Scilly, Tolman, or hallowed stones, conjecturing that whoever passed through these acquired a kind of holiness, and became more acceptable to God; also that the cavity might be a sanctuary for the offender to fly to; but chiefly, that such were intended and used for introducing proselytes, people under vows, or going to sacrifice, into their more sublime mysteries. But might they not answer another purpose still? In ancient Greece there was a custom of returning oracular answers by a voice from a secret place, without the inquirer seeing who spoke to him. This was to give the greater sanction to what was delivered, as though it was some Deity who spoke. And why should not these artful Druids have practised a juggle of this sort? They were consulted about future events, and they might choose, on certain occasions, to give their answers from these cavities."

"I know not," further observes Watson, "whether the rock basins cut on the Tolman were used on this occasion, but there are a few worked into the Rocking-stone, which help to prove that the Druids used it."

Mr. F. A. Leyland, the Halifax antiquary, speaks of the rock in question thus:—

"In the sheltered glades that once spread their branches over the now barren wastes of Warley, stood the singular Druidical monument—the rocking-stone, for the most part still remaining. The cover of this remain which still rests on its shaly pedestal, is completely honeycombed with deeply-worn basins. After a careful and personal survey of the rocks in the parish of Halifax, we are enabled to say that the remain furnishes the only instance throughout our extensive division of so many basins being crowded together in the same space."

The footpath from Slade to Height Lodge has this redeeming feature, *i.e.*, it leads within a few paces of the Rocking-Stone.

* * * * * *

Sauntering on we now catch a glimpse of Warley Moor Reservoir—Fly Flat, which, when constructed, wiped out the upper length of the aforementioned original path from Low to Nab Water—and a minute later gain the high road, from which we deviated

E

Rocking Stone, Warley Moor.

beyond Lumb Mill. Grouse again flush up and in language seemingly clear request us to retreat, but we turn a deaf ear to their expostulations and stride buoyantly along the iron track laid the length of Fill Belly for the protection of the road from heavy stone traffic. Approaching us is a woman, and there is a mutual recognition. We now call to mind the keeper mentioning a possibility of our meeting a daughter whom he expected before noon.

"My word! yo've had a tidy trudge this mornin'," we remark, by way of greeting, making no pretence to refinement of speech, but adhering to our native twang.

"Eea! but it doesn't seem far when aw can com' across th' moor, as nah, when it's soa vary dry. Av yo' com'd bi th' Slade?"

"We 'av; an' 'ad a good long stop theer too."

"They'll keep a body as long as they con, aw kno'; aw guess they're booath middlin?"

"Aye! th' first class! yo're father's champion. Fancy! 87 year old, wi' all his faculties an' as straight as a pickin'-rod; som' on us 'll 'av alter'd i' shape afooar we've rock'n sooa monny mile-stooans."

"Yond's 'im, isn't it, gooin in at th' fold top?"

"Aye, he *wod* com' gate'ards wi' us as far as th' Fill Belly. But we mooant detain yo'; yo'll be o'pins ta get yo're clooas aght i' this nice druft. Good mornin'!"

"Good mornin'!"

Unconsciously almost, we find ourselves repeating, as we saunter on, this earnest plea of Hartley's:—

"Dooant forget the old folks,
They've done a lot for thee;
Remember tha'd a mother once,
Who nursed thi on her knee,
A father too, who tew'd all day
To make thi what tha art,
An' dooant forget tha owes a debt,
An' strive to pay a part."

Warley Moor Reservoir (Fly Flat), from West.

CHAPTER VI.

FLY FLAT: PAST AND PRESENT.

Now we command a goodly view of Fly Flat Reservoir, with Cock Hill moor rising in the background. How shallow the water looks; so low that little islands of black heath protrude above its surface, seemingly making it possible to hop, from one to another, to the embankment on the far side. Half-a-mile distant these projecting mounds appear speckled. We focus our telescope upon them and watch with interest a few black-headed gulls—a large family of which make Fly Flat their habitation from year to year. Some basking in the sunshine, others uttering a wailful note, are gracefully cleaving the air. Round the reservoir are bunches of ling tied at short intervals along the top of the iron fencing to the Corporation territory. These tufts serve as danger signals to grouse in low flight. Those little stacks of root on the beach have been gathered from the deep peat fissures, now the reservoir is low, which is evidence that at one time this was a forest. Authorities tell us the trees were white birch. "An' rare an' gooid firewood it is," declare gleaners of the fuel, "specially to stick under th' uven o' th' bakin' day."

Much as we love the country and fresh air, we do not envy the man in charge of the reservoir. Each morning duty calls him to inspect and try the valves, etc. This from Height Lodge means a trudge of one and-a-half miles over the bleakest of moorland, and often in weather far less congenial than the present fine spell; in fact:—

Whether it rains or whether it snows,
Whether it freeze or whether it thaws,
Whether it's calm or whether it blows;
Whether it's cold or whether it's hot,
He weathers the weather, whether or not.

We remember once traversing that self-same track, and observing a rugged stone bearing this inscription:—

"A sinner saved by grace."

Mr. Watson, our friend the keeper, is of opinion that the rough carving was the work of a navvy, since he remembers first seeing it directly after the reservoir was completed. We raise our telescope westwards, and perceive Boulsworth peeping over the head of Cock Hill, eight miles away as the crow flies, and crowned with a cluster of strangely weather-worn rocks. Here, at Near New Fly, where the Halifax Corporation warn us against trespassing, a pack-horse road formerly entered the moor to Luddenden Dean. This also the reservoir obliterated. Old people tell us it was no uncommon sight when they were children to see twenty or thirty galloways—many piebald—with tinkling bells, and panniers laden with lime, file down the moor.

But the forenoon is slipping away, and we must stride on. For three-quarters of a mile forward the road is practically level, skirted on the left by a few farms, a ruin,—Old Fly,—and one or two deserted cottages adjoining a beer-shop—Delvers' Arms.

What a hive of industry Fly was less than forty years ago! Even comparatively young people remember the time when fifteen quarries were in full swing in the neighbourhood, employing more than three hundred men and requiring between fifty and sixty horses. It seems incredible, so marked is the change. We look round and wonder where men and horses came from. At present there are two small quarries in operation, together employing five men. From one of these quarries we hear the ring of tools in passing. As to the population in the vicinity just three couples remain, including revered friends, upon whom we are about to call.

By diligent research aforetime we have ascertained that during this wave of prosperity three fatal accidents occurred. Strange to say each unfortunate person bore the christian name John. The first was John Holgate, whose horse "Jerry," on May 4, 1860, tripped him in the delph-gate, and the loaded cart ran over him. The second, John Dawson, who was struck by a flying stone in a blasting operation on October 13, 1864. The third, John Whitaker, who was killed instantly on February 6, 1869, by a stone, loosened by thaw after strong frost, and weighing about fifteen cwts., falling upon him.

CHAPTER VII.

SAM AND BETTY—THEIR REMINISCENCES.

As we approach Far New Fly, (/\ 1418-3) the wicket-gate is thrown open, and we are greeted by one of the best natured souls we know.

"Good mornin' to yo'!"

"Good mornin', Betty!"

"Aw said it wer yo' as sooin as yo' com' i' th' seet t'other side o' Squires. Ahr Sam said it worn't, an' 'e wod o' threeap'd me aght on't, but aw 'firm'd it dahn it wer' yo. Yo' 'appen 'avn't seen owt ov a stirk as yo've com' on th' rooad, av yo'?"

"We 'avn't, Betty. 'Av yo' lost one?"

"Now, *we* 'avn't lost one, but a man thro' Foorside call'd abaht hawf-an-hahr sin seekin' one—a leet-rooan'd 'n. Nub'dy seems ta a' seen it i' th' rooad onywheer, sooa'e thowt it 'ad 'appen made across th' moor ta th' Fly 'ere; but we 'avn't seen owt on't; vary likely it's whandered somewheear Den'ome way. Th' châp look'd bother'd a gooid bit, but aw advised 'im ta make 'issel content abaht it; it'll'd turn up all reyt. Aw guess yo're middlin?"

"We are, thank yo', are yo' th' same?"

"Well, nobbut sooa; Ee's like an old rake et's used op wi' 'aytime; th' rumatic i' this reyt arm payns me a gooid bit; but ther's vary oft summat wrang wi' th' system, mooar or less."

"That's vary true, Betty."

> "If all our life were one broad glare
>   Of sunlight, clear, unclouded;
> If all our path were smooth and fair,
>   By no soft gloom enshrouded;
> If all life's flowers were fully blown.
>   Without the sweets unfolding,
> And happiness were rudely thrown
>   On hands too weak for holding—
> Should we not miss the twilight hours,
>   The gentle haze and sadness?
> Should we not long for storms and showers
>   To break the constant gladness?"

"It's a long time sin aw heeard yo' recite afooar. Them's grand words an' true un's an' all yo've just repeated. Ahr Maker kno's whaats' best for us fooaks, doesn't He?" Aways wi yo forrard inta th' 'aase, whol aw 'av a word wi' Stan'orth; yo'll find ahr Sam in; 'e's just dun milkin', aw think, bi th' clomp ov 'is clogs dahn i' th' mistel. Aw's' bi on in a minute or two an' yo's 'av' a bite o' summat t' eyt befooar yo' gooa ony further."

At Betty's bidding we step into the house; indeed we should feel strange lingering on the threshold. Betty's, to us, is home.

No Sam is visible, but in regions below and above the uproar of much poultry we hear the clatter of his clogs, and presently his tall form appears.

"Good mornin', Samson!"

"Hallow! is it yo'? Aw thowt aw'd heeard a fraysh fooit com' in. Good mornin!"

"It's nobbut us, yo' see."

"Nobbut! Aw call yo' som'dy o' consequence. It worn't yo' at wer comin' on th' other side o' Squires abaht ten minits sin, wor it?"

"Vary likely; we've bin stopped lookin' rahnd a bit."

"Then aw've lost. Aw'd a bit ov a tiff wi' th' wife as ta whether it wer' yo' er net; shoo stuck in't shoo wer reyt. 'Av yo' seen owt on her?"

"We've just met her on bi th' watterin' trough. Shoo said shoo'd be back in a minit or two; she whanted ta 'av a word wi' Stan'orth."

"Oh, it's William, et's fettlin' a tooathry slate-st'ns on th' delph-hill et shoo's whantin' ta see. Ther's a partic'lar friend o' her's gooan off sudden-like dahn Oxenhope way, an' shoo'll be axin' 'im when th' funeral is; shoo'll mooast likely be bid, an' shoo's hooapin' et it willn't be o' Wednesday: th' day she gooas to Halifax wi' th' butter an' eggs. An' ther's been a weddin' an' all dahn i' their quarter et shoo's interested in; shoo'll vary likely mention that to 'im as well, tho' aw dooan't think shoo'll make ony inquiries es to whaat th' bride—that's whaat yo'll call th' woman, aw suppooas?—'ad on; shoo'll be th' mooast con-sarned es ta whether they're yequally yooaked together or net."

"An' es like es net shoo'll awther tak' er send 'em a pund o' butter an' a shillin'orth o' eggs for a weddin' present," we put in.

"Shoo *might*, es yo say, bi back in a minit or two, seein' et shoo's seen yo' com', or it *might* bi longer. But aw'll just whash mi 'ands an' fill th' kettle, then th' watter'll be comin' on; shoo must o' taen th' ladin-tin wi' 'er!"

" Then yo' arn't short o' watter i th' spite of it net 'avin' raain'd all this time ? "

" Now, that run et th' end o' th' 'aase keeps up well ; of cooarse, if this druft continnys, it'll get thinner, but th' well's never bin dry sin th' day we com' ta th' spot thirty year sin."

A stream of vapour pours from the kettle hanging on the reckon as Betty's parting words with Stan'orth come floating on the breeze. Fortunately the time of the interment suits her convenience, and the wedding arrangements meet with her approval.

The open Bible—symbol of yesterday's thoughts—lies on the table, and it is gently removed. Tea mashed, we urge the use of pint jugs, since we must "av a bite o' summat ta eyt;" but the best crockery is brought from the oak cupboard in the corner. Protestations are futile ; we only receive for answer " Yo' dooan't com' every day fooaks," and "draw up ta sich as E 'av." " Ahr Sam," we are pleased, decides to join us, and " 'av an odd peck, mooar fer th' sake o' th' cumpany." He draws up his customary chair—a massive piece of oak, a typical model of that our mothers used to suddenly place us in when—when—when quite little toddlers, only minus the two finger-holes at the back, and one, saucer-size, in the seat.

" Draw up ta sich as E 'av," indeed. What lack we ? Good wholesome home-made bread, rich cream and fresh butter—" th' fat o' Fly land,"—with eggs direct from the manufacturers. No necessity for an apology, surely. But then the remark is characteristic of Betty.

Thirty years—half man's allotted span almost—spent at an altitude of 1,418 feet, six miles from the nearest town (Halifax), and two-and-a-half from the nearest village (Wainstalls), means incalculable privations, and our friends Sam and Betty can relate many such. Betty's shopping expeditions on numerous occasions have only been accomplished under fearful difficulties. She recalls times when returning from the stores, shoulders laden pannier-fashion, having to make headway over Knowl Hill in the teeth of a terrific wind, she has found it necessary to crawl on all-fours for a considerable distance, and sometimes with one or both hands full. We have often seen her burdened with loads suited only for Balaam's friend ; certainly never for woman. This was invariably due to her willingness to oblige others. Once we remember being here, just prior to her departure to Wainstalls Co-op. Her nearest neighbour—a native of Bradford—called and enquired : "Ya'r barn ta Cou-op, bean't ya ? bring me a paand o' lard en tow pennorth o' dried eeast, will ya' ?

an' E meean't forget th' bacca—fower arnces ; yar owd mon's nearly famish'd ; 'e 'asn't 'ad a pipe o' three daas. Ya' weean't bi bock till 7 o'clock ? Well, neear eed ; it weean't bi th' first time E'v 'ad ta baake i' th' lamp leet."

Well on her road, another intercepts her and desires her to call at Mrs. Smith's for a pair of clogs " thro Charles, " a third wants " a bunch o' rheubob an' two pund o' apples," should she meet with a greengrocer. We see a fourth reclining over a farm-yard gate, and hear the solicitation :

" It's a grand day, Betty ! Aw been lookin' aght for yo ever sin nooin. Yo're makin' for th' Co-op, aw reckon ? We 'avn't a spooinful o' suegar i' th' 'aas ; wod ya mind bringing me an odd pund, just to put me on whol ta-morn, an' two pund o' suet, if th' mayt's com' ; an' yo'll ax Walter to change theease checks, willn't yo ?—ther's five paands' 'orth."

To stem this tide our friend years ago deemed it expedient to make some restriction, and it was mutually agreed that henceforth she should be recompensed ; the "checks" for goods brought "fro' th' Co-op." should be hers. More facilities are afforded to-day. Lately, a local farmer established (or purchased) a milk-round in Halifax, and travelling daily accepted these commissions, much to the relief of Betty, whose age, though somewhat indefinite, cannot be less than seventy-six, according to her own reckoning.*

* * * * * *

Our friends recall many memorable snow-storms, one in particular: Shortly after noon, many years ago, snow fell thick and fast, and was driven by a piercing east wind. The storm continued through the night. In its early stages a woman, one Susy Greenwood, living at Spring Mill, less than a mile-and-a-half away, called " just for a tooathry minutes, wol th' storm 'bated," but it was more than a week before she could proceed home. The morning following the blast it was found the drifts nearly covered the house. Doors and windows were blocked, and only a tiny opening near a bedroom lattice was left. The occupants were not greatly disconcerted by such sharp changes in the weather, since, taught by long experience :—

All was safely gathered in
Ere the winter storm begin.

An out-building had little room for more, for it was piled to the roof

*Betty's birth certificate was obtained to qualify her for the old-age pension, and it shows she was born Jan. 27, 1827, being christened Elizabeth Hindle.

with coal, coke, and peat. The "paraffin man" had recently paid his monthly visit and left double the usual quantity; the provender cart, in the nick of time only, had also brought its load of food for live-stock, as well as goods for the household. A flitch of bacon and a ham hung from the ceiling, and what was of greatest importance, from Sam's point of view, was a store of tobacco, sufficient to last a pretty lengthy siege.

Two days after, Sam set about digging a cave in the snow. A three-legged table, the identical one we have feet under, was placed therein, laden with good things, and around it were seats arranged for four—Sam, Betty, their daughter Betsy, and the imprisoned neighbour, Mrs. Greenwood. When about to partake of the viands spread, Betty stood at the "door" and gave a hearty invitation to all within sound of her voice, and a dark figure just then appeared over the riggin of the snow-house and made reply "Aw'm comin'!" Little did she count on any from the outer world being within earshot, and certainly not Stan'orth, their old friend from Oxenhope, who had "scratted up th' edge just ta see if they were all alive at th' Fly." Another chair was introduced into the snow circle, and the five immensely enjoyed the novel experience.

* * * * * *

No one for miles around, it is safe to say, is better known or more highly esteemed than Betty—Mrs. Sunderland, to give her what she would call her "Sunday name." Few, however, identify her by this. Inquire for "Betty o' th' Fly," and the least urchin living within three miles will direct you. It will come as a surprise to some of her nearest neighbours even to learn that "Betty" is not her christian name, but Elizabeth, which, she explains her father disliked, preferring "Betty." She was well advanced in life and had twice appeared at the altar before her true name was revealed to her.

If we mention Parliament's present dealings with half-timers we rouse Betty's ire. She declares that before she had attained to the age children are now permitted to work she had earned a little fortune, only she never had a pay-day. Her parents were hand-loom weavers and oat-cake bakers. At the age of four she wound bobbins for them; at eight she had the management of a loom; at eleven we see her on certain days tramping the outlying district round Bents Side, Warcock Hill, Cliviger, in Lancashire, where she was born and "pooatering out" (Betty's term for delivering) to customers havercakes. In her teens for a short spell we find her installed as toll-keeper at Stiperden, about a mile from home,

which necessitated much night work, whereof she relates more than one unpleasant experience. In addition to this she had the " caring " of little ones and farm duties. Next she was in service, and finally came the event of a woman's life—marriage. Between fifty and sixty years she has had cattle in her keeping. The points of a cow she sums up in lines we have often heard her repeat :—

" She's but short in her face, fine in her horn ;
She'll quickly get fat, without cake or corn ;
She's clean in her jaws, she's full in her chine ;
Heavy in flank, and wide in her loin,
Broad in her ribs, long in her rump,
Straight, and flat back, with never a hump ;
She's wide in her hips, calm in her eyes,
Broad in her shoulders, thick in her thighs ;
Light in her neck, small but her tail ;
Broad in her breast, good at her pail ;
Fine in her bone, silky of skin,
Greasy without, all soundness within."

Yes, throughout each chapter of the life of our friend Betty the dominant notes are labour—downright honest labour—and love. " Wark'll 'urt nubdy, fooaks," she tells us, " if yo've nobbut 'ealth an' strength ta do it." No great heroine, perhaps, as heroines go, but how applicable the lines :—

"The roughened hands that never shirked,
The plain, brown hands, that planned and worked,
They clasped each cross, with trust and prayer,
And burdens bore more than their share ;
Aye, ugly, coarse, unlovely quite,
They look to our defective sight,
But to their mission dutiful,
In God's eyes they are beautiful."

Her trust in Providence is superb,—beautiful.

" She's read the Psalms of David for nearly eighty years,
They've been her staff and comfort, and calmed life's many fears."

And often she finds comfort to her soul in her favourite hymn (375 in Sankey's), which she sings with touching pathos :

" When the storms of life are raging,
Tempest wild on sea and land ;
I will seek a place of refuge
In the shadow of God's hand."

" He will hide me where no harm can e'er betide me ;
He will hide me ! safely hide me
In the shadow of His hand."

" So, while here the cross I'm bearing,
Meeting storms and billows wild,
Jesus for my soul is caring,
Nought can harm His father's child."
" He will hide me, &c."

* * * * * *

After that substantial " tuck-in," surely we shall have no further " call " (Betty's term for appetite) till the day is far spent; leastwise this is our verdict as we measure our height under the bread-creel, give a tug at our vests, and request our bill. Our friends' looks warn us from pressing the point. An expression of thanks, even, is immediately stifled.

" Yo're as welcome as th' flaars i' May," Betty assures us.

" An' it 'll sooin bi aght nah," observes " Ahr Sam." " Let's see! it's getten whaat, th' 29th ? "

" Twenty-ninth ! "

" Then yo're fer orf ? " " Well, yo've little time bi' th' 'and, fer th' gate yo've set ta travel. It's nah on th' strooak ov eleven, aw see bi th' old-cased clock; but then it's cloise on hawf-an-hahr fast bi Calvert's whew."

" Aw declare it gooas o' wheels ! " interposes Betty.

" My opinion o' th' weather ? Accooardin' to them delph-mates o' mine et went on a bit sin ther's nooa raain i' th' seet yet. They say th' glass 's well up; they tapped it afooar they coom ta ther wark, an' it wodn't budge a 'air's breadth; an' it wer' fair on fair."

Sent off with " Ahr Sam's " best wishes for a fine day and " a grand aght altogether," we again saunter on, accompanied by Betty as far as Woodcock Hall, that she may complete a tale of vital interest, though when we part her " pooak (sack) isn't awf emty," she says, which translated means, " to be continued in our next." Here a stone, half buried in decayed bent-grass, divides Haworth Parish from what was Warley Township prior to its being taken over by the Halifax Corporation in 1900. We watch our friend round the bend and catch her parting blessing, intermixed with the remark :—

" E'v two or three pooaks E'v never oppen'd yet ! "

CHAPTER VIII.

VIEW FROM NAB HILL—LOST IN COCK HILL SNOWSTORM—OXENHOPE WORTH VALLEY LINE—A DELIGHTFUL CONCERT.

HEATHER-CLAD delph tippings crowning Sawood Hill (Nab Hill, 1,450 feet), remind us of this upland's former glory. Given a clear day, a charming and extensive view is obtained here. Unfortunately, bright as is the morning, distant headlands are hidden in haze. To aid us in describing them let us hark back to June 20, 1897, when the nation commemorated Queen Victoria's reign of sixty years ; then, to quote the clerk's record in the register at Haworth Church, on the Coronation day of Charles II, (April 23, 1661), " heaven and earth conspired to make it glorious." This, our late Queen's Diamond Jubilee day, we elected to spend the sunny hours up here in quietude, " far from the madding crowd," and we were privileged to enjoy the prospect now partially obscured.

Over our left shoulder Stoodley Pike rears its sturdy column on the south-western sky-line ; westward Boulsworth blots out Lancashire's proud eminence—Pendle Hill (1,831 feet)—but we catch a glimpse of it from a point a few hundred yards more eastwards. North-west, and to the right of Jackson's Ridge, we behold the flat summit of Ingleborough (2,373 feet). Veering slightly north are Penygant (2,273 feet) and Fountains Fell (1,944 feet), apparently near neighbours to Ingleborough, yet respectively six and ten miles apart. Still further north, over the hills around Skipton and beyond the Embsay Moor, are Great Whernside (2,310 feet)and Little Whernside (2,384 feet). Nearer we locate Keighley, and beyond, Rombalds Moor, crossing which we see the road (1,247 feet) to Ilkley like a grey cable. Coming nearer is Oakworth village, well nigh hidden in woodland. Through the prominence of its conservatories we single out the home of the late Sir Isaac Holden, Bart. Nearer still is seen what constitutes modern Haworth, Messrs. Merrall's Mills standing out conspicuously. Above is old Haworth, and notwithstanding its being " set on a hill " from our point of vantage, it is wholly hidden, save the church tower and blue roof rising over a clump of trees. Of the moors so dear to the Brontë family, only a remote corner is seen.

Rising to the right of Oxenhope, is Leeming and Sawood (locally "Sa'ard") beautified in the foreground by a sheet of water (Leeming Reservoir) owned by Bradford Corporation. At our feet, as it were, taking a zigzag course across the waste, is the open conduit which conveys water gathered on the moors to Thornton Reservoir.

We recall days, not very many years ago, when bilberries, in season, were plentiful here at Nab Hill. How the then fruitful bushes became so black is a mystery, since they have not suffered fire. On Sam and Betty's authority, "it 'appened all i' one neet," which seems to confirm a belief that they were scorched by lightning. We remember two of us once gathering 13 pints in one day, which we accounted a wonderful achievement; for the tiny fruit bulks exceedingly slowly. Darkness was upon us and our cans were barely full; we would they were up to the brim. On our way home (we then resided at Halifax) we called at Betty's. Fortunately she had just returned from the stores and could supply us with the pound of currants we requested. These made up the deficiency, and, with a thin layer of bilberries on the top, was highly satisfactory to our minds. Arriving home, a neighbour insisted on our selling her a pint of freshly-gathered bilberries, direct from the moor. Here was temptation for a practical joke, and we knew no one we would sooner make its victim. Before her eyes, in the gaslight, we measured out the luscious-looking morsels. "Wo'dn't their Jim enjoy his teah ta-morn 't neet when he coom hooam? That he wod!" And we suppressed a smile. The following morning she declared "them wer' queer bilber yo sell'd mi yusterneet," and we confessed our deceit.

Those were delightful moorland excursions. And how we relished victuals carried six miles and dried by exposure to the sun. And no tea ever tasted so good as that made by old Sarah Ellis, who, with her husband Jacob—a decent and respected couple—occupied the cottage we now see in ruin (see illustration page 81), midway down Nab Hill.

* * * * * *

"A barking dog seldom bites." Hence we march on fearless of the black shepherd's dog "Laddie," advancing up the hill towards us, the while signalling to his master below that strangers are approaching.

Once two little girls (this story is not legend, but literally true) from Cold Edge were on a visit to relatives near Oxenhope, and when passing Nab Water farm here (⩚ 1264-7) two women were stood outside. One greeted the children very cordially, but the other knew them not.

"Whaw! doesn't ta know 'em?" enquired the first, in astonishment.

"Now! who are they?"

"Whaw! tha' caps ma. It's Sarah an' Martha o' Mary's o' John's o' George's o' John's o' Will's o' Tim's at Nan Scar Top."

This was enlightenment; their identity was established.

Here the road sweeps to the right; and some four or five hundred yards further winds to the left. To cut off the elbow we mount steps over the fence and strike a path parallel with the conduit. Two dogs drowned in this water are buried in a field at Withins in Cold Edge. Over their tombstone is this inscription:—

> Here lie the remains of Wallet and Dart,
> Who in their last race made a capital start;
> But, their owners lamented, they never got through it,
> For, alas! they were drowned in Thornton conduit.
>
> These dogs were drowned on March 31, 1891.

We do not, and indeed never did, possess a spark of poetic genius, as is evident in the above lines; but we were foolish enough to comply with the request of one we had a special regard for, and "framed" a verse, and so we fear we must bear the ridicule thereof to the end of our days.

Notwithstanding that on one hand is "New York," a single-decker habitation, and on the other "New Leeds," a cottage long in ruins, we feel a sense of loneliness. One human being only do we see, a woman who, ceasing to spread clothes in the croft, with shaded eyes endeavours to recognize the wayfarers; but we are too far distant apparently. We signal with handkerchief, but there is no response until a nearer view reveals our identity, and vigorous greetings are exchanged as we cross the allotment corner and step again on the road.

Soon we descend Hill House Edge ("Th' Hill 'ous Edge") and land on Cock Hill road, where a mile "stoop" built in the corner of the fence tells us we are nine miles from Halifax, a hand pointing the direction we have come. The Cock Hill road face of the post indicates the way to Hebden Bridge (Halliwell Sutcliffe's "Ludworth") and Keighley (Sutcliffe's "Heathley"), but the mileage is obliterated. Originally, we remember, it read, "To Hebden Bridge, 6 miles," "To Keighley, 5 miles."

Cock Hill.—Lost in a Snowstorm.

Glancing up towards Cock Hill Moor—dreaded in winter by drivers and frequented in summer for health-giving breezes—our minds wander back to that winter's night when Benjamin Foster lost his life. Returning

home to Denholme from Crimsworth, horse and cart laden with pieces, he was overtaken by a snow-storm. With benumbed hands he held on behind the cart for aid and shelter, trusting to the instinct of " Jumper," his horse, to pilot him across the moor. Alas! horse and cart were precipitated into a deep morass. With fractured knee, presumably the result of a fall in a battle with death, the poor fellow was found the following day. He had strayed a mile from the road, having gone in the direction of Fly where, it was thought, he saw lights. His corpse was covered with snow. Lying across his breast was his dog " Shep," extremely weak, but kindly treatment brought it round, and it lived four years longer.

It has been the writer's privilege to see a painting of this faithful dog. " Jumper " also lived some years, and travelled many times by the scene of his calamitous experience. The story is told on a tombstone in the old burial-ground of Denholme Wesleyan Chapel :—

> To the memory of Benjamin, the son of Matthew and Hannah Foster, of Denholme, who lost his life on Cockhill through the inclemency of the weather, February 4th, 1831, aged 22 years.
>
> Say, sprightly youth, dost thou on life presume,
> Observe the date, and tremble at this tomb,
> To health, nor strength, nor youthful vigour trust,
> Behold! here, death hath laid them in the dust.

Our photograph gives a vivid impression of the exposed road over Cock Hill moor (/\ 1424-8). Quotations from Emily Brontë's *Wuthering Heights* and Halliwell Sutcliffe's *Man of the Moors* explain the presence of the " stoups." In Chapter III of the former novel we read :—

" I had remarked on one side of the road at intervals of six or seven yards, a line of upright stones continued through the whole length of the barren; these were erected and daubed with lime on purpose to serve as guides in the dark, and also when a fall of snow like the present confounded the deep swamps on either hand with the firmer path; but, excepting a dirty spot pointing up here and there, all trace of their existence had vanished, and my companion found it necessary to warn me frequently to steer to the right or left, when I imagined I was following correctly the windings of the road."

Sutcliffe, in his work, introduces Chapter X with :—

" Between Marshcotes (Haworth) and Cranshaw (Oxenhope) the highroad runs for a mile and a half. From Cranshaw to Ludworth in Lancashire is a very good six. The hill rises sharp after you pass Cran-

Cottage Ruin, Nab Hill.

F

shaw Church and the wild, wind-swept burial ground ; and well towards the top, soon as you gain the open moor, a grim line of " stoups " guards the right hand of the way. It is an eerie road to travel, especially if night has fallen and brought you no company. The stoups, huge blocks of millstone-grit, whitewashed at the base, blackened at the top, seem to stand out from the darkness, to move towards you almost. Year after year they have stood there, pointing the way to travellers : if snow be thick on the highway, their black crowns show clear against the white ; if the moor lie black, their white bodies point the way of safety."

Once in a saunter over Cock Hill from Hebden Bridge to Oxenhope, we counted the whitewashed " stoups," and, accepting nothing in our reckoning save whole posts or pillars (there are other objects " daubed with lime "), found they totalled 185—179 on the left-hand and 6 on the right.

Oxenhope.

Crossing Cock Hill road, we proceed down a rough-bedded lane leading us past the little cosily-situated church of Oxenhope, founded by a Rev. Joseph Brett Grant—Charlotte Brontë's Donne in *Shirley*. It is said he begged practically the whole of the £1,300 it cost to build, and the novelist intimates he wore his shoes to the uppers in tramping the country to that end. The Rev. W. H. Gunyon is the present vicar.

From a little book entitled *The Wild Moor*, written by a Rev. James Whalley, curate of Cross-Stone, Todmorden, and published in 1869, we cull this quotation, which has reference to the church here :—

> " Nothing could have been more admirably chosen than the present site, embracing everything which either taste or convenience requires. The church stands upon an eminence overlooking the little hamlet, and commanding an extensive prospect of the surrounding country. The general outline of the building is in strict harmony with the scenery, and reminds us more of a structure of long bygone times than one of modern days. There is something quite unique in the whole design—something peculiarly suited to the circumstances of the locality. Though the style be adapted to and may be admired for this immediate district, the church will not bear to be made a model for too enlarged imitation. From whatever point of view it be looked at, there is a picturesqueness of effect, and antiquity of appearance about it, for which the architect deserves much commendation. The building is in the very severest style of Anglo-Norman architecture."

The church was consecrated Oct. 11, 1849, and dedicated to St. Mary the Virgin, the Bishop of Ripon preaching on the occasion from Psalm cxxii., 1. To celebrate its jubilee in 1899, Mr. Wilkinson Whitham, Moorhouse, Oxenhope, defrayed the cost of six bells, which were placed in the

"STOOPS," COCK HILL MOOR LOOKING TOWARDS OXENHOPE.
(*Photo by W. Edmondson, Haworth*).

Oxenhope Church.

square tower, an erection apparently much out of proportion to the church. The door is slightly ajar, and stepping up the pavement spanning the small God's acre—so much in harmony with the little edifice—we doff our caps and enter. How very dark it seems ; while we are seated, though, light appears to break through the loophole windows, and these lines occur to us :—

> " Lo ! God is here ! let us adore,
> And own how dreadful is this place ;
> Let all within us feel His power,
> And silent bow before His face ;
> Who know His power, His grace who prove,
> Serve Him with awe, with reverent love."

* * * * * *

With feelings of thankfulness for this side-glimpse and the rest, we journey on. Now we enter Oxenhope, distinguished by an Upper and Lower Town. Two cottages, dignified a street, perpetuate the name of the founder of the Church. Round the first bend near the National School a post points the way " To Stanbury," along a good road to our left (Shaw Lane), which mounts over Haworth Moor ; beyond, its descent becomes exceedingly rough and narrow, with an ugly rise at the finish. Formerly this latter section was the pack-horse route from Stanbury to Halifax. On our map it is named " Water Head-lane," and most appropriately. To vehicles it seems impassable because of its uneven and rocky bed. Though we hope presently to pass through Stanbury, on this trip we choose the more circuitous route, through Upper Town. As we saunter along there falls on our ears the " Glory Song," and we are tempted to peer through an open door. A mother, with baby reclining at her breast, sweetly sings, keeping time with the rocker :

> " When all my labours and trials are o'er,
> And I am safe on that beautiful shore,
> Just to be near the dear Lord I adore,
> Will through the ages be glory for me."

No doubt she feels it, for every word is given expression. To whom are they more applicable than a mother ? we ask ourselves.

We turn aside to view the commodious premises of the Wesleyans. On the walls of the Sunday School, erected, we observe, in the Queen's Jubilee, 1897, is a string of names and initials which we impose upon ourselves the task of counting—twenty-four names, fifty-four initials. Apprehending their significance we think of the Master's injunction in Matt. 6. Next moment thought counsels us to " judge not, that

Oxenhope, from North.

ye be not judged," so after admiring the exterior of the chapel, built in 1890, we move on to where four roads meet and a post directs us to Keighley, Denholme, Hebden Bridge and Haworth.

Worth Valley Line.

We take the Haworth road until near Oxenhope Station, where we strike a path to our right and follow the stream—Bridgehouse Beck. We linger a few minutes while a five-coach train is being drawn from a siding and backed to the platform. A handful of passengers take their seats, the engine's shrill whistle sounds, and next moment "puffer" and carriages disappear round a curve. In a trice also vanishes the solitary servant on duty, and the station is as tranquil as a graveyard, if we discard two individuals loitering near the weigh office, and a nigger-like visage bobbing above the side of a truck and tilting coal into a cart alongside.

Tradition says that when the first train coughed its way into this terminus (April 13, 1867), as a remedy for its sufferings an old woman prescribed "a peggy-tub o' draff an' mayl;" it had had a terrible struggle from Keighley with the directors aboard, once, if not oftener, having actually to run down to Keighley for a re-start. We have also heard that the booking office at Damems was once put on a dray, in mistake for a hen-house; and it is on record that the plan of the line was swallowed by a cow! "Bill o' th' Hoylus End"* tells "*Th' history o' Haworth Railway*" in these lines:—

"They had a meeting th' other neet,
Fair o' th' top o' Wuthering Street,
To see what things they'd got complete
Concerning Haworth railway.

Wen Penny Wabbac tuk the chair
(He lukt to be i' grate despair),
He sez, good foak, are yo' aware
Wat's happened to the railway ?

Wi' persperashun on his bra,
He sez, good foak, I'll tell yo nah;
Owd Blue Beard's nasty wizen'd kaa
Hez swallow'd plan o' th' railway.

Wi' theas remarks poor Wabbac sat,
When Jonny Broth doft off his hat,
His een they blazed—like some wild cat—
Wi' vengeance for the railway.

*William Wright, better known as "Bill o' th' Hoylus End," a born poet, of Keighley, died 21st August, 1897, aged 63. His photograph, which is in Keighley Public Library among local characters, is, we are told, a faithful likeness of the man. Judging from appearances we should not consider him the choicest of companions. He was "quite a Mark Twain in his way," writes one. An old Keighleyite tells us Bill liked to be styled "the Yorkshire Burns;" and it was assumed he had notions of imitating the Scot's bard, for he always wore a Scotch cap. In one thing, forsooth, he was successful, for excesses kept both in the gutter.

He sed, mi blud begins to boil,
To think, 'at we sud work an' toil,
An' even th' cattle cannot thoyle
To let us hev a railway!

On hearing this the Haworth foak
Began to think it wur no joak,
An' wish't 'at greedy kaa ma choak
'At swallow'd plan o' th' railway."

" They gat ower this, an' th' gert job wur done,
An' th' next thing to argue wur wen it sud run;
So thay sent Joe o' Stirks araand wi' his bell,
An' gave him strict orders 'at he wur to tell
'At th' inspector hed been, an' examined it throo,
An' come to th' conclusion 'at th' railway wud do."

But it would appear some had misgivings, since this author also declares :—

" Thar's owd Mally Brook hez been daan to look,
An' shoo's sore disappointed, thay say;
Shoo's omost gone crakt for shoo says it weant act,
For they nobbut can run it one way."

Despite "owd Mally's" assertion, and the multitudinous mishaps which befel the railway in its construction, according to "Bill o' th' Hoylus End's" version, in his wind-up we read :—

" Hasumever thare hopes hes not been in vain,
For th' days arrived an' yonder's train;
An' thaasands o' foak are flocking to th' spot,
Th' gent fra his hall, th' peasant fra his cot;
For all are determined as th' weather is fine,
To hev an excurshun up th' Worth Valley Line.

They land up i' Haworth, an' sports at is seen
Wur niver yet equalled it reign o' the Queen;
Such processions wi' music yo niver saw th' like,
Thay wur bands fra all nashuns (excepting Black Dyke);
An' Sham o' Blue Bills sed he'd kick up a shine,
For na they hed oppen'd th' Worth Valley Line.

Thare wur Jim o' th' Damems, an' Will o' th' Gooise Coit,
An' th' lads at wur in that puddin exploit;
Thare wur Ned daan fra Haworth, an' Ike fra Loin-ends,
Along wi' thair aristocratical friends;
They repaired to Black Bull, of saand puddin to dine,
That day at they oppen'd th' Worth Valley Line.

I' all nooks an' corners an' chimla tops,
Wur floatin' gert banners on mighty big props,
An' stampt on each flag in figures so nice,
Sum an inscripshun, an' sum a device;
But th' nicest i' th' lump at swung on a band,
Wur " Welcum to Haworth fra ivery land."

Yor welcome, yor welcome, all men upon earth,
Yor welcome to the Valley of Worth;
Fra th' Humber to th' Mersey, fra th' Thames daan to th' Tyne,
Yor welcome to travel th' Worth Valley Line."

* * * * * *

Beyond the station we are conducted past an old mill and over a wooden foot-bridge spanning the brook. A path mounts the embankment and across the railway, but we follow the stream o'ershadowed by woodland. Nature is about to assume her "coat of many colours."

> "The sun shines on the open flowers,
> That neath his gaze their lovely charms display;
> Decking with gorgeous tints this earth of ours,
> Gladd'ning man's sight and making nature gay."

Beech and sycamore are, as usual, first in leaf, and the oak, this year of grace at any rate, is likely to outstrip the ash. We may therefore anticipate a droughty summer if there be truth in the rhyme :–

> "If the ash is out before the oak
> The earth is certain to have a soak;
> If the oak is out before the ash,
> The earth will only get a splash."

We note a few bleared specimens of Wordsworth's pet flower, the lesser celandine, of which the Lakeland poet sings :—

> "I have seen thee high, and low,
> Thirty years or more and yet
> 'Twas a face I did not know;
> Thou has now, go where I may,
> Fifty greetings in a day."

As Good reverentially observes :—

> "Not for worlds on worlds in phalanx deep
> Need we to prove a God is here;
> The daisy, fresh from Nature's sleep
> Tells of His hand, in lines as clear
> For, who but He, who arched the skys,
> And pours the day-springs living flood,
> Wondrous alike, in all He tries,
> Could raise the daisy's crimson bud,
> And fling it, unrestrained and free,
> O'er hill and dale and desert sod?
> That man, where'er he walks, may see
> In every step the stamp of God."

A Delightful Concert.

For a short while we sit and listen to a minor chorus of feathered songsters, the principals having relinquished song till evening draws on. One sweet voice chants a pleasing ditty :—

> "Come up, come up, it seems to say,
> Where the topmost branches sway."

In reality the dear little thing is all the time longing to be rid of its audience. Much more at ease, a robin hops boldly to the front, sings a short air in staccato, takes up another position in the tree, and repeats the strain. Twittering swallows flash by, flit in and out of the branches o'er-hanging the stream, at each dip diminishing the cloud of midges dancing over the water. As a grand finale, the instant we vacate our seat, rival cuckoos, in their respective keys, make the vale re-echo with their malicious, mocking calls. We have attended many concerts not nearly so pleasing.

* * * * * *

A winding path leads us a second time across another wooden bridge over the stream, and again two ways present themselves. We reluct-antly forsake that continuing down the dale, and branch to the left. For the third time we are conducted over the brook; this time by a narrow stone foot-bridge, locally known as " Donkey Bridge," "Saddle Bridge," or " Brearley Bridge," the latter, we believe, through people of that name once tenanting the farm we noted a minute ago on our left. Passing beneath the railway, we ascend a shady and pebbly lane and enter fields. Haworth,—old Haworth—that historic world-famed spot, now appears in view three-quarters of a mile ahead; its narrow and steep thoroughfare seems cleared for our reception.

A most pleasant and enjoyable walk that along by the stream from Oxenhope, we muse, as we gain the highway (/|\ 716-3). Besides shortening the distance somewhat from Oxenhope to Haworth, we have avoided a rise of 64 feet.

CHAPTER IX.

HAWORTH—TURBULENT TIMES.

THE cuckoo's call still reaches us, but dies away as we proceed along Sun Street,—the southern end of the village immortalized by the Brontës. We hear the chime of Haworth Church clock and consult our watches for comparison. Twelve-thirty! Usually we have an aversion to meeting an outflow of millhands, but this noon, somehow, the rattling of clogs on the pavement is music to our ears. A well, near the Haworth end of the street, denotes the site of the ducking-stool of olden times. A little further, on our left, is Emmott Hall, one of the oldest buildings in Haworth, and formerly the home of the owners of the bulk of the land in old Haworth. Opposite, and conspicuous on the slope, is Hall Green Baptist Chapel, erected in 1824. The stiff rise from Haworth Station to old Haworth—a matter of 220 feet—is divided into sections. To here—end of Sun Street—it is called Bridge House Lane, and forward, Main Street. Mrs. Gaskell, Charlotte Brontë's biographer, travelling by road from Keighley to Haworth (there was no railway line then), says on reaching this juncture, "The old stone houses are high compared with the width of the street, which makes an abrupt turn before reaching the more level ground at the head of the village, so that the steep aspect of the place in one part is almost like that of a wall."

We saunter up the middle of the narrow street, and so avoid the fragmentary side-path. Once, though, with eyes intent on the sign of the Black Bull suspended over the street, we unconsciously wander thither, and nearly measure our length on the pavement. We are thinking of unruly Patrick Branwell Brontë. He and the Inn are inseparably associated. St. Michael's Church lies in close proximity, as also once did the village stocks, the demolition of which we regret, since to us a church and public-house—and there are five inns within a stone-cast—seem incomplete without the stocks,* particularly here at Haworth, remembering its notorious ruffian days. Would that the relics had been

*Since our saunter, the Stocks have been re-set on the old site.

PATRICK BRANWELL BRONTË'S CHAIR IN THE BLACK BULL,
Still in the possession of the Sugden's, who kept the Inn in Brontë days.
(*Photo by J. J. Stead, Heckmondwike*).

Donkey Bridge, Oxenhope.

preserved and as efficiently protected as those, dated 1697, at Illingworth —a hamlet across the valley north-east of our own village—near to the old prison (erected A.D. 1823), over whose portal is Paul's exhortation: "Let him that stole steal no more, but rather let him labour, working with his hands the thing which is good, that he may have to give to him that needeth." A Mr. John Cotton, of Birmingham, referring in verse to old-time punishments—the stocks, ducking-stool and pillory—says:—

"And corporal punishment no longer thrives,
Save through the cat, which now alone survives;
Each mode has served its turn and played a part
For good or ill with man; but while the bane
Of drunkenness corrupts the nation's heart—
Discrediting our age—methinks the reign
Of stocks, at least, were well revived again."

Haworth Church—Turbulent Times.

We mount seven broad steps (opposite /\ 779-0) at the east end of the church, and observe the figures of St. Michael and St. Gabriel looking down upon us from high pedestals. Passing through a semi-circular gate-way we enter the churchyard and saunter up the flagged footpath, which is public. On each hand are iron rails dividing two portions of the ground. A subtle influence seems to hang about us. First thoughts take us back to the time when, at the death of the Rev. James Charnock (the Haworth Church register states that he died May 25, and was buried May 31, 1819, aged "57 and three-quarters"), the Rev. Patrick Brontë was appointed incumbent of Haworth by the Vicar of Bradford. The Vicar's choice was opposed by the trustees; his right of patronage they disputed, since the funds from which the clergyman's stipend mainly proceeds are vested in the hands of the trustees, who have the power to withhold them if a nominee is sent of whom they disapprove. Mr. Brontë was told by those assuming authority that to himself personally they had no objection, but as the nominee of the Vicar he would not be received. He retired, saying that if he could not come with the approval of the parish his ministry could not be useful. A Mr. Redhead, who had taken duty during the illness of Mr. Charnock, and who was well liked, was next chosen. But he also was rejected. Mr. Brontë said Mr. Redhead was so opposed that after only three weeks' possession he was compelled to retire. Mrs. Gaskell tells the story as related by two survivors. "The first Sunday he preached Haworth Church was full; most of the people wore the wooden clogs

Old Haworth, from South-east.

of the district. While Mr. Redhead was reading the lesson the congregation began to leave, making as much noise as they could with clattering and clumping of clogs. Mr. Redhead and clerk were soon the only pair left to continue the service. This was bad enough, but the next Sunday was worse. Again the church was packed, not to the aisles, as before, and during the lesson a man rode in astride an ass, with face turned towards the tail, and as many old hats on his head as he could carry. He urged the beast down the aisle, and the screams, cries and laughter drowned Mr. Redhead's voice, and he retired during the uproar. Hitherto they had not proceeded to anything like personal violence; but on the third Sunday they must have been greatly irritated at seeing Mr. Redhead, determined to be brave, ride up the village street accompanied by several gentlemen from Bradford. They put their horses up at the Black Bull, the inn close to, and went into the church. People followed, accompanied by a sweep they had copiously plied with drink. They reared him before the reading desk, and with blackened face he nodded stupid assent to all Mr. Redhead said. At last, prompted by some mischief-maker, or from tipsy impulse, he clambered the pulpit stairs, and attempted to embrace Mr. Redhead. Some pushed the sweep against Mr. Redhead as he tried to escape. They threw both him and his tormentor down where the soot-bag had been emptied in the churchyard, and Mr. Redhead escaped into the Black Bull, the doors of which were barred, the people raging without and threatening to stone him and his friends. One of my informants was landlord at the time. Such was the temper of the mob, he avers, that Mr. Redhead was in danger of his life. This man planned the escape for his unpopular inmates. The Black Bull is near the top of Haworth's Main Street, and at the bottom, close by the bridge on the road to Keighley, is a turnpike. Giving directions to his guests to steal out by the back door (through which probably many a ne'er-do-weel has escaped from good Mr. Grimshaw's horsewhip), the landlord and the stable-boys rode the horses belonging to the party from Bradford backwards and forwards before his front door among the excited people. Through an opening between the houses those on the horses saw Mr. Redhead and his friends creeping away, and striking spurs they dashed down to the turnpike. The clergyman and his friends mounted in haste, and had travelled some distance before the people found their prey had escaped.

This was Mr. Redhead's last appearance at Haworth for many years. Long afterwards he came to preach, and he good-humouredly told a

HAWORTH OLD CHURCH, SCHOOL AND PARSONAGE, AS IN THE BRONTË DAYS.
(By kind permission of Mr. J. H. Widdop, Haworth).

Main Street, Haworth.

large congregation of the circumstances just described. They gave him a hearty welcome, for they owed him no grudge ; but on the former occasion they had been ready enough to stone him to maintain what they considered their rights."

"When Mr. Redhead was repelled, a new difficulty arose," wrote "A Yorkshire Gentleman" to Mrs. Gaskell. "Someone must move towards a settlement, but a spirit had been engendered which could not be easily quieted. The matter was referred to an arbitrator (my informant's parent). A meeting was convened, and the business was settled by the Vicar tendering his resignation. Their next choice now fell on Mr. Brontë, whose promptness and prudence had won their hearts, and on Feb. 25, 1820, a procession of seven farmers' carts came over the hills from Thornton—where Mr. Brontë had faithfully ministered five years—to Haworth, carrying the goods and chattels of the new incumbent."

* * * * * *

We think we see the vehicles arrive at the Rectory, and whilst they are being unloaded, hear the children scamper in ecstasy through their new home. To all outward appearance a bright and happy career was before them, but how true :—

> "We know not what awaits us,
> God kindly veils our eyes."

Haworth Church.

CHAPTER X.

BRONTË FAMILY'S SORROWS—HAWORTH CHURCHYARD—BRONTË SERVANTS' TOMBS—THE RECTORY—EPITAPHS—THE BELFRY—INSIDE THE CHURCH.

BARELY had Mr. Brontë become settled in his new sphere when dire trouble visited him.

On Sept. 15, 1821, nineteen months after the removal, his dear wife, the saintly mother of his six children, died in her 39th year. On May 6, 1825, the eldest child Maria, aged 11, whose beautiful character as "Helen Burns" is portrayed in *Jane Eyre*, joined her mother. The following month the second daughter Elizabeth, aged 10, was laid by their side. For seventeen years after this death withheld its icy hand. In 1842 Miss Branwell,* an elder sister of Mrs. Brontë, who kept house at the parsonage, passed hence. This alarming intelligence reached Charlotte and Emily whilst at school at Brussels.

It has been said that in every flock there is one black sheep, and Mr. Brontë's household proved no exception, his only son, Patrick Branwell, chiefly through intemperate habits, being the cause of many a heart-pang. His course, however, was speedily run, death claiming him September 24, 1848, at the age of 31.

Mrs. Gaskell has described him as " very clever, perhaps the greatest genius in this rare family, the hope, darling, and pride of the gifted sisters, the great favourite of his aunt, and the brilliant and talented boy of his father."

Three months later, Emily Jane, aged 30, the acknowledged author of *Wuthering Heights*, was snatched from the sorrowing family circle.

* In the Haworth edition of Mrs. Gaskell's *Life of Charlotte Brontë*, Mr. Clement K. Shorter gives Miss Ellen Nussey's description of Miss Branwell :—

" Miss Branwell was a very small, antiquated little lady ; she wore caps large enough for half a dozen of the present fashion, and a front of light auburn curls over her forehead. She always dressed in silk. She talked a great deal of her younger days, the gaieties of her native town, Penzance, in Cornwall, the soft warm climate, &c. She very probably had been a belle among her acquaintances ; the social life of her younger days she appeared to recall with regret. She took snuff out of a very pretty little gold snuff-box, which she sometimes presented with a little laugh, as if she enjoyed the slight shock and astonishment visible in your countenance. In summer she spent most of the afternoons in reading aloud to Mr. Brontë, and in the winter evenings she must have enjoyed this, for she and Mr. Brontë had sometimes to finish their discussion on what she had read when we all met for tea ; she would be very lively and intelligent in her talk, and tilted argument without fear against Mr. Brontë."

Her death scene is wondrously strange, strange as the book she wrote :
" She rose, dressed herself as usual, making many a pause, but doing everything for herself, and even endeavouring to take up her sewing ; the servants looked on, conscious of what the catching, rattling breath and the glazing of the eye too surely foretold ; but she kept at her work, and Charlotte and Anne, though full of dread, still had faint hope. Many a time they dropped their sewing, or ceased writing, to listen with wrung hearts to the failing step, the laboured breathing, the frequent pauses with which their sister climbed the short staircase ; yet they dare not notice it in words, far less by the caressing assistance of a helping arm or hand. Medicine was tendered her, to no avail ; she even recoiled at the offer ; in sooth ! she had not granted permission for a doctor to come near her, but he prescribed in accordance with symptoms observed by Charlotte. Towards noon she grew worse and her words were scarcely audible. Death had stamped its mark upon her brow ere she turned to Charlotte and faintly sobbed ' If you will send for a doctor I will see him now,'—but too late ; two hours more and the languished form had ceased to suffer." So writes Mrs. Gaskell.

" Never in all her life had she lingered over any task that lay before her, and she dare not now," says Charlotte. " She sank rapidly, she made haste to leave us. Day by day, when I saw with what a front she met suffering, I looked on her with an anguish of wonder and love. I have seen nothing like it ; but, indeed, I have never seen her parallel in anything. Stronger than a man, simpler than a child, her nature stood alone. The awful point was that, while full of ruth for others, for herself she had no pity ; the spirit was inexorable to the flesh ; from the trembling hand, the unnerved limbs, the fading eyes, the same service was exacted as they had rendered in health. To stand by and witness this, and not dare to remonstrate, was a pain no words can render. She made no complaint ; she would not endure questioning, she rejected sympathy and help."

How exceedingly dear in life Emily was to Charlotte ; " I think Emily seems the nearest thing to my heart in the world," she says. And after her death, how deep her lament. " If there were no hope beyond this world, no eternity, no life to come, Emily's fate and that which threatens Anne, would be heart-breaking. I cannot forget Emily's death-day ; it becomes a more fixed, a darker, a more frequently recurring idea in my mind than ever. It was very terrible. She was torn, conscious, panting, reluctant, though resolute, out of a happy life."

But to our woeful story. At the end of another six months, Anne—author of *The Tenant of Wildfell Hall*, *Agnes Grey*, and many poems—was called to her reward. Her ashes lie in Scarborough Parish Church yard. She went to Scarborough in the hope of recovering health. Charlotte's forebodings regarding her now only sister were too surely realized, for four days after leaving home (May 24, 1849) she passed away. Thoughts of removing her remains to Haworth were entertained but relinquished, Charlotte "deciding to lay the flower in the place where it had fallen, thinking not of the grave, for that is but the body's goal, but of all that is beyond it."

Anne's kindly spirit is shown in an incident, penned by Miss Ellen Nussey, Charlotte's devout friend of more than twenty years, who accompanied her and her sister to Scarborough.

"On the 26th (two days after her arrival at Scarborough), she drove on the sands an hour, and lest the poor donkey should be urged to a greater speed than her heart thought right, she took the reins and drove herself. When joined by her friend, she was charging the boy—master of the donkey—to treat the animal well. She was ever fond of dumb things, and would relinquish her own comfort for theirs."

Anne's yearning to live is manifested in these, her own lines :—

"I hoped that with the brave and strong
My portioned task might lie ;
To toil among the busy throng,
With purpose pure and high ;
But God has fixed another part,
And He has fixed it well ;
I said so with my bleeding heart,
When first the anguish fell."

"Thou God has taken our delight,
Our treasured hope away ;
Thou bid'st us now weep through the night
And sorrow through the day.
These weary hours will not be lost,
These days of misery,
These nights of darkness, tempest tost,
Can I but turn to Thee.

And mourning her weakened state, she prays :—

"If Thou should bring me back to life,
More humble I should be ;
More wise—more strengthened for the strife—
More apt to lean on Thee ;
Should death be standing at the gate
Thus should I keep my vow ;
But Lord, whatever be my fate,
Oh, let me serve Thee now."

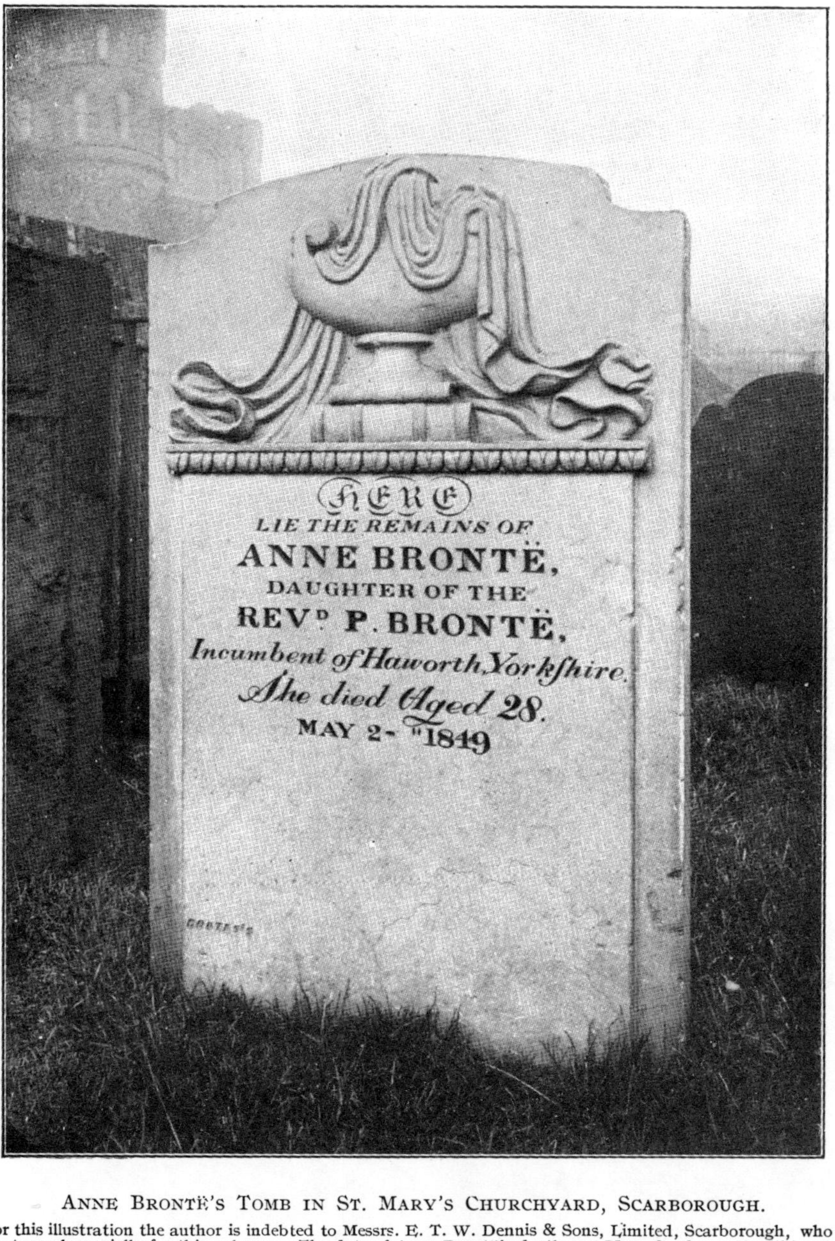

ANNE BRONTË'S TOMB IN ST. MARY'S CHURCHYARD, SCARBOROUGH.

For this illustration the author is indebted to Messrs. E. T. W. Dennis & Sons, Limited, Scarborough, who took the photograph specially for this volume. The date of Anne Brontë's death was May 28, 1849. It will be noticed that in place of the figure 8 is a dash. The line bearing the date is not, like all the other wording, cut into the stone. The stone is painted white, the graven letters being blacked in. After the painting, the date line, being thus obliterated, was presumably forgotten for a time and then was painted in wrongly. The dash after May 2 is now cut in the stone. We have a partial clue to what has happened to this stone in a letter of Charlotte Brontë's dated June 23, 1852 :—

> " The duty to be discharged at Scarbro' was the chief motive that drew me to the East Coast. I have been there, visited the churchyard, seen the stone, there were five errors, consequently I had to give directions for its being re-faced and re-lettered."

Was ever a tombstone so fated ?

Two only of the family remained, Charlotte and her father, and the latter was almost blind. A ray of sunshine still gleamed through the portals of the benighted home. Charlotte's novel, *Jane Eyre,* written during a year under most adverse circumstances, and first published Oct. 16, 1847, literally bounded into popularity. But the joy derived from this was comparatively short-lived. Scarcely six years passed before the Authoress, Mr. Brontë's last child, the praise of whose work "went unto all the earth," was called hence. Only nine months before, on June 29, 1854, the bells had rung out Charlotte's union with the Rev. A. B. Nicholls, B.A.

Left in solitude on that lonely hearth, Divine grace only could possibly sustain the pair. Surely it needed hearts devout and wills resigned as Job's to say :—

> "We cannot Lord Thy purpose see,
> But all is well that's done by Thee."

> "Earth to earth, and dust to dust,
> Calmly now the words we say ;
> Left behind, we wait in trust
> For the resurrection day.
> Father, in Thy gracious keeping,
> Leave we now Thy servant sleeping."

The dejected father lived over six years more, bearing his sorrow and affliction. On June 7, 1861, at the age of 84, his summons came. So Mr. Brontë survived the whole of his household.

Haworth Churchyard.

Now we roam the churchyard in search of epitaphs quaint and interesting, such as we have read of in similar old graveyards. First we note, immediately within the railings on our left, an upright stone with an E-flat cornet in high relief thereon. The mouthpiece and valve-tips have been broken off, notwithstanding the grave is protected by railings almost as high as the headstone. Beneath the cornet we read of a :—

JOHN DAWSON HOPKINSON,
of Bents, who died August 3rd, 1860,
in the 27th Year of his Age.

Below the instrument is a floral wreath and an open book which contains the whole of Luther's hymn in D, each note being most distinct,

even to the trumpet call, which is carved in microscopic characters. Presumably the young man was a musician of repute.

No doubt the sexton could help us make our visit here more interesting. We will hunt him up. Only one dwelling likely is visible, and on this we keep an eye, hoping someone will appear at the door, wide ajar. But no! Therefore we approach it. A man in holiday garb responds to our delicate rat-tat. To our delight it is the sexton. Yes, he will be pleased to conduct us through the yard and inside the church. Our first impulse is to visit the graves of the Brontë servants. Re-entering the yard, we turn sharply to the right, and step lightly over the tombs till we stand in front of the Rectory, and opposite the middle of the garden we see a double vaulted grave, guarded in like manner to that which first attracted our attention.

Brontë Servants' Tombs.

Between this and the garden wall is a table-tomb. On it we read first of the death of a *George* Aykroyd, and *Susannah* Wood, aged respectively 76 and 90, and below:—

Also, of Tabitha Aykroyd, of
Haworth, who Died Feb$^{y.}$ 17$^{th.}$ 1855,
in the 85th Year of her Age.

Charlotte Brontë, Mrs. Gaskell and Miss Nussey together give us a remarkably good picture of the old servant Tabby.

Mrs. Gaskell says that "About this time (1825) an elderly woman of the village came to live as servant at the parsonage. She remained there as a member of the household for thirty years, and from the length of her faithful service, and the attachment and respect which she inspired, is deserving of mention. Tabby was a thorough specimen of a Yorkshire woman of her class, in dialect, in appearance, and in character. She abounded in strong practical sense and shrewdness. Her words were far from flattery; but she would spare no deeds in the cause of those whom she kindly regarded. She ruled the children pretty sharply, and yet never grudged a little extra trouble to provide them with such small treats as came within her power. In return, she claimed to be looked upon as a humble friend; and many years later Miss Brontë told me that she found it somewhat difficult to manage, as Tabby expected to be informed of all the family concerns, and yet had grown so deaf that what was repeated to her became known to whoever might be in

or about the house. To obviate this publication of what might be desirable to keep secret, Miss Brontë used to take her out for a walk on the solitary moors where, when both were seated on a tuft of heather, in some high, lonely place, she could acquaint the old woman at leisure with all that she wanted to hear.

Tabby had lived in Haworth in the days when the pack-horses went through once a week with their tinkling bells and gay worsted adornments, carrying the produce of the country from Keighley over the hills to Colne and Burnley. What is more, she had known the 'bottom,' or valley, in those primitive days when the fairies frequented the margin of the beck on moonlight nights, and had known folk who had seen them. But that was when there were no mills in the valley, and when all the wool spinning was done by hand in the farmhouses round. 'It wur factories as had driven 'em away,' she said.

To a visitor at the parsonage it was a great thing to have Tabby's good word. She had the Yorkshire keenness for perception of character, and it was not everybody she liked."

'She was nearer seventy than sixty,' and had lived with the Brontë's some ten or twelve years, having become, as Charlotte expressed it, "one of the family," when a painful incident befel the faithful, trusty old soul.

"She had gone out (writes Charlotte) into the village on some errand, when, as she was descending the steep street, her foot slipped on the ice, and she fell. It was dark and no one saw her mischance, till, after a time, her groans attracted the attention of a passer-by. She was lifted up and conveyed into a druggist's near; and, after the examination, it was discovered she had completely shattered and dislocated one leg. Eventually, she was removed back to the parsonage, where, as soon as the immediate danger to the old servant's life was over, Miss Branwell, out of consideration for Mr. Brontë's slender purse, and with pure economical motives, urged her removal to one of her sisters living in the village, arguing that 'the savings she had accumulated during many years' service formed a competency for one in her rank of life. Or if, in this time of sickness, she fell short of any comforts which her state rendered necessary, the parsonage would supply them.' So reasoned Miss Branwell, the prudent, not to say conscious aunt, whose argument in the end proved effectual; but previous to its being put into execution, the decision was communicated to the girls. There were symptoms of a quiet but sturdy rebellion that winter afternoon in the small precincts of Haworth Parsonage. They made one unanimous and stiff remon-

strance, Tabby had tended them in their childhood ; they, and none other, should tend her, in her infirmity and age. At tea-time they were sad and silent, and the meal went away untouched by any of the three. So it was at breakfast ; they did not waste many words upon the subject, but each word they did utter was weighty. They 'struck' eating till the resolution was rescinded, and Tabby was allowed to remain, a helpless invalid, entirely dependent upon them. Herein was the strong feeling of duty being paramount to pleasure, made most apparent."

And Miss Nussey tells us that "Tabby, the faithful, trustworthy old servant, was very quaint in appearance, very active, and in those days the general servant and factotum. We were all 'children' and 'bairns' in her estimation. She still kept to her habit of walking out with the children if they went any distance from home, unless Branwell was sent by his father as protector. In later days, after she had been attacked with paralysis, she would anxiously look out for such duties as she was still capable of. The postman was her special point of attention ; she did not approve of the inspections which the younger eyes of her fellow-servant bestowed on his deliveries ; she jealously seized them (when she could) and carried them off with hobbling step and shaking head to the safe custody of Charlotte."

* * * * * *

Leaving Tabby's grave, we thread our way among crowded tombs, keeping near the southern side of the Rectory garden wall, and slightly past midway we halt at a square, dwarf monument. This records the death, in 1835, of William Brown, sexton for twenty-seven years, and his wife Mary. John Brown, who died in 1855, and who presumably stepped into William's shoes and served twenty years ; again Mary is the name of the widow. One Joseph Hardaker, an old Haworthite, undoubtedly, had one or both these sextons in mind when he penned the following lines, which we cull from Mr. J. Horsfall Turner's *Haworth, Past and Present* :—

"O, sexton, ye are such a soul,
Ye little care for whom ye toll ;
If ye can drain the arvill bowl,
With many more,
Ye'll for a moment sigh and growl,
Then all is o'er.

Before the corpse, in solemn pace,
Full oft I've seen ye pull a face ;
As though ye were to truth and grace
Nearly allied ;
That few would think ye mean or base,
So deep ye sighed.

But think ye, old case-hardened blade,
Knight of the mattock and the spade,
Some lustier brother of the trade,
Perhaps ere' long,
May lig you where you've thousands laid,
Nor think it wrong."

But the name we are most anxious to see on this, the Browns' tombstone, is that of Tabby's assistant, and here it is :—

Also
of MARTHA, daughter of
John & Mary Brown,
Haworth,
who died Jany 19th 1880, in
the 52nd Year of her age."

THE RECTORY.

Here, beside Martha's grave, we obtain a goodly view of the Rectory, notwithstanding its being partially obscured by a tall hedge of budding thorns and variegated holly, which serve as a shelter for the inner fringe of rhododendrons, the lawn and its central flower bed. Shooting above the whole are the mountain ash, sycamore, oak, and a couple of firs. Here imagination finds play. As we look down at the window left of the entrance (the room between the door and the new wing of the building was Mr. Brontë's study) we picture the spare form of Charlotte, sitting near the light, and, with strained eyes bent over her manuscript ; we see the slim figure of her younger sister Emily as, on a beautiful summer's evening, she bounds across the lawn, plants her little buffet in a shady nook and becomes absorbed in the study of the strange characters about to be introduced into her most wondrous book. We seem to hear the low growling of Emily's dog " Keeper " (" Tartar " in *Shirley*) which has disobeyed orders and is about to receive chastisement. "He loved to steal upstairs, and stretch his square tawny limbs on the comfortable beds, covered over with delicate white counterpanes." Now she is dragging him down the staircase, held by the " scuff of the neck, his hind legs set in an attitude of resistance." She belabours him till his eyes are swollen, and afterwards is led to his accustomed lair to have his swollen head fomented and cared for by the very Emily herself. The faithful dog, true to his instinct, bore its mistress no malice for the punishment received, but loved her yet the more, and at her funeral walked first among the mourners and moaned for nights at the door of her room.

Glancing up at the window above Charlotte's study, our minds wander to that Easter Saturday, half a century ago, when the life of Mrs.

Nicholls was ebbing away; in her state of delirium, moments can be counted by heart-throbs. For an instant she wakes to consciousness and whispers "Oh! I am not going to die, am I? He will not separate us; we have been so happy." A little while and her spirit wings its flight where

"More than conquerors at last,
Here they find their trials o'er;
They have all their sufferings past,
Hunger now, and thirst no more;
No excessive heat they feel
From the sun's director ray,
In a milder clime they dwell,
Region of eternal day."

Epitaphs.

Though our guide has been sexton ten years he fears he is acquainted with few interesting epitaphs. Since, however, we come from Halifax, he thinks one on a tombstone between Tabby's and the church will interest us. This is the inscription :—

UNDERNEATH, in silent repose,
Waiting for the resurrection of the Just,
Are interred the *REMAINS* of the aforenamed
Rev. MICHAEL COUSIN.
He was a native of this Parish, and died
at HALIFAX, Nov. 6, 1852, aged 70 Years.

With a mind honest and independent,
a soul devout and ardent; and with a
physical frame unusually robust and
vigorous, he untiringly spent forty-eight
years of his life in proclaiming the glorious
gospel of the blessed God.

Beside this it is recorded that :—

"Beneath this ſtone doth lie
As much Virtue as could die,
When on earth did vigour give
To as much beauty as could live."

Yet another near by extols the virtues of one who "departed this life without a blot upon his character." We never yet met such an one, and passages of Scripture flashing across our minds confirm the thought. Paul's declaration rings in our ears: "There is none righteous, no not one, for all have sinned," and we think of Job's admission :—

"If I justify myself, mine own mouth shall condemn me. If I say, I am perfect, it shall also prove me perverse," and John's affirmation, "If we say we have no sin, we deceive ourselves, and the truth is not in us."

One inscription reminds us that :—

> " This world's a city, full of crooked streets,
> Death is the market-place, where all men meet ;
> If life was merchandise that men could buy,
> The rich would live, the poor must always die."

On an upright stone, beside the path in the newer portion of the ground, we read of a Joseph Redman,

> Who for 36 years was Clerk of this
> Church, and who died July 8th, 1862,
> Aged 66 years.

With a little show of pride our conductor, Mr. Widdop by name, says that Joseph was his grandfather. In the old yard (now inaccessible to the public), and near the Black Bull, is a roughly-hewn stone, which bears the simple inscription :—

J. S. 1796.

Tradition, according to our guide, says the initials are those of one who, for sheep stealing, was hung at York and his body was brought here in a cart.

There, is the little square back window of the Black Bull, through which, it is said, Patrick Branwell (at the inn and in the village he was Patrick ; at home he was Branwell) used to make his exit when his father came seeking him. The next minute the incorrigible son might be found squatting composedly by the kitchen fire in the parsonage. Now, led close to the church on the south side, we are shown a grave, simply a flag 2 feet 6 inches square, where lie interred a family of six of the name of Murgatroyd, their ages being 86, 88, 95, 85, 70 and 85—an aggregate of 509 years. "Old milk and porridge undoubtedly had a part in the longevity," we remark, and the sexton agrees. Only one grave in this portion of the yard remains to be opened, and then the entire old ground will be closed for burial purposes ; the part behind the Black Bull was closed some years ago. It is calculated that not less than 40,000 lie buried here. The first interment registered was in 1645, but on a rude stone, four yards left of the path leading to the south entrance, are the figures 1640 ; there is no further inscription to account for their presence. Beneath the figures is a record of the death of one Pighells (the christian name is broken away), "who died April 17th, 1769." "The day of the month we first saw light," we tell the sexton.

"All big folks are born in April," we receive in reply, a statement we are unable to substantiate.

* * * * * *

Now we turn our attention to the church, which was built in 1879, on the site of an older one, the demolition of which was strenuously opposed. The only remnant of the original building is the tower, which was left intact.

THE BELFRY.

We suggest a climb to the belfry, but first copy the characters, crumbling with age, on the wall of the tower :—

These characters are chaos to our minds. Whitaker, in his *Loidis and Elmete*, gives this explanation :—

"Not every antiquary knows that the formula of prayer 'bono statu' always refers to the living. I suspect this singular Christian name has been mistaken by the stone-cutter for Austet, a contraction of Eustatius, but the word Tod, which has been mis-read for the Arabic figures 600, is perfectly fair and legible. On the presumption of this foolish claim to antiquity, the people would needs set up for independence, and contest the right of the Vicar of Bradford to nominate a curate at Haworth."

The Rev. T. W. Story, the present Rector, in his *Notes on the old Haworth Registers*, tells us that the latter inscription purports to be a translation of the former, and is in more modern characters. He criticizes Mrs. Gaskell's remark that the date 600 was before the preaching of Christianity in Northumbria, and states that the district in which Haworth is situated was still British and Christian at that date. He says, however, that the positive evidence will not bear investigation, pointing to *Mayall's Annals*, wherein it is stated : "There appears to have been a church here as early as A.D. 600 ;" and to Kelly, who says : "A church has been here since the 7th century, and in the present building there are stones bearing date 600, leading to the supposition that these stones formed part of a structure which existed at that time." "We may be sure," says Mr. Story, "that Kelly had never seen the stones referred to, or he would scarcely have regarded inscriptions in

modern characters as evidence that the stones formed part of so ancient a structure. One of the stones referred to bore the inscription :—

Hic olim fuit Monachorum
Cœnobium ad honorem
Sancti Michaelis et omnium
Angelorum dictatum.
Auteste fundatore, Anno Christo Sexcentissimo.

This is the translation : 'Here formerly was a monastery dedicated to the honour of St. Michael and All Angels, Autest being the founder in the year of Christ, six hundred.' Here we get Autest again, no doubt the same person for whose welfare we are requested, by the inscription on the tower, to pray. Yet the Latin inscription on the tower does not say 600, and it is evidently by a mistake that the last word of that inscription has been so translated ; and it is an inconceivable coincidence that the Latin should have been misread as 600, and all the while there really had been a Monastery founded by an Autest or Eutest in 600. The word Tod in the Latin inscription having been mistaken for 600, the idea arose that there was some kind of a church here at that date, and from that the other inscriptions came into existence. The conclusion is, that while it is a mistake to say that Christianity did not exist in the district in 600, and therefore that Monastic establishments were impossible, on the other hand the evidence of the inscriptions as showing that such an establishment existed then at Haworth is valueless. The real date of the old tower is not very easy to ascertain. It has been made higher three or four times, and the pinnacles, which must have been carried up with each successive elevation, are said to be like those of decorated perpendicular buildings of the Plantagenet period. A little window in the west of the oldest portion of the tower is also said to belong to the 'Early English decorated period.'"

* * * * * *

While we are looking about the tower and porch the belfry door is opened. Ingress we find somewhat embarassing, so low and narrow is the entrance. But later, progress seems even more hazardous. However, we manage to wriggle our way up side-ways : this passage was never meant for anything approaching to aldermanic proportions. Reaching the belfry chamber we count six bell-ropes, and note this gilded inscription :—

"This peal of bells was hung by William Wood, Joseph Redman being the architect, and was opened and prizes given, March 10th, 1846."

Another flight of steps scaled, and we are in the belfry. How the wind whistles about our ears! Match after match is whiffed out before we are enabled to decipher this inscription on one of the bells :—

C. and G. Mears, founders, London,
These bells were raised by subscription.
Rev. Patrick Brontë, Incumbent.
Mr. George Feather, Mr. James Lambert,
Churchwardens.

Conversation ends abruptly while 1-30 is being chimed, and now taking extra precautions we make the descent. As we reach the open and liberty, we expand our chests in breaths of grateful relief. Making our exit from the churchyard our attention is arrested by these words on a stone :—

" Time was I ftood as thou doft now,
And view'd the Dead as thou doft me ;
Ere long thou'lt be as low as I,
And others ftand and look o'er thee."

Glancing up at the tower, on the west side, we observe a sun-dial, which gives this counsel, " Remember thy latter end," and is dated 1840. Yea, all round we seem to hear the prophet's warning " Set thine house in order, for thou must die and not live."

We think of David's lamentation, " Our days on the earth are as a shadow, and there is none abiding ; " of the musings of the writer of Ecclesiastes, " Man goeth to his long home, and the mourners go about the streets " ; likewise the grave surmisings of Job amid his distress, " Man dieth, and wasteth away ; yea, man giveth up the ghost, and where is he ? " " They shall lie down alike in the dust and the worms shall cover them."

Our guide listens attentively whilst we cite the closing lines of Laycock's *Thee and Me*, an address to the rich man :—

" But deawn i' th grave, what spoils o' th' sport,
No ray o' leet can shine,
An' th' worms below can hardly sort
Thy pampered cla fro' mine ;
So when this world for th' next tha swaps,
Tak wi' thi under th' stone
Thi cooat ov arms, an' bits o' traps,
Or else tha'll ne'er be known.

But up above there's One 'at sees
  Through th' heart o' every mon ;
An' He'll just find thee as tha dees,
  So dee as weel as t' con ;
An' aw'll do th' same, owd friend, an' then,
  Wi' o' eawr fauts forgiven,
P'raps thee an' me may meet again,
  An' boath shake honds i' heaven."

Inside the Church.

Now the church's black oaken door yields to the sexton, and we enter the vestibule. Time will not admit of our dwelling on its architecture and decorations, so we content ourselves with things pertaining mostly to the Brontë's. Passing into the sanctuary, the first feature to attract us is the Brontë tablet and we copy the inscription :—

In Memory of

Maria, Wife of the Revd. P. Brontë, A.B., Minister of Haworth ; She died Septr. 15th, 1821, in the 39th Year of her age.

Also of Maria, their daughter, who died May 6th, 1825, in the 12th Year of her age.

Also of Elizabeth, their daughter ; who died June 15th, 1825, in the 11th Year of her age.

Also of Patrick Branwell, their son ; who died Septr. 24th, 1848, aged 31 Years.

Also of Emily Jane, their daughter ; who died Decr. 19th, 1848, aged 30 Years.

Also of Anne, their daughter ; who died May 28th, 1849, aged 29 Years. She was buried at the old Church, Scarborough.

Also of Charlotte, their daughter ; wife of the Revd. A. B. Nicholls, B.A. She died March 31st, 1855, in the 39th Year of her age.

Also of the aforenamed Revd. P. Brontë, A.B. who died June 7th, 1861, in the 85th Year of his age, having been Incumbent of Haworth for upwards of 41 Years.

" The Sting of Death is Sin, and the Strength of Sin is the Law ; but thanks be to God, which giveth us the victory through our Lord Jesus Christ," 1 Cor. XV. 56, 57.

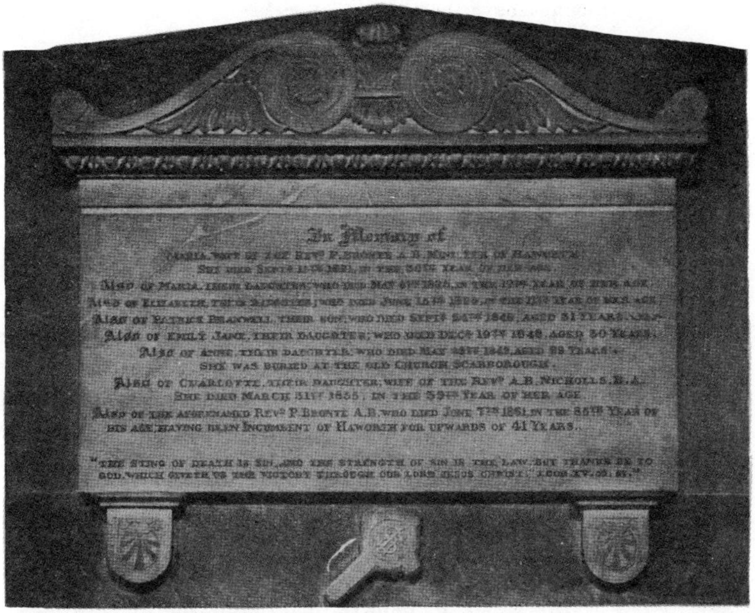

BRONTË MEMORIAL TABLET.
(*Photo. by F. Shuttleworth*).

A tablet in the Baptistry commemorates the death, Sept. 2, 1842, of William Weightman, M.A., curate here for three years, who died by an attack of typhoid fever at the early age of 26. He was held in high esteem by the Brontë sisters: the Baptistry window contains portraits of the Butterfield family, of Cliffe Castle, Keighley.

On the south side of the church is a stained window of six lights, illustrating the text, Matt. xxv. 35-36:—

> "For I was an hungered, and ye gave me meat:
> I was thirsty, and ye gave me drink:
> I was a stranger, and ye took me in:
> Naked, and ye clothed me:
> I was sick, and ye visited me:
> I was in prison, and ye came unto me."

The sexton reads aloud the passages of Scripture as the pictures are arranged:—

> "I was a stranger, and ye took me in:
> I was sick, and ye visited me:
> I was in prison, and ye came unto me:
> I was an hungered, and ye gave me meat:
> I was thirsty, and ye gave me drink:
> Naked, and ye clothed me:"

This window is dedicated

To the glory of God and the pleasant memory of Charlotte Brontë
by an American citizen.

On the floor, near the chancel, a brassplate some 20 inches by 16, records the deaths of Emily and Charlotte, though all the family, with the exception of Anne, Mr. Widdop tells us, are buried beneath our feet.

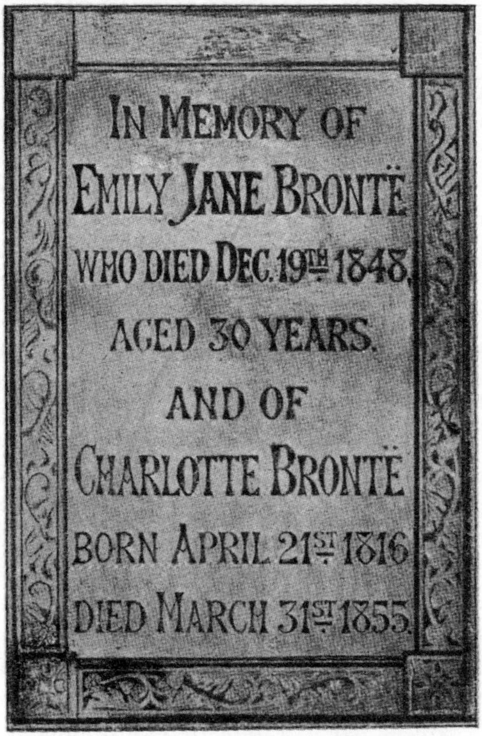

BRASS PLATE OVER BRONTË VAULT IN HAWORTH CHURCH.
(*Photo by J. J. Stead*).

At the base of the chancel arch is inscribed :—

To the Glory of God,
In the faith of Jesus Christ,
This Stone was laid
By Michael Merrall, Esq.,
of Law House,
On Christmas Day, 1879.

Mr. Widdop remembers very well when he, a boy of nine, sat on the south side of the old church and heard Mr. Brontë preach from the three-decker pulpit. We are curious to learn how the ancient relic fared when supplanted by the elaborate alabaster one we are now admiring; we feel sure it will have been accorded an exalted position in the realm of antiquity. To our astonishment we are informed it rests in the hayloft of an old barn at Stanbury.

"We purpose passing there presently, can we get to see it.?"

Nothing so sure as this, we are told, assuming that the tenant of the farm is not away from home; sometimes he attends Skipton cattle market on this day—Monday.

The sexton proceeds to describe the old church's interior and speaks of there having been two aisles in place of three, as now, with graves the entire length of each. The pews were high-backed, in black oak, and the owners' names were painted on the doors.

Time, we feel, is pressing, yet we are tempted to linger over a superb alabaster copy in high relief, of Leonardo da Vinci's painting of the Last Supper, presented by the late Rector's wife, Mrs. Wade. We study those who "left all and followed Him." How eagerly they rise from the table, and turning towards the central figure, their Master, on His declaring that "one of you which eateth with me shall betray me," inquiring "Is it I?" seemingly yearn for a reply. There is an unmistakable trace of guilt on the countenance of the one who clenches "the bag" as he pitilessly hisses "Is it I?" "Is it I?"

Returning along the nave we are about to take leave of the sexton when his good lady appears and informs him that another party wait to be shown round.

After mapping out our saunter to Mr. and Mrs. Widdop, and showing that to-morrow afternoon we hope to arrive back at Haworth on our way home, they very kindly concede to our request and offer us cups of tea, at which we are elated. Promised entertainment in the Church School-house where curates of the Brontë days lodged! Delightful thought! We hasten to express our thanks for the privilege. Since we are going beyond Stanbury, we are advised to be sure and call upon "Owd Timmy, t' owd 'and-loom weaver."

"Owd Timmy!" We have read of him, and shall seize the opportunity to make his acquaintance.

CHAPTER XI.

GRIMSHAW'S CHAPEL—BRONTË WATERFALL—GRIMSHAW'S PULPIT—
"T'OWD GENTLEMAN'S GRAVE—STANBURY—
A LANCASHIRE TYKE.

THE church clock chimes 2-15, and we wonder whether the remaining hours of light will see us to the end of our day's saunter. Hitherto the road has mostly been familiar to us, but now, like one of old, "we know not whither we go," and must, we presume, trust largely to our map.

The substantial meal obtained at our friends at Fly has not sufficiently subsided to justify another, but we feel we shall act with discretion if here we lay in "victuals for our journey." Accordingly, we repair to a confectioner's and purchase such provisions as we deem will meet requirements, and for the nonce we leave this magnetic shrine, striking out by West Lane, as appropriately named as Main Street, of which it is a continuation. As we round the curve we view on our left, Parson's Fields, much travelled by the Brontë sisters in their visits to the moors. A street recently formed takes the name of the illustrious family. For a moment we admire an imposing Bethel well back from the road, and the inscription, though in relief characters, for dullards like ourselves is a mental exercise :—

BAPTIST CHAPEL,
BUILT MDCCLII.,
ENLARGED MDCCLXXV.,
REBUILT MDCCCXLIV.

Places of worship in Haworth are plentiful ; so, too, are public-houses. We halt again, opposite a similarly-placed sanctuary to that just mentioned, but not nearly so pretentious. Here we look in vain for a date. We suspect, however, this is the Wesleyans, "th' old body," founded by the Rev. William Grimshaw, many years Vicar of the Parish, and a remnant of whose original chapel we observe in the yard beside the chapel-keeper's house. Inscriptions at the back are the only clue to

the fact that the chapel was built by Grimshaw. They read as follows :—

The 1st Chapel was
Erected by the Rev[d].
William Grimfhaw,
A.B., Minifter of
Haworth Church,
A.D. 1758.

TO US
To Live is CHRIS[t]
To Die is Gain.
A.D. 1758.

The latter was Grimshaw's favourite text. It seems a pity these tablets, which adorned the front of "The 1ft Chapel," should be placed at the back of the premises. In all probability Charlotte here gathered food for that account in *Shirley* of a lively prayer meeting held in Briar Chapel, at the conclusion of which she says "The roof of the chapel did *not* fly off; which speaks volumes in praise of its solid slating." The present chapel, we ascertain, was built in 1846 and will seat 800.

In 1746 Charles Wesley preached in Haworth, his brother John the following year, and two years after came George Whitfield. Grimshaw's became the chief buildings in a "round," the primitive name for circuit—of 120 miles, extending from Otley to Whitehaven. In this area in 1775 there were three itinerant ministers and 1,344 members; now there are 30 circuits, in charge of some 80 ministers, with a membership of over 17,000.

BRONTË WATERFALL.

A little further, and a road branches away up to Haworth Moor. A post points the way "To the Cemetery and Waterfall," and again down a sharp incline "To Colne."

Brontë waterfall sounds alluring, but the Fall itself is, mostly, disappointing. At present we should find a mere trickle of water amid moss-covered rocks. The walk thither, though charming, breezy and exhilarating, is deceptive, for from here—a quarter-of-a-mile outside Haworth—it is not less than two miles. Once when the moors were purple we visited the Fall, approaching it by Oxenhope and over Haworth Moor to Waterhead Lane top, thence to the left along a rough, clayey cart-track skirting the moor most of the way. One or two farmhouses intervene, and last is an unoccupied one in ruins. Here the road tapers to a footpath in which we continued until dividing at a sign warning

" LITTLE MILL " (EAST SIDE), STANBURY.

visitors against wandering, save on the moors, " By order of the Bradford Corporation." No guide was requisite to direct us to the Fall. Instinctively we took the well-trodden downward course fringed with high bracken and beset with ugly boulders and slippery places, behoving us

BRONTË CHAIR.

to ponder well the path of our feet. At intervals we found good footing, and halted to view the woodland in Sladen valley*—Halliwell Sutcliffe's Hazel Dene, wherein is his " Hazel Mill," locally known as " Little

*A reservoir is here now (1913) in course of construction for Keighley.

Brontë Bridge.

Mill." Very shortly we heard a faint splashing of water, and in a few seconds more we were gazing up at the Fall, not in bewilderment, but in utter disappointment. We were then unaware of its small gathering ground. We sat in the "Brontë Chair"—a rock naturally planted at the foot of the Fall and beside the path—and watched the water ripple down and lose itself in Sladen Beck. Here the stream is spanned by a crotchety-looking stone foot-bridge, which is known as "Brontë Bridge." Just above is a large moorland sheep-pen.

After heavy rain or sudden thaw, the Fall must be decidedly pretty. It was on such a day that Charlotte Brontë visited it for the last time, Writing to a friend on Nov. 29, 1854, she says :—

"I intended to have written a line yesterday, but just as I was sitting down for the purpose, Arthur called to me to take a walk. We set off, not intending to go far ; but though wild and cloudy, it was fine in the morning ; when we had got about half-a-mile on the moors, Arthur suggested the idea of the waterfall ; after the melted snow, he said it would be fine. I had often wished to see it in its winter power, so we walked on. It was fine indeed ; a perfect torrent racing over the rocks, white and beautiful ! It began to rain while we were watching it, and we returned home under a streaming sky. However, I enjoyed the walk inexpressibly, and would not have missed the spectacle on any account."

Mrs. Gaskell tells us that "She (Charlotte) did not achieve this walk of seven or eight miles (in reality, less than five the double journey) in such weather with impunity. She began to shiver soon after her return home, in spite of every precaution, and had a bad lingering sore throat and cold, which hung about her, and made her thin and weak."

* * * * * *

But let us jog on. Old Sol now plays hide-and-seek behind dark clouds, and we have forebodings. We proceed along the turnpike Colne-wards, descend the sharp hill to Sladen Bridge (/\ 640-3), and immediately rise towards Stanbury village, seen on the hill's crest directly after leaving Haworth, a mile separating the two places.

At the corner of Stanbury Cemetery, midway up the incline, a seat offers welcome rest ; but we pass by, for a tramp holds full possession. While the man snores we behold his face, dotted with blue as a clown's is painted. Surely he is unconscious of his appearance. Evidently the work of some practical joker, we muse. What a snapshot ! Bone of our bone and flesh of our flesh, our hearts beat for him. Poor fellow !

BRONTË WATERFALL.
When "Summer suns are glowing."
(*Photo by J. J. Stead, Heckmondwike*).

Brontë Waterfall.
"When winter holds her sway."
(*Photo by J. Rushworth, Balby, Doncaster*).

BRONTË WATERFALL.
"A perfect torrent racing over the rocks, white and beautiful."—C. BRONTË.
(*Photo by F. Shuttleworth, Haworth*).

Brontë Waterfall, from near Brontë Chair.
"Bursts of thunder rend th' encumber'd air."
(Photo by F. Shuttleworth, Haworth).

" No matter how wayward his footsteps have been ;
No matter how deep he has sunken in sin ;
No matter how low is his standard of joy,
Though degraded and loathsome, he is somebody's boy."

* Grimshaw's Pulpit.

Prior to passing through Stanbury—Halliwell Sutcliffe's "Ling Cragg"—we seek a glimpse of the pulpit of old Haworth Church. We make our wishes known to a typical Yorkshire farmer who is *not* at Skipton market, as was feared.

"Aye, sartenly ya con see t'owd puppit if ya wish to ; just bide wheer ya ar till E fetch a stee," and the farmer bounds across the road into a modern laithe, returns shouldering a ladder, with one end of which he thrusts open the folding doors of an old-fashioned barn. Rearing the ladder against the loft, we are requested to mount.

"Ya'll waant a leet, E daar saa, afaar ya con see it graadly," observes our friend.

Matches will not give a satisfactory view of the pulpit that we dimly see pushed into the remotest corner. Its custodian comes to our aid with a candle, which is handed up the ladder. Before we can apply a light something brushes past us and whisks across the loft, making our flesh creep. A second later fears are allayed as we catch sight of pussy vanishing through the open door.

We can scarcely conceive that the black old hexagonal box, so thickly coated with dust and mould, was once the central figure in Haworth Church; nor that from its desk John Wesley expounded the Gospel. "My pulpit, I hope, shall be always at yours and your brother's service, and my house, as long as I have one, your home," wrote Mr. Grimshaw to Wesley, in August, 1747, and we read that on several occasions Wesley availed himself of the hospitality.

Sharing lodgings with the pulpit is the under portion of the sounding-board, round the rim of which we read with difficulty :—

"For I am determined not to know anything among you save Jesus Christ and Him crucified. Grimshaw, B.A., 1742."

The farmer awaits our descent with a heavy boot firmly planted on the lowest rung of the ladder, and arms outstretched lest we come to grief. He is interested when we tell him we live within a mile of Luddenden Church, where Grimshaw is buried, and compliments us on our memory as we repeat the inscription on the brass tablet marking his tomb :—

* Since our saunter the pulpit has been restored and placed in Stanbury Mission Church.

TO THE HONOR AND GLORY OF GOD
AND
IN MEMORY OF
WILLIAM GRIMSHAW, B.A., CLERK.
INCUMBENT OF HAWORTH,
✝
DIED 7TH APRIL, 1763,
AGED 54 YEARS.

GRIMSHAW'S PULPIT SOUNDING-BOARD.

We are told the present farm is rented by Mr. G. S. Taylor (lately deceased, and for whom our informant worked over forty years), of Silsden, a trustee of Haworth Church. This, says our farmer-friend, explains the consignment of these relics to this quarter. He remembers the sounding-board as it stood over the pulpit, a white dove on top, Upon the bird children used to fix their eyes, expecting every moment to see it spread wings and fly across the church.

Yes, and he recalls also Patrick Brontë very well, for he christened him " i' t'owd chutch, ower sixty yeear sin'."

" T'OWD GENTLEMAN'S " GRAVE.

Describing our route we are advised not to omit visiting " t'owd gentleman's " grave, just across the valley and near to Griff Mill—

GRIMSHAW'S PULPIT.

Halliwell Sutcliffe's "Goit Mill." On our map we are pointed to the field where "t'owd gentleman" is buried, and are shown also where "owd Timmy" lives; for later reference we make a pin-hole in the map where his dwelling is. We hear with interest the story of "t'owd gentleman's" eccentric choice of burial-place, which we proceed to visit, going along a narrow lane branching off immediately on our right. Entering fields, we readily locate the grave through the description given us. Crossing the stream by a wooden foot-bridge, we find it necessary to trespass to reach the spot. Fenced by a dry wall some 16 feet by 12 feet, and 4 feet high, and lined by thick thorns with no opening save at the foot of the grave, is an upright head-stone, on which is inscribed:—

In
MEMORY
OF
Mr. JAMES MITCHELL, late
PROPRIETOR and *OCCUPIER* of
Oldfield House, who died on the
27th *day* of *January*, 1835,
Aged 72 *Years*.

Over the tomb is the identical stone—3 feet 6 inches by 2 feet 6 inches, and 2 feet thick—set in motion by the farm-hands at Oldfield (seen amidst trees above) at the dictation of their master, who affirmed that where it stopped there he would be buried. Old residents say the stone first rested in the bed of the stream below, which we think plausible enough; but our own impression is its course would be arrested probably where the grave is, since the large pear-shaped mound surrounding the tomb is situated in the centre of a clough and appears to be artificial.

A Nonconformist minister performed the act of burial, and a large concourse of people from far and near came to witness the funeral.

STANBURY.

Retracing steps we saunter through Stanbury village, described by one tourist as "a strange medley of buildings, barns, cottages and chapels, hustling each other for position." Legend says Cromwell passed through this hamlet, and halting, inquired its name.

"Bury," said affrighted natives.

"Then let Bury stand!" answered Cromwell, and his men resumed their march. In this wise Stanbury is said to have derived its name,

STANBURY, FROM SOUTH.

though the Rev. T. W. Story, in the publication already referred to, says Stanbury was Stanbury hundreds of years before Cromwell was born.

" T'OWD GENTLEMAN'S " GRAVE.
(*Photo by J. Bradley, Stanbury*).

A LANCASHIRE TYKE.

We are barely clear of the village when our steps are arrested by a voice behind shouting :

" Heigh ther ! "

We recognise the figure—a Lancashire tyke—and guess his purport.

" Aw wodno' be sure wen yo' went by on yon' at it wur yo' ; but e gye ! aw wur na far orf. An' yo' com' o'er *T'Stairs " ? he asks, feigning interest in us.

This is our addresser's wily mode of attack ; at heart he hopes to

*An old road some three-quarters of a mile north-west of Cock Hill, and leading from Hebden Bridge to Haworth.

realize the price of a pint of beer. He pleads hunger when we appear reluctant, and seems stunned when we offer a tea-cake procured from a neighbour; yet he accepts it with thanks, bids us "good day," and turns towards whence he came, gulping down with evident relish the buttered "muffin." We have had him in hand before, and sometimes have envied his happy-go-lucky life. In summer a hay-maker, and when the harvest is ended he may be found anywhere within twelve miles of Keighley spreading manure, or doing odd jobs about farms. Hartley's "Jolly Beggar" fits him splendidly:—

"Aw'm as rich as a Jew, tho aw havn't a meg,
But aw'm free as a bird, an' aw shak a loise leg;
Aw've noa haase, an' noa bairns, soa aw nivver pay rent,
But still aw feel rich, for aw'm bless'd wi' content,
Aw live, an' aw'm jolly,
An' if it is folly,
Let others be wise, but aw'll follow mi bent.

Mi kitchen aw find amang th' rocks up o' th' moor,
An' et neet under th' edge of a haystack aw snoor,
An' a wide spreadin' branch keeps th' cold rain off mi mop,
Wol aw listen to th' stormcock, at pipes up o' th' top.
Aw live, an' aw'm jolly, &c.

Aw never fear thieves, for aw've nowt they can tack,
Unless it's thease tatters at hing o' mi back;
An' if they prig them, they'll get sucked, do yo see,
They'll be noa use to them, for they're little to me.
Aw live, an' aw'm jolly, &c.

Tho' philosophers talk, an' church parsons may praich,
An' tell us true joy is far aght of us raich;
Yet aw nivver tak heed o' ther cant o' ther noise,
For he's now't to be feared on at's nowt he can loise.
Aw live, an' aw'm jolly, &c.

CHAPTER XII.

"Owd Timmy": His Home and Loom.*

Past the bar-house at the far end of the village we diverge from the turnpike, and looking away to the moors, stroll up a narrow road to the left a short distance, when another branching of roads occurs. A male invalid resting on a seat at the junction raises a smile upon detecting a pin-hole through "Owd Timmy's" house, as we hold our map up to the light, while assuring us the way to our right will lead us to "t'owd 'and-lume weeaver's." So on we trudge.

As we near the farthest cottages at Buckley Green Bottom, we note on the walls of the far one :—

R.
G. M.
1832.

Ivy creeps up by the curtainless window, partially covering the house-front and gable-end, clambering on to the roof and finally throwing a green mantle round the chimney. Stunted Jerusalem lily plants (Imantophyllum) adorn (?) the window inside; but for these we should imagine the house untenanted. The once green door is closed, and minus sneck. A stout piece of tree-trunk does duty as threshold.

We sincerely hope "Timmy" is at home, though we hear not the clatter of the loom, and there are no signs of life about the place. Gentle taps with knuckles bring no response, nor knocks with an umbrella. Are we foiled in our errand, after all? We hammer away in earnest, but only succeed in bringing "Timmy's" neighbour to her door. She is confident Timmy is in, and perhaps his deafness has prevented him hearing us. Some fine folk with a carriage-and-pair have just left and he was knocking about then, she adds. Again we pommel the door. Maybe he is upstairs doing something to his loom, or he is "picking up

*Timmy's loom and all necessary apparatus are lodged in a special room at the Keighley Museum.

TIMOTHY FEATHER ("OWD TIMMY") HAND-LOOM WEAVER, STANBURY.
(*Photo by F. Shuttleworth, Haworth*).

dropped ends," suggests his neighbour. We have thoughts of a ladder, but are recommended a clothes' prop, and one is brought us. This novel plan works admirably. Two or three slight taps on the chamber window, and there is a responsive rap on the pane. Now we hear the slow, irregular clomping of clogs down the staircase, a shuffling behind the door, a fumbling of hands, the withdrawal of a bolt and the door swings open. There before us with white woolly locks stands a pure, primitive type of an old-time hand-loom weaver. In stature short of five feet, and, as Mr. Keighley Snowden observes, "in the strong old face we catch a look of Mr. Gladstone and Dr. Temple."

"The smile that won't come off" is surely that of the old weaver's, we muse, as he greets us, and motioning, invites us to "draw tat owd cheer nar t' fire," while apologetically observing "E see it's neear art es a toucher; but ya'll 'appen net feel cowd if E oppen t' daar a bit en put t' draw-tin op?"

After scrambling on to the table amid a jorum of pots, pans, tins, etc., securing two early spring chickens from amongst the window plants and politely transmitting them to the open air, we settle down to converse with "Little Timmy," as he is familiarly referred to in the neighbourhood. No one ever calls him Timothy, he tells us, or addresses him as Mr. Feather, "cept fine fooaks."

We think our presence may hinder work, and intimating this are at once set at ease.

"Naa, ya'll na'an 'inder maa fra ony wark. E's na'an ower 'tic'lar thrang just naa; E's raather short o' waft."

Timmy's dwelling baffles description; many have attempted it, but only two we have read of have succeeded with any success; *our* pencils are incompetent.

Mr. Keighley Snowden, after a visit to Timmy's, invites *Yorkshire Weekly Post* readers to "Step into his cosy house and admire a fine disorder; a picturesque interior; an old curiosity shop. There is an eight-day clock with other time-pieces, of which the only one going is a cuckoo clock, with naked weights and pendulum. There are four bird cages, two cases of stuffed animals, two oak chests, a chest of drawers, a long table, three or four old carved chairs, and his bobbin-winder, all packed into 15 feet square; and the floor is strewn with bowls and tins, and the table littered with all of a bachelor's kitchening—jugs and mugs and basins, syrup tins and a porridge thible, old spoons and forks thrown anyhow, a teapot, plates, a clay pipe, and a dusty tea-caddy. Three

sickly plants survive on the window-ledge, and the walls are covered close with pictures. Another clock and two more cages in the weaving chamber. The loom fills half the room, and the bed disputes the other half with meal-tubs and old lumber. There are no birds in the cages now ; he could not keep them singing after his brother died, not understanding them. When all the clocks were going, and all the larks and throstles sang, and the loom resounded too, this was a lively house."

And one Arthur Melton, writing in the *Sunday Chronicle*, says :

" Photographs do injustice both to the man and his loom. Was there ever such a living-room as this kitchen, which, with the staircase, occupies all the ground-floor of the cottage ? It is a picture in itself. His furniture dates back to the days when solidity was more highly thought of than cheapness. That old oak chest, which would look well in the vestry of an ancient church, has tempted many a collector of antiquities. So has the high chest of drawers with the inlay and the fluted angle pieces. There is a grandfather's clock in the corner, a spinning wheel by Timmy's armchair, and a table and delph-rack against the furthermost wall which hold pottery that everybody wants to buy as relics of the old hand-weaver's cottage. You might as well ask Timmy to sell you his head !

Under the window is a dresser which proclaims what a fine, crusted old bachelor Timmy is. It is covered with tins. Preserve tins, fruit tins, coffee tins, tins of all sizes and of all shapes—what a collection ! You could imagine a conscientious Yorkshire house-wife, with a craze for tidiness, sweeping the whole lot into a sack and pitching them outside. There are kindly women who would tidy things up a little if Timmy was willing. But that independent old man declares he will do his own tidying, and the woman who attempted to re-arrange his domestic possessions, and reduce his larder of tins to order, would find that behind Timmy's mild manner is concealed a tongue that scarifies."

* * * * * *

And, certainly, to transform Timmy's cot into the ideal home, an assiduous housewife would for days have a thoroughly good time. But the comfort of being unworried with the thoughts of cleaning down ! What bliss !

Little talking is necessary on our part. Timmy rattles away. Our pencils have to hasten to keep pace, but he heeds us not, nor even offers comment upon what we are jotting down.

Timothy Feather's Kitchen; "A Picturesque Interior."
(*Photo by J. J. Stead, Heckmondwike*).

"Ya cum ta luke et ma lume an' see ma weeav, beant ya?" inquires the old man, his face radiant.

To catch our reply the little man inclines an ear, and we shout in unpolished phrase:

"Aye, that's partly es mission."

"Ya'r art fishin'? E'm feeared ya'll net leet ower mony raand 'ere."

Deafness is a sad affliction, and we hasten to express sympathy.

Timmy's misapprehension of our answer calls to mind an incident equally amusing. We knew the man personally; indeed we are linked on to the lineage. He, too, was a hand-loom weaver, over 90 years of age and very deaf. One morning he was "out for an airing," as he termed it, and met his grandson, who saluted him thus:—

"Well, gronfayher! ha're yo' gooin on wi yo'r 'and-loom?"

"Yos!" responded the old man, "aw allus thowt aw shud like ta gooa up in a balloon."

"But," shrieked the boy in his ear, "aw think yo' dooan't kno' whaat aw say."

"Oh now," came the still more bewildering reply, with a shake of the head, "aw dooan't think it *wod* pay."

* * * * * *

"Which waa an ya cum?" next inquires Timmy.

"From Haworth," we shout.

"Then ya'll a met yon fine fooak i tha'r carriage?"

We nod an affirmative.

"Thay've bin o' purpos ta see ma, en ta pleease 'em E've wovven 'em a fow picks. Eaah! See ya whaat thay've laft ma!"

Here he dives into his pocket and brings forth a florin and a shilling.

"Tha'r vary guid fooaks, deant ya think saa? Thay've laft an order beside for sum cotton, but E deant kno' when thay'll get it, fer E ca'ant weeave fast enif; E've three twelve yards an' one twenty et E caan't fit op. Ya'll be able ta mack art ha' mich thay waant, E think thay've writn't on that paaper on't kist lid. Eaah!"

On the back of the "paaper" (a grocer's bill to Timmy for £2, promptly settled) is pencilled an order for twenty yards of cotton. On our intimating this to Tim he declares "'t ay'll 'av ta waat thar turn, saa's they're net laaikly fer gettin' 't ower saain." "But," adds he, smilingly looking up in our faces, "if thay deaan't get it thay weaant av ta pay for't, will thay?"

"E'm naa scholar," laments Timmy, "Naan o' ya'r fooak cud read

or write, an' tha wur ten iv us—all 'andlume weeavers—an' E'm t' ony one laft."

He has some faint recollection as a lad of reading and writing being taught at "Scar Top Sunday Schewl, then a low-raam'd biggin." Brothers and sisters are all gone, Timmy goes on to tell us, the last, a brother, dying three years ago at the age of 92. Sixteen years back a sister died, and since then he has lived alone.

We suggest a wife by way of gleaning his views on matrimony.

"Did ya saa E sud be mare cumfort'ble if E'd a woman ta taa care o' ma? E's naa daat thay're vary useful i' thay're plaace, makin' a meeal an' suing yar buttons on, but E think E'll be able ta wither ma bit o' time aart es E am. E's ya saa, E cud weeav mony a bit whol E's botherin' makkin summat t' eyt. A man gat on talkin' es ya're dooin' wun daa, an' he'd nubbat just gat wed naaither a fow weeaks afoor, but he said he'd laaike ta sha'ack a looise leg ageean."

Timmy cannot definitely state his age,* but says "Yar fooak allus said E wur born twenty weeaks after t' Crow Hill flood (Sep. 2, 1824).

As we chat, the fire glows while steam and some solid substance threaten to dislodge the lid of the pan on the hob, reminding us of the story told of the little one who apprised its mother that "th' sheep-heead wer' tuppin' th' dumplins aght o' th' pan."

"It's nobbut a bit o' meeat E's simmerin' et E bought this mornin' iv a butcher et cums raand iv'ry Monday," explains Timmy, seeing we manifest concern; and he adds "E caan't chew it es E used ta cud; E's baart teeth."

"Do you have porridge sometimes, Timmy?"

"Whaat did ya saa? Do E iver av ma porridge? Eaah! iv'ry mornin', an' thay're t' best meeal E get i' t' daa."

"Then yo' smook a bit, Timmy," we remark as he produces a black short clay and charges it with shreds of tobacco from his waistcoat pocket.

"E av a pipe naa an then. It's naa'en a yar sart o' bacco E reck'n. E'er niver used ta baa mare na tue macks—leet an' dark—naa, e'ers a scaare or tue diff'rent saarts."

His tobacco alight, and meat attended to, we ply him with questions thick and varied. Contrary to expectation we find he has seen the sea.

"Bin ta Liverpool waance, an' Marcum Baa three times," he tells us.

* According to the baptismal register at Haworth Church, Timmy was born Jan. 20, 1825, and was baptised July 25, the same year, by the Rev. Patrick Brontë. He died Nov. 30, 1910.

"A saail? Eaah! E paid a shillin' et Marcum ta gu on t' watter, an' E rade reyght aht, an' it niver tuke naa hod o' ma; it macks sum fooak pick up (vomit), ya kno'. Eaah!"

He has lived about here all his life, and under this same roof ever since he was a lad. "E starts wark when E likes, an' E gives op when E likes," says he, "but E've a full daa's 'aliday et t' Sunday."

Timmy abhors Sunday visiting, and will not on that day talk of his loom, or allow any to see it. He has grown very devout in his latter days, we afterwards learn, though he "wur niver whaat ya ma call a bad'n." And we find he is, in principle, a temperance advocate. He "never did apply hot and rebellious liquors to the blood," and wonders why men should. His greatest delight in his younger days was jumping and clog-dancing; "an' mind yo," says he, "a brother o' mine an' ma cud clatter it." He relates with pride how he once saved his native village, Stanbury, from disgrace at the hands of the Haworthites in a jumping-match, by cutting a rival's mark by over two feet! He has had his likeness "ta'en maany scooas o' times. E'er caame tue men o' 'orseback wun daa, an' thay tuke baath t' inside an' t' aartside o' t' biggin', an' maa an' all es E wur weeavin. But E tuke naa naatice iv 'em; E wur ower thrang et t' time. Ya con buy ma fer tuppence on a paast-card, aaither i' Stanb'ry, Ha'orth, Keeathla or Bradfo'd, thay saa. Eaah!"

We intimate our intention of bringing him before the Halifax public, and wonder if he repels.

"Naa! net E marry. Ya con print whaat ya laaike an' mak t' shap o' ma an' all fer ought E care," says Timmy, "but E's licked whaat ya con fynd ta saa. Whaat paaper did ya saa ya wur gain ta put it in?"

"*Halifax Weekly Courier*," we shout.

"E caan't reead, ya kno', but that young woman next daar es vary guid, she'll reead it ta ma iv E ax her."

We promise to forward a "paaper." Now we are conducted upstairs.

"That's whaat E calls a swift-top, says Tim, seeing we are interested in a cocoanut-like wooden article on three legs, and he demonstrates its use.

How desperately cold in winter must be this "oppen-ta-thack" chamber. Sleeping, storage, lumber and workroom combined. Here are sacks of corn and meal to feed the eighty odd poultry which their owner declares keeps him "fra rickettin, when short o' waft or warp."

Timmy now adjusts his spectacles and busies himself, humouring his lifelong friend at certain points in preparation to "weeave a fow picks" for our edification. That we may have a "front seat" during the

performance we are requested to "lift t' owd spooil-reel ower tuther side o' t' bed, an' put it daahn under t' little end winda art o' t' rooad; an' mynd ya dean't mucky ya'r claase." He strides nimbly into the belt-seat and like an organist about to play, plants thick clogs on the treadles, grasps with right hand the shuttle-string, urges "t' 'and tree" by a gentle push, and we are treated to an exhibition of manual labour the like of which it may never be our lot to see agian. As the old frame shivers it seems to wearily chant :—

"Nick a ting, nock a ting;
Wages keep pocketing,
Working for little is better nor laikin',
Twist an' twine, reel an' wind,
Keep a contented mind;
Troubles are oft of a body's own makin'."

"Ya wadn't laaik ta due that fer a fow shillin' a weeak, wad ya?" queries Tim in a little breathing space. "Fooaks dean't kno' thay're born naa o' daas; E cud tell ya sum taails et 'd cap ya, an' mak ya feel fayn ya warn't livin' saventy yeear sin', when E wur a lad. Eaah!"

Deep notches in "t' 'and tree," (sleyboard)—the imprint of finger and thumb of the left hand—tell of the 540,000,000 times it must have been pushed and pulled these sixty years of 250 days of ten hours each, in the weaving of 234,780 yards of stuff, reckoning sixteen picks to a quarter-inch. This, according to Mr. Snowden's calculations.

"Did ya saa whaat langth wur ma warp when E first gat it?" This et E av in naah wur fower 'underd yards lang when E started on't five or six weeak sin. E laaiked tue or three weeaks bafaar then, but E macks nowt o' laaikin; E'd raather 'av full wark! Eaah! E daar saa E'll 'av wovven a 'underd yards fra it naah; but it's all gaan, an' iv E'd es mich agaan ready E cudn't ableage iverbody et waants sum. Fooaks 'r plump weearisome; thay're fit ta pool ma aht o' t' 'ahse fer 't." Eaah!

"Haa mich do E sell ma cotton a yard, did ya ax?" "Waal, E 'av sell'd it at savenp'nce-awpney, but thay rase ma t' waft a awpney a pund, abaat three weeak sin', an' E'm faarst ta charge eightp'nce naah; E caan't work fer nowt, ya kno'; Naah!"

Again to his loom he entertains us to another "fow picks," then, as if mindful of other visitors, he springs from his seat, remarking "E meean't weeav ower mich; E deean't kno' when E'll gat ony mare waft."

Placing an order for cotton which we request sending by carrier to Halifax, we descend the stone stairs, Timmy following at our heels.

TIMOTHY FEATHER'S LOOM IN KEIGHLEY MUSEUM.
The picture on the wall, nearest the loom, depicts Timmy's Kitchen, and he in his arm-chair, smoking.
(*Photo by Messrs. Hall & Siggers, Keighley*).

" Ya'll av ta waat ya'r turn, ya kno' Eaah! But ya'll 'appen baa this waa agaan bafaar E con gat it wuvven ? "

We are exceedingly pleased to have made the acquaintance of Stanbury's celebrity, and we make known the fact to him. Timmy seems to half apprehend and with a look of astonishment wonders why " fooaks mack sich o' doo 'av 'im."

If there is an item in Timmy's home we covet as a memento it is the warming-pan hanging on the wall. It reminds us of the woman who recently visited a friend of ours who had become possessed of a warming-pan, and it hung lustrous at the hob-end. The visitor, known for her inquisitiveness, seeing the round shimmering object with long wooden handle, seriously inquired :—

" En which on yo's leeanin' ta play th' banjo ? "

John Hartley speaks of its usefulness and laments its doom :—

That old warmin' pan, wi' its raand brazzen face,
Has hung theear for mony a day ;
'Twor mi gronny's, and th' haase wodn't luk like th' same place
If we tuk th' owd utensil away.

We ne'er use it nah—but aw recollect th' time
When, at neet, it wor filled wi' red cowks ;
An' ivery bed gate weel warmed, except mine,
For they said it worn't meant for young fowks.

When old gronny deed, 'tworn't mich shoo possest,
An' mi mother coom in for all th' lot ;
An' shoo raised up a duzzen, misen amang th' rest,
An' shoo lived whol shoo deed i' th' same cot.

Aw'm th' maister here nah, but aw see plain enuff,
Things willn't goa long on th' old plan ;
Th' young'ns turn up their nooses at old-fashioned stuff,
An' make gam o' mi old warming pan.

But aw look at it oft as it glimmers i' th' leet,
An' aw seem to live ovver once moor
Them days when mi futer wor all seemin' breet,
An' aw thowt nowt but joy wor i' stoor.

Aw'm summat like th' pan, aw've aght lasted mi day,
An' aw'st sooin get mi nooatice to flit ;
But aw've this consolation—aw think aw may say—
Aw'st leeave some, at aw've warmed up a bit.

" T' owd weeaver," however, is loth to part with any household chattels, no matter how trivial and worthless they may appear ; fancy prices even are no inducement. The more covetous one becomes the more tenaciously Tim clings. Hence we warmly congratulate ourselves on successfully securing a brown meos-pot, reminding us of Betty Rothery's

days, one of two score and more such crockery hanging on the rafters.

* * * * * *

Five-thirty ! How the time has sped since we left Haworth. Timmy's clocks are unreliable ; he declares "e'ers naan iv 'em raat." We are about to depart and are being advised by him the nearest way to Withens when two ladies and a gentleman in a conveyance pull up at his door. Curious to watch their proceedings we remain a few minutes. The same reception is given these strangers as was extended to us. It is apparent this is not their first pilgrimage here. Two of the party bound up the stairs, beckoning their friend to follow without so much as consulting the proprietor. We should protest, but Timmy looks calmly on, seemingly accounting it nothing strange. Another "fow picks" are requested, and Timmy cheerily complies. For two or three minutes it is difficult to say which makes the biggest racket, the loom or the audience.

To see Tim weave is not the chief motive of the new arrivals. They have come to photograph him, and we further linger to see him pose. Spool-reel, swift-top and armchair are requisite to complete the picture, and these are quickly placed outside the cottage door. Timmy has undergone the process such a number of times that he knows exactly what is required of him, and the instant the photographer is ready he betakes himself to his armchair, sitting as if winding a spool. This time, however, it is desired he should present a front view, and omit the winding pretence. A strong breeze is blowing, tantalizing both photographer and subject. Everything is in apple-pie order when, alas, a wuthery gust overturns the reel, and well-nigh dethrones Timmy in his endeavour to save his slouch hat, which is lifted off his white head, and balances in the air as if undecided whether to ascend further. When again in its owner's clutches it is subjected to sound bangings against the lintel of the door by way of cleansing. In the meantime the reel is righted, and once more all are ready, Timmy this time making secure his hat by pulling it nearly down to his ears. For about the seventh time the operator dives under the black cover, and re-appearing, bids one of the party ask Timmy to "look a little more pleasant." The appeal is warranted ; we should never have thought him capable of so grave an expression.

"Now that is much better, Timmy ; keep like that, please," remarks the photographer from force of habit, forgetting for the moment Timmy's deafness.

"That will do, thank you!"

Timmy understands and vacates his seat.

"E daar saa ya'd laaike ta saa ma wynd an odd spooil bafaar ya gaa," volunteers "t' owd weeaver," addressing us all.

We nod assent, gather up the "scenery" and step inside again. The reel is dressed with a fresh cotton hank, and in a trice Timmy has sifted the end of the thread, fixed on the spindle of the swift-top an empty spool, and is making the wheel hum, his forefinger inserted between the thin worm-eaten spokes. At the conclusion of this performance Timmy is liberally rewarded, and shortly after the party drive away towards Haworth.

"Ivry daa's alaaike a'most," says Tim, turning his attention to us, "e'ers allus sum'dy cumin ta luke et ma, aither fine fooak er poor fooak. E caan't seea whaat thay con seea i' aither maa ert' owd lume. Thay've bin even fra Lundon ta luke et ma. Eaah! But av caarse thay dean't cum o' purpus saa far; thay've laaikely cum ta Haworth an' fooaks tells 'em abaat ma, ya kno'. Eaah! Es E wur tellin' on ya when yon fooak caame, ya mon gaa threw that gaat an' past yon rocks an' ya'll cum ta tue lang, lowish biggins, baath farms. E'ers naa wun lives at 'em naa. At t' back iv 'em e'ers an owd cart-track; ya mon keep tul it an it'll laad ya raight up ta t' Withens; ya caan't miss but 'it!"

It occurs to us that Timmy, with his knowledge of the district, may be able to locate "Th' Lad o' Crow Hill"—a stone-post said to have been set up to denote the place where was found the body of one who, like Benjamin Foster, was lost on the moors in a snowstorm. On our return to-morrow we hope to pay the "lad" a visit, and information respecting "his" whereabouts will prove useful.

"'Lad o' Crow Hill'!" echoes Tim. "Eaah! E've bin at it maany scaar o' times." Pointing north-west in the direction of chimney-like objects on the sky-line, he continues:—

"Ya saa yon row o'—E deaan't kno' whaat ya'll call 'em, but it's wheear sheuters caar when thay're on t' maar; thay luke laaike chimlays fra 'ere."

"Shooting covers," we suggest.

"Eaah! E daar saa that's thar naame. At t' back iv 'em is an owd delph—ya con saa tippins, luke ya! 'T' Lad' es abaat tue or three 'underd yards farther back, at t' flat o' t' maar, an' abaat a 'underd an' fifty yards fra t' edge."

"Haa far wod ya call it fra 'ere?" we ask, attempting to frame a sentence in Stanbury dialect.

"E sud think it'll naan baa abaan a mile an' a 'awf es t' crow flies, but it'll taa ya, E daar saa, an 'aar an' a quarter ta traance it." If ya wur gaain straat awaa, ya'd 'av ta gaa daan past Pondin reservoy an' up past Pondin Hall yonder, luke ya! Eaah! it's a ruffish gaat, but ya'd fynd yar waa E've naa daat."

We shout "Good afternoon" into Timmy's ear, though it is turned six, and by a firm grip of his hand endeavour to make him feel the thanks we are at a loss to express otherwise.

"Waal! E haap ya'll land saaf ta yar jarny's end 'afaar dark," is "t'owd weeaver's" benediction. "Ya've cum a lang waa an' ya've a lang waa ta gaa yet. It's laaily fer bin a grand neet, saa that'll baa e yar faavor ower t' maar. Gooid daa! E'll send yar cotton on when E 'av it ready. Gooid daa!"

* * * * * *

A while ago the inner man called for attention, so as we wind up the craggy moorland (Timmy's poultry-farm) we munch victuals stowed in our pockets. Thoughts are largely occupied with things seen and heard during our sojourn at Timmy's. What a genial old man he is, to be sure. The very essence of patience and contentment. His happy state calls to mind Halliwell Sutcliffe's summary of life in an interview in the *County Monthly* some time since. Asked if he had a theory of life he wished to illustrate, the Bingley novelist, probably having in his mind's-eye "t'owd weeaver," since, as we believe, they are no strangers to each other, said :—

"I have no theory of life, except that farm life—the life of tilling and ploughing—is the only sane one," adding, "I am sincerely convinced of the evil tendency of what we call 'progress.' Steam, it seems to me, has done more to degrade man than any discovery the world has known ; it has substituted hurry for patience, and greed for the old quiet wish to earn as much as mind and body needed for ordinary comfort ; it has drawn men to the towns, and the towns have always been a sort of cancerous growth ; it has substituted the hideous conditions of the factory for the same healthy handiwork that was done in country cottages. There's no doubt at all that the period preceding the introduction of the steam engine was the happiest that the working man has known ; he had the sane life then, and farmed and sowed, and reaped in the intervals of weaving, or of combing. He was, in his own quiet way, a rich man, for he could grow on his bit of land enough to keep himself well fed, and, in addition, he had the wages of his handicraft."

CHAPTER XIII.

A KINDRED SOUL—WITHENS ("WUTHERING HEIGHTS").

RATHER than risk our shins in the stile whose flanks bow to each other, we prefer climbing the crumbling wall, first placing, on a safe top-stone, our "little brown jug," which we feel as proud of as those folks on the way to Bradford possessed of a negative of "t'owd weeaver." Forward through three small meadows, and we enter the old cart-track close beside "t' bottomest" of the "tue lang lowish biggins" pointed out by Timmy. We are in luck's way for a man approaches; surely a rarity at this time of the day in so outlandish a spot. He tells us the present "biggin" is called Lower Height, and the one immediately above is Upper Height (⩚ 1161.5); they are indicated on our map, but no names are given.

LOWER HEIGHT.

We intimate that friends beyond Walshaw Dean Waterworks await us; indeed are expecting us every moment. Observing we are strangers in a strange land, our friend imparts most acceptable information. Like Timmy he rattles away, and it is only necessary for us to occasionally respond. We make a mental note of most he says though, and afterwards couple it up.

"Whaw! aw've just 'ad an aghting ovver theer misel ta day, an' my

word, it is a thrang place ! " he goes on to tell us. " But they'll nooan be workin' when yo' get theer—vary few at ony rate—they'll 'av ligged away aboon an' haar sin'. When yo' get ta th' first Withens—ther's three Withens, all farms, th' Lower, th' Middle, an' th' Heigher—yo'll 'av a job ta tell et ther is, or ever wor, a rooad et all. Ther's nubdy lives et ony o' th' buildin's naah, nor 'as ther fer some time, yo'll nooatice. When yo' get ta th' Heigher Withens—we can just see it under th' 'ill edge thro' 'ere—yo' mun tak ta th' left an' follo th' wall—th' top side on't—ta wheer it turns dahn th' moor, then yo' mun twist up t' th' reight. Ther' is a bit of a sign of a track forrard, but it's sooa faynt yo'll 'av ta booath put yo'r specs on an' strike matches ta find it."

We smile at the humour, but our countenances belie our feelings, for we are really seriously concerned. In less than three hours darkness will be upon us, and we have yet " a trudge of two haars an' a hawf, nice gentle gooin," we are told.

" An' yo've been on yo'r rooad ovver twelve haars, yo' say ! whaw, yo'r 'ardly aght o' th' seet o' 'ooam yet. Yo' see yond farest hill-point ? " looking southwards across Haworth Moor, " yond's th' Nab Hill et yo'll 'a com' dahn this mornin'. But yo'r ankshus ta get on yo'r way aw see. Well ! it's grand naah, tho' it luck'd a bit like rain abaht three o'clock. Yo'll just pike ovver th' moor afooar dark aw think. Now ! aw dooan't think yo'll see another face this side yo'r destinashun, 'cept it be a tooathry navvies sidlin' abaht as yo' goa past th' works. Well, good neet ! "

" Good neet ! "

* * * * * *

We guessed he was from Halifax the moment he spoke. Soon the moor ridge cuts off all sight of our friendly instructor as he descends to Stanbury. The three Withens now appear in view, and in a few minutes we are passing the Lower Withens (⩚ 1223-2) ; we now rise through fields, in which we fail to trace the path marked on our map, to Middle Withens* (⩚ 1292.3), and forward to Higher Withens (⩚ 1376.9). Emily Brontë's " Wuthering Heights," and Halliwell Sutcliffe's " Lost Withens."

* This property, consisting of farmhouse, barn, and about fifty acres of land, was left in trust in 1723 by one David Midgley, to " clothe with food and convenient blue clothes and other necessary wearing apparel, ten poor children of the township of Haworth, to be from time to time made choice of at the discretion of his said trustees and their heirs, which children should be then under the age of seven years if the rents and profits of the said premises would extend to the same."

A tablet in Haworth Church records the deed in these words :—

" David Midgley, Lord of the manor of Haworth, left a farm for ever to clothe yearly ten poor children (in blue) belonging to the said parish."

Top Withens ("Wuthering Heights").

The Rev. T. W. Story, in his *Notes on the old Haworth Registers*, commenting on the above bequest and quoting from a copy of the will included in the registers, says "this was to be done yearly, and every year for ever, at the Feast of St. Martin the Bishop, in winter," adding that "though the bequest is still carried out, the actual date at which it should be done is ignored." He points out that "the Feast of St. Martin the Bishop" falls now on Nov. 11th, and further observes that "David Midgley meant the children to be better equipped with clothes near the beginning of winter than is now the case."

After that climb of 451 feet from Timmy's we welcome the sound of running water, but are puzzled to know whence it comes. A little searching, however, and we discover a spring a few feet away, literally hidden in a drapery of herbage, and we drink freely.

There! an excellent substitute for the cup of tea we dearly should have enjoyed with our open-air lunch.

And this, the Top Withens, is "Wuthering Heights," the name of Heathcliffe's dwelling. The building, however, indicates the situation only of "Wuthering Heights;" we are told, Law Hill, Southowram, near Halifax, where Emily Brontë was teacher from September, 1836 to March or April, 1837, is recognised as the original externally. Notwithstanding, we will make comparisons. In Emily's masterpiece we read that "'Wuthering' is a significant provincial adjective, descriptive of the atmospheric tumult to which its station is exposed in stormy weather. Pure, bracing ventilation they must have up here, at all times indeed. One may guess the power of the north wind blowing over the edge by the excessive slant of a few firs at the end of the house, and by a range of gaunt thorns, all stretching their limbs one way, as if asking alms of the sun. Happily the architect had foresight to build it strong, the narrow windows are deeply set in the wall, and the corners defended with large jutting stones."

The building before us comprises mistal, barn, house—which at one time had a thick coating of plaster—and peat-house, substantially and firmly planted end-on to the hill-side. While subjected to "the power of the north wind blowing over the edge," it is considerably more exposed to the storms of the east which drive across Haworth Moor. The narrow windows are deeply set in the wall. The panes originally were evidently leaded and diamond-shaped, for a last remnant hangs partly torn from a mullion. We peer through this opening, knowing the place is unoccupied, and behold a weird hearth. A rudely-

constructed table and seats, a dinted enamelled kettle, and heaped-up ashes in the rusty grate suggest occasional visits by shepherds. Crouching in the cramped house porch we try the door, but find it securely fastened, as are also those of the barn and mistal. Access is only obtainable to the lofty peat-house, now serving as shelter for moorland sheep. There appears to be no date on the building. Across the yard, where grass springs up between the rough pavement, are two tiny fenced strips—probably sheep folds, but suggesting an old-time garden—at the top of which a group of young sycamores bend their slender limbs northwards, as if imploring mercy from the elements; at the bottom, beside an outhouse lit with leaded panes, a "gaunt thorn" inclines in the direction of its more youthful associates, and like a decrepit person with bent body, and ready for the call, seems reconciled to its fate. We are tempted to rest on the slab beneath the tree, while we look down the dale into wild expanse. Before us is a sweeping stretch of Haworth Moor, and beyond the eye wanders over the north side of the Worth Valley. Anyone approaching from Haworth (in a bee-line over three miles distant), say on a visit to Brontë Waterfall, would be under the ken of our glass till they dipped into "Hazel Dene," a mile below. We would fain linger, but time forbids, and the wind blows chill.

CHAPTER XIV.

WALSHAW DEAN—A DISPUTED FOOTPATH—THE RESERVOIRS.

" UP ! let's trudge another mile."

LO ! there is no "way out" from "Wuthering Heights" forward. Gaps filled up and gates made fast temporarily impede us, but over the wall we spring, first exercising care for the safety of the precious relic reminding us of Timmy, alighting on the skirt of the moor, where we now observe the doorway affording ready housing for the peat. Having regard to directions received, though pinning our trust more especially to our map, we "tak ta th' left 'and, an' follo' th' wall" for some 200 or 300 yards, where we strike a moorland path,* the right to use which we afterwards find was long contested. Proceeding, we keep parallel with the fence to the end as directed, and as our map indicates, now "twist op th' moor ta th' reight." True, friend, "ther' is a bit ov a sign ov a track forrad, but it's sooa faynt, yo'll av ta booath put yo'r specs on an' strike matches ta find it." We feel the force of this as we advance.

* After a deal of newspaper controversy, and meetings to discuss the question of right of footpath, the following amicable settlement was arrived at in May, 1908 (three years after our saunter), between Mr. B. Lipscomb, agent for Lord Savile, and the representatives of Halifax Corporation, Wadsworth, Heptonstall and Blackshaw Parish Councils, Todmorden Rural District Council and Oakworth Urban District Council :

" It is mutually agreed by all parties represented at this meeting that, without prejudice to the rights claimed by any party, the public shall be allowed to cross the Walshaw Dean Valley on foot, and unaccompanied by dogs (except such dogs are under control by being in leash), by means of the Corporation roadway from Blake Dean, and over the embankment of the Middle Reservoir, and on the inner side of the Corporation boundary wall to a point near Black Clough, and thence over the moor to Withens on a way to be defined by stones or otherwise.

This arrangement to be subject to immediate determination by either Lord Savile or the Corporation when in the opinion of either the use of such footpath occasions any nuisance or damage, and in the event of such determination all parties will be thrown back upon their rights as they exist to-day, as if this arrangement had never been made.

It is further understood that upon such days as the use of the path would certainly cause annoyance and damage, Lord Savile will endeavour to arrange that a notice shall be posted at Shaw Dike, and the Wadsworth and Stanbury boundary, to warn persons from using the path. Suggested notice to be posted at Shaw Dike and Wadsworth and Stanbury boundary : "Walshaw Dean to Stanbury path. The privilege of using this footpath is subject to the public taking no dogs except as aforesaid, and causing no damage or nuisance. A red flag will be flown upon this pole on those days when the use of the path will certainly cause damage and inconvenience, and the public are therefore warned not to use the path while the flag flies."

Mr. Halliwell Sutcliffe, replying to a request to sign a petition maintaining a public right of way, wrote: " It is both a pleasure and a duty to me to sign the copy of the memorial. Far too many tracks over the moors are being lost sight of now-a-days, and you are right in thinking that I have a special interest in the path you mention. It runs through what is to me—and, I know, to many others—the most beautiful and characteristic moorland in the West Riding."

Presently the dry wiry grass gives place to patches of black earth, over which the path appears more distinct. Twenty minutes' walk from "Wuthering Heights," and we have reached the summit of the moor—1,457 feet—our highest point. On our right is Withens Height—1,500 feet. Not a habitation or soul within sight. On every hand nothing but wild waste. Not a sound save the eerie wails of a pair of whimbrels far out of gun range, the timorous birds obviously regarding us as violators of their peace and tranquillity. It was Robinson Crusoe, we believe, who in a soliloquy sighed :—

"Oh solitude, where are the charms
That sages have seen in thy face ?
Better dwell in the midst of alarms
Than reign in this horrible place."

But we differ in our present soliloquy :—

"Who does not love to tramp the moor,
Knee deep in purple heath !
Or press the springy emerald floor
That decks the dale beneath ?
Who does not love the mountain peak,
Its awful solitude ;
Where not a murmur dares to break
Upon its quietude ?"

A sharp whistle changes our trend of thought, and for a moment we are startled. Are we then under the observation of a keeper? And is that his warning to keep to the footpath? No, we conclude, it is only the shriek of an engine at the works in the dale, and we press on. For a short distance the moor is almost dead level. Gradually there opens out to our view Walshaw Dean, the site of three new reservoirs for Halifax. As we commence the descent we see the two lower basins a mile, perhaps, ahead. Down, down, down we trudge over the bent-covered peat-clods, picking every step, lest we should come to grief in one of many treacherous channels. At the head of the Dean, away up on our right, we observe the partially completed embankment of the top reservoir. As we descend the wind subsides, while :—

"Sunk to a curve, the day star lessens still,
Gives one bright glance, and drops behind the hill."

We arrive near the embankment of the middle reservoir. Through the construction of the reservoirs our path forward is wiped out. Claiming right-of-way, we proceed past the works ; we have no alternative.

Yonder at the bottom of the Dean, on the far side of the valley, is the home of our friends and our haven of rest. Only two miles away, but O! how far it seems. Passing through a broken space in the new boundary wall, we cross on planks the deep newly-paved conduit, and standing between the rails encircling the whole works, endeavour to take in the situation. With the rising moor as a back-ground, and commanding the two lower reservoirs, is the new Waterman's Cottage, already dubbed the "Councillors' Hotel." What a vast enterprise is set up here betwixt the hills, and yet, amid it all, no life that is apparent. Upon closer observation, right down in the bed of the reservoir we perceive figures moving about. The 16 travelling cranes, 15 locomotives, 6 portable engines, sand machine, and the numerous 6 in. and 4 in. pumps which we saw mentioned in the *Halifax Weekly Courier* a short time ago, are standing idle. We were then told the scheme would approach £300,000, as against Mr. Tempest's contract for £200,000; this through "extras" which had cropped up chiefly in the trenches—where a foundation was expected at a depth of 60 feet, but in many places has necessitated an excavation double that depth—the "beaching" and removal of peat. The maximum number of men employed since the first sod was cut—September 17, 1900, by Ald. W. Brear, then Mayor of Halifax,—was 600. At that ceremony the Mayor predicted 1908 would be ushered in before the huge reservoirs would be completed.* The storage capacities of the basins are :—

Top reservoir	...	204,945,000 gallons.
Middle reservoir	...	244,354,000 ,,
Lower reservoir	...	159,971,000 ,,

an aggregate of 609,270,000 gallons. The drainage embraces an area of 2,325 acres.

We travel at a forced pace down the iron track, adapting our stride to the irregularly-placed sleepers which carry seemingly insecurely-fastened rails. Occasionally the line leaps, in bridge fashion, yawning spaces, but over these eerie-looking structures we dare not venture. We have steered clear of pitfalls thus far, and we would not wittingly subject ourselves to danger. So at each such chasm encountered we quit the line, scramble along the edge of the embankment, and where convenient rejoin the track. Again we halt to survey the gigantic undertaking. Deposited here and there among the ling are a number of out-of-date horse-trams, on which we read "18 inside and 22 outside,"

*The opening took place 1st October, 1907.

" Passengers are requested not to stand on the platform," and " Lime Street." How very unique their situation, transmitted from the heart of Liverpool to this solitary wilderness ; but what luxurious cabins they make for navvies !

It was a commercial traveller, we have heard say, who boarded one of these cars at Hebden Bridge Station, where it awaited conveyance hither, and becoming absorbed in his paper, sat for an incredible time, then alighted, and inquired what time the tram was due out!

Again down the track we plod our way. Serenity floats in the air ; all is still as death. Twice our feet are arrested by audible sounds, and we listen breathlessly. We could affirm we heard voices in huts near at hand, but no ! not a whisper ; our ears must deceive us, and we trudge on. A little further and we distinctly hear a babbling of tongues ; this time it is no delusion. Rounding a sharp curve approaches a small party of both sexes in holiday attire ; they presumably have chosen the tranquil evening hours wherein to view the works—when the implements are laid aside and the toilers have retired. We comment upon the weather and pass on. As we reach the embankment of the lower reservoir our minds hark back to the Thursday following Shrove Tuesday, 1902—an ideal winter's morning—when these bleak hills were clothed in a white mantle. We then stood on this spot admiring the landscape. A navvy, we remember, pronounced the scene " just lovely ! "

Now we enter a comparatively straight stretch of shining metals, running through fertile meadows which look pretty in the gathering twilight. Wordsworth's poet's darlings—the dearly-cherished daisies—have long since

" Shut ther' een an' sed
" Good neet " to th' dew an' gone to bed."

The dandelion is tucking in the strings of nature's hood, veiling its glossy face from the raw evening wind, while buttercups and hemlock, with their respective yellow and grey crowns unswayed by breeze, tower high above the more lowly associates, as if " watching o'er their flock by night."

" A blackbird singing far away
Seems to praise the dying day
In sweet celestial melodies."

Presently we catch a glimpse of Blake Dean Trestle Bridge—700 feet long and 105 feet high—which spans the valley at the head of Hardcastle

Craggs, that glorious rendezvous of thousands of trippers, and paradise of nature students.

* * * * *

This bridge was sublet to, and built by, Geo Greenwood, Hebden Bridge. He is the son of Nimrod Greenwood, landscape gardener and assistant land surveyor, formerly of Lower Saltonstall, who, prior to the construction of Widdop reservoir (1872-8), spent three years in the service of the Halifax Corporation registering the rainfall in the vicinity of the reservoir, lodging during the time at the Pack Horse, a hostelry we hope to pass to-morrow, on our way to Widdop.

George's sister has vivid recollections of visiting her father when up in those regions; once with her mother and her brother George, aged eight. They had walked from Lower Saltonstall to Luddenden Foot station (3 miles), where they purposed catching a certain train to Hebden Bridge; but as it had gone, they started on shanks' pony to cover the 7½ miles separating them and father. It was a very warm day, and told heavily on the children. Upon reaching the place opposite the bridge—within three-quarters of a mile of the Pack Horse—George gave out; he declared he couldn't walk another stride. Just then his father appeared, coming to meet them, and the little fellow, forgetting his tiredness, jumped up and ran for all he was worth.

Trestle Bridge, Blake Dean.

(Photo by Messrs. Westermans, Hebden Bridge).

As the bridge had become insecure, the Walshaw Reservoir Contractors began taking it down on August 14, 1912, and the demolition took until the second week in November following.

CHAPTER XV.

RIDGE NOOK—"COMFORTABLE APARTMENTS"—FORMER VISIT RECALLED—A RUDE AWAKENING—"SIX O'CLOCK MAIL"—WINCING SCENE THROUGH A GLASS—BLAKE DEAN CHAPEL—ANNIVERSARY DAY—A NIGHT BEFORE A PEAT FIRE.

DIVERGING from the railroad, we strike a temporary path, descend sharp into the hollow of the valley, and gain a macadamized road near Alcomden Bridge at Holme Ends. Until now we have not trod road worth the name since leaving Stanbury. Crossing Alcomden Water, contaminated by the works above, we steer along a road forking to the left, somewhat resembling a carriage-drive, and on the face of a precipitous slope. This road was made (1892-4) by the Halifax Corporation, in view of constructing Walshaw Dean Reservoirs. No longer are we strangers in a benighted land; we tread familiar ground. For long years no smoke ascended the chimneys of the old dwellings which we dimly see nestling near the stream; now these are tenanted by navvies. The day's washing hangs languidly on lines strung from post to post over the greensward, an ancient yew at the corner of the croft keeping guard, as it were. Darkness is hastening, but what of that? The fact creates no fears, since but two or three meadows divide us from Ridge Nook, where friends are waiting to welcome us. A few sheep, grazing by the roadside, startled by the click of the gate which crosses the road, disappear in the shadow of a plantation. Scaling the pasture on our right, rabbits scurry hither and thither, their white tails discernible only for a moment; we might be animated scare-crows judging by the fear we seem to inspire in them, but, Bunny! thou need not scamper thus, for:—

"We're nooan bahn to try to catch thi!
We've noa dog wi' us to worry
Thee, poor thing—we like to watch thi.
Life to thee, we're suer, is sweeter
Nor thi flesh to us could prove;
May thy lot an' ours grow breeter,
Blest wi' liberty an' love."

Our destination we see faintly outlined in the twilight. As we draw near we perceive a white object moving slowly towards us, and we salute a man in clean smock. Our " Good evening " evokes a prompt " 'ow do ? " Though strangers to him, we hasten to point out we are not to the tenants of the farm, at which light dawns upon him.

" Aw fancy yo're th' party et they've been expectin' ever sin' long afooar dark, um ? "

" Very likely," we reply.

" Then aw'd advise yo' ta be sharp an' shew yo'rseln. They've a mack o' geen yo' op. Aw'm just bahn ta seeal theease two stirks—it's rayther ta cold fer 'em ta lig aght yet—an' fas'en th' hens op."

While the man attends them, we make our way through the farmyard. How very sincere our welcome.

" Aw been hark'nin' fer a fresh fooit comin' doun th' fold ever sin' teah-time," says our friend Mrs. Parker, meeting us at the porch and extending her hand in greeting. " My word ! yo are lat. Com' yo'r ways in, fer aw'll be bun for't yo're booath tir'd an' 'ungry."

Dismissing the need for any anxiety on our behalf, and depositing our treasured meos–pot in the keeping of our friend to be forwarded to another friend at Hebden Bridge, we accept the hearty invitation, hanging our caps on pegs of the dried stem of a fir tree, suspending from a beam, as we walk in.

Another Betty ! the fourth introduced in our saunter thus far. Old-fashioned ourselves in many things, we have a special regard for " Betty," and such old-time names. Like " Betty o' th' Fly," our friend Mrs. Parker here rarely hears her " Sunday name ; " she says " wi fock et knaw mi best aw seldom get ought but ' Betty o' th' Ridge.' " Supper is ready, and we beseat ourselves before a well-laden table. Mr. Parker, in his homely manner, joins us, having just finished milking—9-30. A white-shaded oil-lamp lights up the cosy primitive scene. We are pressed to " get a gooid supper ; " and we assure our friends we shall ; we have " call " for it, to quote our other friend, Betty. The meal ended, we accede to the wishes of our host and draw chairs round the glowing fire of coal, coke and peat. We must necessarily relate experiences of our day's saunter, to which our audience listens attentively. The long walk and bracing air, however, soon lure " tired nature's sweet restorer, balmy sleep," and it is comforting to follow in the train of the lighted candle being carried up the narrow wooden staircase. When one is thoroughly tired out, what signifieth it whether one's place of

Trestle Bridge, Blake Dean—Walshaw Beyond.

rest be that of a tapestry-draped bedstead, an old-fashioned shut-up contrivance, or a deal plank? Strange surroundings, and the tick of the clock on the mantel-piece, keep us awake for a time, and we are recalling our first visit to Ridge Nook here, many years ago.

A party of us, some our friends who were intimate with our host and hostess, started out early the third Sunday in August, a beautiful morning it was, to visit Blake Dean Sunday School Anniversary, known far and wide as "th' Bonk Charity," or "th' Ridge Charity;" and we made this our head-quarters. At each meal-time tables were spread with home-made comforts. The scene, as we lay awake, is remarkably vivid.

"The table-cloth, though coarse,
Was of a snowy white;
The vessels, spoons and knives
Were clean and dazzling bright;
So, down we sat,
Devoid of care,
Nor envied kings
Their dainty fare."

While we fared sumptously, the farmyard and precincts swarmed with hungry folk, impatiently waiting their turn. "Mon! they're fit ta eyt th' bit o' th' furnatur when they land op 'ere," a waitress declares, and we remember no more till awakened by what seems to us, in our yet semi-conscious state, as the roaring of some terrible monsters fighting. We have a presentiment that something fearful is about to happen, and that we shall be drawn into the conflict; we are not sure we do not ejaculate some absurd remark in our fright. Gradually, however, sense is restored, assisted we think, by the odour of frizzling bacon below. What a relief to find we are still in the land of the peaceful. Yonder across the valley, a quarter of a mile away, is the cause of our nightmare. Through the bedroom window we see struggling up the incline two locomotives, and between them three trucks packed with workmen, bound from "Dawson City,"* for the water-works. The engines puff and snort in their efforts to proceed. Small wonder that rude awakening, we remark later, since at home our rest is never disturbed by train nor tram, and rarely by motor;† and we are not usually roused so early—half-past five. Before our toilet is completed, clearing the Trestle Bridge is another living freight. Hastening outside we focus our glass upon the train. The dangerous postures of a few of the men are appalling. Some sit dangling their legs over the wagon sides, others

*A temporary village of navvies' wooden huts at White Hill Nook, near Heptonstall.
†There is now a Motor-bus Service between King Cross (Halifax), Mount Tabor and Wainstalls.

on the square wooden buffers. And the trucks totter and jolt, threatening each moment to pitch every traveller overboard. But all hold on calmly, and apparently extract as much comfort out of their Irish clays as is possible ere the trip is run, and the time for work comes round. A little nearer and we hear their confusion of tongues. Apprised of the "six o'clock mail," we await its coming over the bridge. It comprises four "coaches," from "Lime Street," each taxed to the utmost with "passengers" outward bound; these also are sandwiched between a pair of locomotives, lest the snapping of a coupling should jeopardise lives.

* * * * * *

It was our intention to return to-day, but as the weather promises well, and our quarters are so comfortable, we resolve to prolong our stay till to-morrow. Unfortunately, there are no means available for trans mitting a message to those expecting us, informing them of our decision.

Blake Dean Chapel

During the day we visit Blake Dean Baptist Chapel, a quarter of a mile below, notable for its anniversary, but most particularly because of its unique situation; we also while away an hour beside the "meeting of the waters" (Widdop and Walshaw Dean), near to.

We delight to puzzle friends telling them we know a Bethel where people, in entering, go "up th' steps into th' bottom, an' dahn th' steps into th' top," Our picture offers the solution. It is possible, however, to enter "th' top" or "th' bottom" and entirely avoid steps.

Over the entrance to "th' top" is the date 1820. Thirteen seats fill the chapel area—which is little larger than two rooms of a cottage house—and eight form the gallery. To one occupying what is known as the "clock seat," it would almost seem possible to shake hands with the preacher in the old-time pulpit opposite.

Round the base of the pulpit assemble the choir—farmers' sons and daughters—who are assisted by an American organ. The chapel, small as it seems, is calculated to seat 200 persons, and on "Charity Day," its capacity is fully taxed. To attend the Anniversary is to receive a lasting impression; not perhaps that one is carried away with the eloquence of the preacher, but the singing! O! the singing! Let the writer bear testimony :—

"Their artless notes were—well;
Grace ran through every line;
Their breasts with rapture swelled,
Their looks were all divine,
Delight o'er all
My senses stole,
And Heaven's pure joy
O'erwhelmed my soul."

The collecting radius, on that day, extends far beyond the chapel walls. On the occasion we paid the Anniversary a visit, we attended service in the afternoon, and at night strolled up to Widdop reservoir (which we purpose passing to-morrow), two miles away, and were on the point of returning when we were approached by a youth who shook a collection box in front of us. The young man intimated his intention of going still half-a-mile further, to where a "school" of gamblers had assembled, and it is said "the sinners gave liberally." After every effort has been put forth, the collections, we learn, average about £11.

Another function, equally pleasing to remember, is the annual "Christmas-party." This is held in the latter part of September or early in October, and on a Saturday, when the moon is nearest full. Experience has shown the unwisdom of providing victuals for a gathering at a time when the roads are dark or made impassable by heavy snows. Close to the chapel is a row of five cottages, now in possession of the navvies, except the one nearest the little sanctuary, and this serves as a Sunday School. To have tea served in that small upper room, and witness its preparation in the ground-floor kitchen is, and has been for long years, one of the anticipated joys of our life.

A slice of an adjoining plantation has, so recently as 1902, been added to the burial ground. According to the inscriptions on stones in the new partition wall, the opening ceremony was performed on October 11, by Mrs. Sutcliffe, Hebden Bridge; Mrs. John Robertshaw, Luddenden Foot; and Ald. Wade, Halifax.

* * * * * *

Our time at Ridge Nook, we reluctantly realize, is all too fleeting. Almost before we are conscious of it the day is gone, night bears down upon us, and once more we find ourselves seated round the hearth. Neighbouring farmers drop in, as it were quite casually, but we have an inkling our advent has been made known. Last night we provided the major part of the evening's entertainment; to-night we retire somewhat in the background and form part of the audience. Indeed

Blake Dean Baptist Chapel.

we could not throw in our lot, however desirous ; we have little in common. No matter what the subject introduced, conversation invariably drifts to farm life, which interests us for a time. A patriarchal individual has at command stories of another order, however, and we incline our ears to the chatty old soul. He delights us with his dry humour, till, really :—

> " As bees flee hame wi' lades o' treasure,
> The minutes winged their way wi' pleasure."

MEETING OF THE WATERS, BLAKE DEAN.

CHAPTER XVI.

BOUND FOR WIDDOP AND BOULSWORTH—PICNIC SCENES—ROUND STONE—JOHN WESLEY'S VISITS—CHALLENGED—DEAR FRIENDS—SHEEP SHEARING.

ANOTHER day dawns—the last in May. What are the weather prospects? Not very promising, we fear, though, when an hour-and-a-half later we lean over the gate (/\ 949-8) leading into the high-road, bidding adieu to our friends, the hitherto clouded sky seems to offer more encouragement. A pair of pewits wheel over our heads uttering plaintive cries, as if jealous for their house and family, and so follow us some distance. High in the heaven the skylark thrills our souls with its melody :—

> " What thou art we know not,
> What is most like thee ?
> From rainbow cloud there flow not,
> Drops so bright to see,
> As from thy presence showers a rain of melody.
>
> Alas ! our journey, rugged and uneven,
> Through prickly moors or dusty ways must wind ;
> But, hearing thee, or others of thy kind,
> As full of gladness and as free of heaven,
> We, with our fate contented, will plod on,
> And hope for higher raptures, when life's day is done."

The morning is beautifully calm ; we would it were a little breezy. We note the spot beside the road where one Whit-Tuesday twenty-four of us—a jovial picnic party from Luddenden Dean—were commanded to "sit down on the grass" while the contents of a lady's boot-box—victuals intended for three—were unveiled. We had tramped all afternoon, over hill and dale, in the streaming heat of the sun, and it was now half-past six. We were well-nigh famished (of a truth, like Cold Edge, 'tis a hungry country this), and intensely thirsty. There had been a tremendous influx of visitors from Yorkshire and Lancashire to Hardcastle Craggs, and refreshment resorts were crowded out. Hence our recourse to provisions in hand. "But what are they among so many ?" one asked, thinking of the Master, Andrew and the lad. The

box was passed round and each "took a little," there remaining we remember, two cracknels. Our appetites were only sharpened the more. "O! for a shower of manna, or even the prodigal's fare," sighed a local preacher amongst us, as we trooped languidly back through the woods. At last we came to a place where business was on the wane, and the sniff of toasted muffins as we ascended the spiral staircase made us quite eager for the onslaught. Not one was abashed. In the words of Tom Twistleton, of Craven :—

"This was naa time for formal pride,
The best amang us cast aside
Wer taast, wer style, an' breedin';
An' lad an' lass wi' au ther might
Were pitchin' into 't left an' right
Like hungry wildbeasts feedin'.

The dainty piles fast disappeared,
An' cups were drain'd an' plates were clear'd,
An' havoc strange were made;
Hed ony hungry plooman seen,
He wod ha' oppen'd wide his een
To watch the parts wi play'd."

To-day we are not likely to suffer short rations any more than the thriving rustic we call to mind. The magnitude of the concertina-shaped bundle dangling at his side as he proceeded to work one morning aroused the curiosity of a passing friend, who, thinking to evoke a laugh at the expense of the owner of the bale, inquired :

"Ar ta gooin fer a wick or a fortnit?"

The lusty labourer was equal to the occasion, and promptly replied.

"If it's mi jock tha'rt alludin' to, this es nobbut mi breakfast; mi dinner's comin' on in a cart."

* * * * * *

Sauntering on, past the old hostelry, the Pack Horse (/\ 984.6), we observe by the roadside a row of hovel-like dwellings with barricaded windows. These were built at the commencement of the waterworks as a speculation, and for a time were occupied; now the one-course brick walls await fresh settlers. A short distance further, between two risings of the road, we pass a wee, small farmstead, Clough Foot (/\ 924.5), the tenants of which look out on a scraggy slope towering high above their level. They are shut in, as it were, amid a world all their own, with one sign only of the outer civilization—a single telephone wire following the course of the stream, and uniting the Waterworks

Offices at Halifax with the keeper of Widdop reservoir, the embankment of which presently comes in view.

ROUND STONE.

High above the reservoir, on the horizon, is poised a large rock, which, viewed from here appears as two, and apparently needs but the strength of a child to topple it over into the water. It is marked on our map "Round Stone." At close quarters the lower and larger portion of the rock reveals the profile of a man with flat brow, Roman nose, open mouth and projecting chin, turned from the reservoir and looking across the moor; the top part is suggestive of a broken earthenware vessel being borne on the man's head.

WESLEY'S ROCK, WIDDOP.

I,

Wesley's Rock.

Up the moor to the right, say 150 yards away, are "ragged rocks, bleak with winter's storm and mottled with tints of brown and green," and upon the largest, even so far off, we read the inscription :—

"J.W., 1766."

Tradition says that John Wesley, in the year stated, preached standing on that rock—known as "Wesley's Pulpit"—but no mention of it is recorded in his journal. Only once do we read of his being in this neighbourhood that year—Thursday, July 30. He says "I preached at Bacup and then rode on to Heptonstall," which latter place is some five miles distant. How exceedingly difficult, in these days, to conceive a Gospel discourse being delivered in so remote a spot, and amid such bleak surroundings. Wesley makes mention of two other occasions when he visited this district, both probably leaving pleasant and vivid recollections. On May 5, 1747, he chronicles, "I preached at Roughlee at five, about eleven at Hinden, and about three at Widdop, a little village in the midst of huge, barren mountains, where also there was a Society. We rode thence about five miles to Stonesey-gate, which lies in a far more fruitful country. Here was a larger congregation at six o'clock than I had seen since my leaving Birstall. They filled both the yard and the road to a considerable distance, and many were seated on a low wall adjoining, which, being built of loose stones, in the middle of the sermon, all fell down at once. I never heard or read of such a thing before. The whole wall and the persons sitting upon it sank down together, none of them screaming out, and very few altering their postures ; and not one was hurt at all ; but they appeared sitting at the bottom just as they sat at the top. Nor was there any interruption, either of my speaking, or of the attention of the hearers." Then on August 25, 1748, Wesley, Wm. Grimshaw and a Mr. T. Colbeck, whilst making their way from Roughlee to Widdop here, were inhumanly handled by "a drunken, cursing, swearing, riotous mob—judge, jury, and executioner—from Colne, armed with clubs and staves." The following day, Wesley penned from Widdop that lengthy and indignant remonstrance to Mr. White, a clergyman, who, he says, "was for some years a Papish priest, and had the living of Colne. It was his manner first to hire, and then to head the mob, when they and he were totally drunk. But he drank himself first into a gaol and then into his grave"*

*Wesley's Journal, June 8, 1752.

Widdop Reservoir, from South-east.

Widdop Reservoir.

Sauntering on and looking ahead we behold on the sky-line a narrow cleft in the hill, where, we presume, the road falls away into Lancashire. As at Fly Flat reservoir, even in this wild sphere trees once gained footing and flourished to a degree, evidence of which is manifest in the roots laid bare in the cutting of the road.

We have arrived at the reservoir embankment (/\ 1056.5), across which there is a public road continuing a zigzag course over the moors to Burnley, six miles; in truth we are "six miles from anywhere," to quote a saying here, the "anywhere" being Hebden Bridge, Burnley, Nelson and Colne. We yearn for a better view of the reservoir, but are checked by a warning-board. To seek permission to enter we must necessarily trespass, since the keeper's house is well within the enclosure. Conscious that the path alongside the reservoir will lead us out again into the highway, and prove, if anything, a shorter cut, we determine to hazard the risk. Alas, we are already detected. News that strangers are abroad is being heralded in no uncertain way by a ferocious-looking brindle mastiff we see strenuously tugging at a chain in the garden in front of the dwelling. Nor will the animal take heed of the remonstrances of the young woman at its side, who endeavours to catch the remark we falteringly attempt, amid the tumult, to transmit across the bywash. It is impossible to be heard while the gruff barking lasts. Foreshadowing the result should the worst happen, we feel just a trifle uncomfortable, but bid our hearts stop fluttering on being assured the dog is secure. To add to the turbulence, a Schipperke terrior scurries out of the house, heedless of the rebukes of an elderly woman, switches over the foot-bridge, and makes towards us most menacingly. Despite its effort to carry off a memento, we simply treat the puny thing with contempt. Tranquillity at last restored, conversation is possible. We are courteously informed that we may proceed on our way without fear of molestation, for which privilege we express gratitude and saunter off, glad to escape the glare of the lion-like brute whose low growl still rolls out. Mentioning our being acquainted with their Teddy undoubtedly has proved an aid to our passport, we are musing, when we hear our names shouted. We look round, but see no one. Now a shutter is thrust up, a head pops out, and its owner hollos: "Wheer ar yo' orf ta this mornin'? Aw hooap when yo' get back yo'll put 't i' th' *Courier*, same as yo' did that ramble ta Old'am two or three yeear sin'." The man has the advantage of us, yet we are told he hails from our

district—is, indeed, comparatively near neighbour to us—and is here at the bidding of the Corporation for repairs. Again a remark is bawled in high pitch, but we are too far away to ken the noddle.

Out of sight and sound, we take a mental snapshot of the sheet of water in whose surface is mirrored the towering stern hills beyond. And engrossed with this scene we do not notice, until quite near, two figures approaching, with radiant faces. Though having no prescience whatsoever of our visiting the neighbourhood, these friends have recognised us, and hasten to greet us. We meant calling upon them, but not to tarry as is their request we should, the journey mapped out, we explain, behoving us to carefully watch the flight of time. We are pressed to stay and have a meal with them, but we assure them we do not suffer hunger, and our bulky pockets are conclusive proofs we are not likely to for many hours. In their home, superbly situated, overlooking the reservoir, we chat on things in common, of friends left behind, once neighbours here, and glean information as to the best ascent of Boulsworth. Shortly we adjourn to the barn and watch shepherds sheep-shearing, an unenviable occupation, one which we immediately associate with Biblical days. We picture Laban, Judah, and Nabal similarly employed, and as the innocent sheep, laid on their backs, submit calmly to the operation, we see forcibly illustrated "As a sheep before her shearers is dumb." One poor comrade we observe lying on the floor has shared a worse fate than those now stripped of clothing. Since sunrise this plump sheep has been found on the moorland heights, stiff and lifeless; how, or by what cause the poor creature met death, there is no evidence to show. We express our sympathy for the loss, and now extend hands in adieu, but our friends insist on accompanying us through the meadows to the highway, where we part, receiving an earnest invitation to "cum when ye can stup a bit;" yea, we are welcome to spend a week or more, whenever we can make it convenient. And shouldn't we enjoy it! Such privilege however, we fear, will not be ours this year of grace, 1905.

CHAPTER XVII.

RAID ON GAMBLERS—PHILIP GILBERT HAMERTON—THE CUCKOO—
TRACKLESS MOOR—ROBIN HOOD'S WELL—
BOULSWORTH'S SUMMIT: THE PROSPECT.

ACUTELY aware that this, our second day's saunter (the third from home), will lead us on to high altitudes, across shelterless moors, we scan the elements and are comforted, for—

"Light and silv'ry cloudlets hover
In the air, as yet scarce warm;
Mild, with glimmer soft tinged over,
Peeps the sun through fragrant balm."

Our spirits thus buoyed up, we step on light-heartedly.

Craggy peaks on our right are now liveried with the blossoming bilberry, and the rugged landscape opposite, in more sombre garb, we deem none the less picturesque.

We are about to pass the last building this side the county boundary. Cards in the window of the farmhouse state that refreshments may be had. Formerly this was the "Travellers' Rest"; the original sign-board is still there, but the words have been obliterated. As a beerhouse the place had a short life after a raid made on a gambling "school" in the vicinity on Sunday, July 9, 1891. That was a remarkably well-designed capture. Not one of some sixty "scholars" suspected the gaily-attired, picnic-like party of men who drove right into the "school" were police. The "crows" picketed on commanding stations *en route* had seen in them no foe. Their straw hats were stylish, and their Havanahs smelt beautifully. Even when the horses drew up, and the party got out, some of the gamblers were entertaining hopes of a good subsequent time at the inn. It was not until handcuffs jingled and staffs were revealed that they realised the true situation. Confusion prevailed, and a stampede ensued. Seven officials, who since the small hours had remained in covert making notes from the time the first "scholar" appeared at 11-50 a.m., now took up the chase.

When the police counted up their prisoners it was found twenty-two were in their clutches. A grey-haired man, with a deep sense of remorse, implored his custodian to "kill me straight off." An additional wagonette, engaged to carry away the "spoil," now arrived on the scene, and quickly the victims were having a trip at the expense of Government. Supt. Fearnside could now cry quits. He was here, and was no doubt thinking of the fine Sunday morning a year before, when he, his groom and another were up here driving, and they chanced upon the self-same "school." The Superintendent dismounted and seized one of the "scholars," whereupon the rest at first made off, but on perceiving the Superintendent was single-handed, they returned. They threatened to pitch both him and his turn-out into the reservoir did he not let the man go. Powerless to cope with so strong a force, Mr. Fearnside had no alternative but to comply. After the lapse of a year, therefore, the net had been cast, and a good haul made, besides fourteen others who at the time escaped, but whose identity was established beyond doubt; one of these was audacious enough to linger and grab what gold was in the ring, leaving silver and copper behind. Tried at Todmorden, three were committed for 21 days; twelve were fined £2 11s. or 21 days; nineteen £2, and fifteen shillings costs or 21 days, and two were asked to pay 21s. Four of them elected to "go down."

* * * * * *

Beyond the inn we pass the site of the "school," and judging by a well-pounded circle in the road, we fear "scholars" still assemble.

Shortly we arrive at a moorland rivulet—locally known as "th' splash watter"—at present crossing the road placidly enough, but in times of flood it must be an awkward obstruction to pedestrians. A stone-post near bears the ordnance survey bench-mark (/|\ 1202.1), and the letters "W" & "E," indicating the division of Wadsworth and Extwistle. Here, too, is the boundary of Yorkshire and Lancashire. In this lone ravine nothing is heard save the bleating of sheep and the meandering water at our feet. We should almost imagine that Emily Brontë, during her brief, frail life, for once outstretched her usual walks, crossed over the moor by the path we trod two days ago, and made herself acquainted with this scene, since in *Wuthering Heights* we read "In winter nothing more dreary; in summer nothing more divine than those glens, shut in by hills and those bluff, bold swells of heath." And in her *Faith and Despondency* she muses :—

"And in the red fire's cheerful glow,
I think of deep glens, blocked with snow;
I dream of moor and misty hill
Where evening closes dark and still."

Though these lines, we know, are also applicable to Emily's immediate home surroundings.

A recent visitor to this neighbourhood, alluding, we should say, to this very spot, writes: "The scenery at one point surpasses in wildness and colour the more famous Dartmoor."

Philip Gilbert Hamerton.

Mr. Philip Gilbert Hamerton, a famous art critic, when 22 years of age erected a camp not far from here—in his *A Painter's Camp* he almost points us to the spot—that he might study direct from nature. For protection he was armed with a five-chambered revolver, and his dog kept him company; and that was all the animal was good for; it was "quite worthless," he says, "the most amiable and hospitable creature imaginable, and would receive a fellow that came to murder me as politely as my most intimate friend."

One night there were prospects of his hut being unpleasantly assailed. Outside were "horrible howls, demoniac laughter, and piercing yells, during which time," says the painter, "my big dog never even growled." In spite of this thrilling episode, and other disagreeable and intolerable experiences, "that month of solitude on the wild hills was a singularly happy time," he records, "so happy that it is not easy, without some reflection, to account for such a degree of felicity. I was young, and the brisk mountain air exhilarated me. I walked out every day on the heather, which I loved as if my father and mother had been a brace of grouse.

As for the solitude and the silence broken only by the wind and rain, their effect was not depressing in the least. Towns are depressing to me—even Paris has that effect,—but how is it possible to feel otherwise than cheerful when you have leagues of fragrant heather all around you, and blue Yorkshire hills on the high and far horizon?" . . . .

"A noteworthy effect of this month on the moors was that on returning to Hollins (his home, near Towneley Park, Burnley), which was situated amongst trim green pastures and plantations, everything seemed so artificial. It came with the force of a discovery. From that day to this the natural and the artificial in landscape have been, for me, as clearly

distinguished as a wild boar from a domestic pig. My strong preference was, and still is, for wild nature."

In his autobiography we read :—

"I regret now that I never met Charlotte Brontë, as she was quite a near neighbour of ours ; in fact, I could have ridden or walked over to Haworth at any time. That village is just on the border of the great Boulsworth moors, where my hut was pitched. At the time of my encampment there, Charlotte Brontë had been dead about eighteen months. She was hardly a contemporary of mine, as she was born seventeen years before me, and died so prematurely ; still, when I think that *Jane Eyre* was written within a very few miles of Hollins (12 from Burnley to Haworth by road), and that for several years, during which I rode or walked every day, Charlotte Brontë was living just on the other side of the moors visible from my home, I am vexed with myself for not having had assurance enough to go to see her."

The artist, in his life's story, gratefully acknowledges the help he received, when in his teens, at the hands of Mr. Edward Alexander, who then lived at Heath Field, Halifax.

* * * * * *

Another sound greets our ears ; surely it is the cuckoo. There ! we hear it again.

Cuckoo ! Cuckoo ! Cuckoo !

Blithe bird, whatever induced thee to wander thus far from the woodlands and bowery glens, thy favourite haunts ? Save for we wayside travellers, thy song is lost on an audience of staring sheep—"wasted on the desert air." Be it far from us to discourage thee in thy gaiety, but welcomed as is thy song, thou hast not everybody's good word. By one writer thou hast been dubbed a vagrant, a lazy, selfish humbug ; thy slanderer, while acknowledging :—

> "At tha brings us glad tidings o' spring,
> An for that art entitled to thanks,"

draws this analogy :—

> "Ther's some men just like tha, soa selfish and base,
> They dooan't care what comes, or what gooas ;
> If they can just manage to live at ther ease,
> Ait an drink, an be donn'd i' fine clooas."

Maybe Cuckoo, like ourselves, thou hast thy faults and failings, but these assuredly are more than counterbalanced by thy gladdening influence ; so cheep up, and sing out thy joyful lay, for :—

> " Not the whole warbling grove in concert heard,
> When sunshine follows shower, the breast can thrill,
> Like the first summons, cuckoo ! of thy bill
> With its twin notes inseparably paired,
> The captive, 'mid damp vaults, unsunned, unaired,
> Measuring the periods of his lonely doom,
> That cry can reach ; and to the sick man's room
> Sends gladness, by no languid smile declared."

Fain would we bask here and enjoy thy sweetness, Cuckoo, but time forbids, and the best of friends must part, so good morning !

" Cuckoo ! "

* * * * * *

We are soon passing through the cleft in the hill we observed a short while ago, and as we conjectured, the road from this point descends. Our map signifies that hereabouts is the surveyor's bench-mark, and we look for the stone, but see none. A little further, on our left, we perceive a rock beside, and level with, the road, and on this is chiselled the "crow-foot"—(⩚ 1276-5)—as we have heard called the arrow-like character.

On each side is sweeping, unfenced moorland. To our right, Boulsworth, " round-shouldered as a bulky grey-beard whose back is bending to the years," rears its head 424 feet above us, while planting one foot, as it were, in the hamlet of Thursden, away down in the hollow yonder, beyond which, towering through haze and murky smoke, we behold mighty Pendle, seemingly quite near, yet as a matter of fact ten miles away as the crow flies. We desire to see Lancashire's proud eminence to better advantage, but from our present outlook are frustrated by a hill-point in the near foreground. Our coveted goal, however, is Boulsworth, apparently less than a mile-and-a-half away. But moorland, like water, is deceptive to gauge. Prior to launching on the trackless expanse, let us take a retrospect of the time. We left Ridge Nook at seven. Three-quarters of an hour later we arrived at Widdop. There we spent a good hour, notwithstanding we purposed at the outset staying but a few minutes, but, bless us, when we are in good company, " how de time scoots away." Since we parted with our friends, another hour has sped. Consulting our watches the hands point to 9-25, so we step on,

striking a bee-line across the moor, towards Halliwell Sutcliffe's "Bluebeard." Now we might be trespassing. We are thinking of three Halifax influential gentlemen once (to be precise, on August 20, 1885) being intercepted on Boulsworth, their names requested, which were readily given, and they were summoned. After an eloquent speech by Mr. W. C. Barber (one of the trio), Principal of the Crossley Orphan Home (now Crossley and Porter), the summonses were withdrawn, and the costs—7s. 6d.—only were inflicted. As Mr. Barber remarked in their defence, even now there is not a stick or a stone, sign-post, hedge, or fence of any kind whatever to warn the pedestrian that he is trespassing.

Robin Hood's Well.

A pleasant breeze sweeps up the moor, blowing straight across from Pendle, whose form is now being gradually unfolded as if for our admiration.

Presently we arrive at a gully, down which flows a fairly broad yet shallow stream ; this on our map, we observe, is called Black Clough. We scramble down the precipitous slope and cross the water to what appears to be a rude cattle-shed—maybe affording shelter for sheep. It offers no such accommodation however, but is used, presumably, as a shooting box. This we note by our map is "Robin Hood's House." Mention is also made of "Robin Hood's Well," but no such thing is visible at first. Being thirsty we are eager to make the acquaintance of the spring. We search, and eventually spy boarding partially obscured by boulders, evidently serving as a covering to something beneath. These we remove—carefully, lest we should contaminate the water—only to find a well, stagnant and muddy, and in possession thereof battalions of red-breasted insects which, at the first streak of light, cease skirmishing, tilt head downwards, and dive to realms unseen. Disappointed, we resort to the brook hard by, and producing our horn-cup drink of its water, which, notwithstanding its incriminating name "Black," is clear as crystal.

We follow up the stream to a point where are a dozen or so sheep-pens. These and the damming of the water close to offer their own suggestion. And we have drunk of the water !

How interesting indeed it would be to while away an hour here watching the shepherd's dogs herd and pen the sheep, then the washing process. To-day, neither shepherd, sheep nor dog is to be seen.

BOULSWORTH.

Boulsworth rises immediately on our left, and we commence the ascent, which we find comparatively easy, and boggy places, thanks to the long spell of drought, are literally dry. Forty minutes' steady climbing from the sheep-pens, and we have reached the summit. We feel half-inclined to throw our caps in the air and shout "Hurrah!" Standing on the highest of the large number of stupendous rocks ("Weather Stones," which we saw so clearly through our glass at Fly Flat), far "above life's turmoil," a strange sense of loneliness possesses us.

Boulsworth somehow to us resembles a large oval-shaped table set lengthwise N.W. and S.E., and having a deep overhanging cover of sheepskin, variegated in shade and colour. We take up a position on this, the south-eastern side of the "table," and admire a glorious panorama. The atmosphere is remarkably clear, so we are particularly fortunate. The ocean of hills tumbling away southwards have a striking similarity to those seen from Slade, though standing out more clearly at 1,700 feet—350 feet higher than the keeper's house. Beyond, Hardcastle Craggs, Heptonstall Church and Stoodley Pike are landmarks in the picture. More to our left is Nab Hill, readily located, Fly Flat, and the buildings thereon; we even single out the grey barn of our friends Sam and Betty. The breeze, so efficacious in cooling us after our climb, fans our cheeks, but is just a trifle provoking as we endeavour to study our map, which we find of infinite value. We tramp across the "table-top" to get a view north. As we advance, the first mass which appears in view is Pendle Hill, as if determined to be noticed, and looking down from its height of 1,831 feet in stern dominion, as it were, upon the series of little hills around, between which are dotted cotton towns :—

"Ambushed by the chimla cheek,
Hid in an atmosphere of reek."

Down the north-western side we look on to a stretch of moorland descending sharply to a plain. This, according to our map, is the forest of Trawden. It may have been a forest at one time, but all traces of it are gone. At present, presumably, it is a wilderness of swamps. On the farther side is Trawden, and a little further back its neighbouring village, Winwall. More west, Colne is seen to good advantage; "a city that is set on a hill cannot be hid." The atmosphere westward is not nearly so good as northward, else we might catch a glimpse of the sea.

Wycoller Hall ("Ferndean Manor" of *Jane Eyre*).

The late F. A. Leyland, in a contribution to the *Halifax Courier* years ago, wrote of standing on Boulsworth one 9th of June, when the mist and rains of the forenoon had suddenly cleared away, and before the sun had had time to raise vapour. Through his telescope he stated he saw the houses on the beach at Blackpool; the steeple of the Catholic Church in Talbot Road, and the wind-mills in the neighbourhood; the Horse-Bank at Lytham, objects at Southport, and the sands that lie between there and the sea; of watching the shrimping boats and fishing-smacks, and observing a large steamer passing, he conjectured, from Fleetwood to Dublin or Belfast, even defining its streaks of colour, its rigging, its paddle-box, etc., and about four o'clock he noticed the inflowing tide.

We direct our glass (certainly not so powerful as Mr. Leyland's) over Wycoller, and endeavour to locate Wycoller Hall, the Ferndean Manor of *Jane Eyre*, but cannot satisfy ourselves that we hit on Rochester's deserted "old house," that "ineligible and insalubrious site." But then *Jane Eyre* herself tells us, "even when within a very short distance of the manor house, you could see nothing of it; so thick and dark grew the timber of the gloomy woods about it."

Due north, nothing obscures the view. How very clear! What a panorama! The hills round Skipton—ten miles away—appear like so many huge mole-hills. Even Great Whernside and Little Whernside, fifteen or sixteen miles in a straight line further back, are faintly visible. More to the left Fountains Fell and Penygant—twenty-two and twenty-six miles distant respectively. Straining our eyes to the utmost, we persuade ourselves we now and again catch a glimpse of Ingleborough, six miles further away.

Whilst enjoying this lovely prospect, promptings within suggest a feast more tangible and substantial. With the dry heath for a seat and a rock for a table, we unpack provisions our friends at Ridge Nook insisted we brought with us, affirming as our pockets were being crammed, "Yo'll whant somat t' eyt fok when yo' get on Buls'orth, er else befooar;" and the prediction is true.

"Some hae meat and canna eat,
An' some therebe that want it;
But we hae meat and we can eat,
So let the Lord be thankit."

The Scot bard's grace we think aloud, and soon a pile of sandwiches has disappeared. But O, how we long for a drink. Even the fragrant weed, with all its accredited influence to sooth, fails to assuage. That which cannot be cured, however, must be endured.

CHAPTER XVIII.

LAD O' CROW HILL—PANORAMA FROM THE HILL—"THREE LAPS"—CROW HILL BOG-BURST—PONDEN KIRK.

HALLOA! Buzzer? Is there a fire somewhere? or is it Calvert's whew we hear? Why, we must have been dozing. And, of a truth, under the mid-day sun and lulled by the mellowing breeze, we have slumbered, and, we believe, soundly too. The mill whistle at Trawden still continues, and directly it ceases, another, in a different key, takes up the strain. We hear them so plainly three miles away; and indeed see the steam thereof being wafted through the air. These whistles are often heard at Ridge when the wind is favourable, though six miles distant and the mass of Boulsworth standing between.

Loth to leave the scene, we rise, turn our backs on the sister county, and set our faces homewards. That nap may cost us dearly; we can ill afford it. Of one thing we are glad; our thirst is partially allayed, so we can trudge on less languidly. Retracing steps we thread our way in and out amongst the "Weather Stones," and proceed along the southern side of Jackson's Ridge—the county boundary line—accepting as guides the division stones and mounds. Tramp, tramp, tramp, now over heathery hillocks, now short stretches of springy turf, and anon patches of green, the swampy nature of which even in average weather would offer many obstacles to our progress, and often turn us far aside. Dikes and ditches are numerous, but these, it is comforting to find, are reduced to mere gutters; their tapering banks are hard, dry and chinky, and our boots leave but the faintest impressions. We are more than ever impressed with the deceptiveness of the moorland. Objects in front, though apparently close at hand, take us almost treble the time we calculate to reach. Not since we set foot on these moors have we flushed a single grouse. Curlews are ever present with us, cutting semi-circles in the air far out of gun reach, and uttering wailful cries. An occasional plover darts up and sharply wings its flight, signalling a somewhat similar, yet fainter, alarm. Gorgeous Emperor moths frequently dance across our path, often in pairs, as if on a joint excursion.

Now we are crossing the head of Walshaw Dean, the extreme source of Crow Hill Beck, which, fed by its manifold tributaries of cloughs and dikes, will shortly be checked by the three reservoirs for Halifax, and made to serve more abundantly than hitherto the requirements

of man. Crow Hill's highest point—1,500 feet—(Sutcliffe's "Dead Lad's Rig") rises clearly a considerable distance away on our left, and we are tempted to set foot there, but having regard for the time, we push forward. This while back we have had in view, and made our landmarks, the delph tippings and shooting covers still far ahead, which we remarked upon when inquiring of "Owd Timmy" as to the whereabouts of "th' Lad o' Crow Hill." "Yo'll fynd it abaat tue er three 'underd yards farther on," said Timmy, pointing to the tippings, "et th' flat o' th' maar, en abaat a 'underd en fifty yards fra t' edge." According to Timmy, then, "th' Lad" cannot be far away, since we are approaching the tippings and the spot indicated. Through age, no doubt, "he" will be black as the peat and difficult to recognise. We stride on. Thrice we are befooled out of our way by what, each time proves, the "Lad's" relatives, and we are on the verge of despairing when we see before us some more prominent object and take heart. As we approach we observe certain initials and the year 1902. This is not, however, the lettering we are hoping to see. Ah! here, facing east, is the original inscription deeply and roughly chiselled :—

LAD
ORSCARR
ON CROW
HILL.

If Timmy had measured the distances quoted us he could not have been much more accurate in his calculations.

The "Lad" stands about five feet out of the boulders in which "he" is embedded, is perhaps five feet broad, two feet thick, and is rough-hewn, apart from "his" head. The wording of the inscription is as confusing as the "Lad's" history is mysterious. Some have conjectured that "Orscarr" was the name of the lad who, according to tradition, met with a similar fate to Benjamin Foster, and was afterwards found at this very spot. Halliwell Sutcliffe in *By Moor and Fell* devotes a page to the "Lad," and says "the country folk call it Laddock Royal, Lancashire Lad, or Lad o' Crow Hill." He tells how the lad, crossing these moors, was caught in a snowstorm and succumbed. No one appears to have missed the lad, and his body remained long waiting identification, but no claimant was forthcoming. Then there arose the question who should bury the corpse. Evidently it was a case for the Parish. Haworth and Stanbury stood obstinate, though the lad was found on their own moors. Trawden, on the other hand, refused, and

Lad o' Crow Hill (Boulsworth in Background).

the authorities waged controversy. Ultimately Trawden—it is said with an eye to business—yielded, and buried the lad where he was found, afterwards claiming the right to push their boundary to this point.

But Mr. Kellner, B.A., of Pannal, explains away this tradition. In reply to a letter of one who had visited the "Lad" he says :—

"The word "Lad" is the old English (Saxon) past participle of the verb "lead." Such participles were used both as nouns and adjectives ; hence "Lad" would be "leader," or guide, and the prominent rock or stone by which people were guided, viz. : the boundary stone. I fear it has nothing to do with the word Lad in its ordinary significance, viz. : a male youth, though this latter word, as well as 'Ladder,' are both derived from and connected with the verb 'to lead.'

The word 'Scar' signifies 'a mark,' and is fairly common in the Yorkshire Dales. Thus 'Timothy Scar,' 'Nan Scar' at Cowling (Keighley Snowden's Cragside of the *Web of an old Weaver*), 'Loup Scar' (Burnsall), and 'Gordale Scar' (Malham)."

In a book of poems by Mr. Gordon Bottomley, of Keighley, are the following, to us, somewhat obscure lines, said to have reference to the "Lad o' Crow Hill" :—

"For a grave on the moor."

"Calmly I lie in heat and cold,
In the new year, in the old.
Ashes to ashes, dust to dust,
Here to live I have no lust ;
Body, rest in the upland bleak,
Forth I go old friends to seek.

Sing me dirges, grouse and plover,
When the moor is painted over
With the purple of the heather ;
Snow in windy, wintry weather,
Lightly press on my body here ;
This is its bed from year to year."

PANORAMA FROM CROW HILL.

Since we are but some 150 yards "fra t' edge," we will sacrifice a few minutes in peeping over. We overlook the Worth Valley. Three-quarters of a mile away, and 300 feet below our present elevation of 1,400 feet, is Watersheddles Reservoir (Halliwell Sutcliffe's "Wild Water"), belonging to Keighley Corporation. "Th' Lad o' Crow Hill," we note, is almost in line with the reservoir's embankment. Yonder across the valley, the turnpike from Haworth winds its way past Ponden

Reservoir (Sutcliffe's "Sorrowful Water"), and over the moor through Wycoller to Colne. Right of the turnpike is Hare Hill, crowned by Tewit Hall, whose Norman tower, over-topping a surrounding plantation, gives it the appearance of a church at a distance, and is an excellent landmark. It is common hearsay, locally, that the tower was erected so that the owner, a contractor, might through a telescope watch his men in the work-yard at Bradford!

Midway down the hill is Oldfield, where resided "t'owd gentleman," whose grave we visited two days ago. Further away, the conservatories of Oakworth House stand out clearly, the village itself being partially obscured in woodland. Beyond Oakworth, over the shoulder of Branshaw Moor, hangs a pall of smoke, and we know that Keighley lies beneath. On the right of the Worth, opposite Keighley, is the village of Thwaites, and a little nearer that of Hainworth. Four or five miles further north-east the sun bathes the heights of Rombalds Moor. We can even see Whorles, a farm house near a plantation of that name, and three miles or so north-west of Keighley, where "Old Three Laps," well and hearty, laid in bed for 49 years. Surely such a life is unprecedented. As a "side-light glimpse," we will relate the story.

"Old Three Laps."

"Three Laps" was William Sharp's nickname, a legacy left him by a miserly father who, it is said, once went to his tailor and requested a suit making of cloth, produced. The tailor found the material somewhat scanty, and pointed out that unless he furnished more cloth the coat would have three laps.

"Then mak' it wi' three laps, or onyrooad," stammered William; and the coat was thus made and worn.

"Old Three Laps," we read in a pamphlet, was the son of a small farmer and manufacturer of a class of worsted goods made rather extensively early in the nineteenth century, and known by the name of "draw boys," in consequence of boys being employed to pull some part of the weaving apparatus. These goods were carried to Halifax market, at that time considered the grand emporium for worsted goods in the Riding. Although employing but few hands, he was looked upon as one of the most extensive manufacturers in the neighbourhood, and finally amassed considerable money.

His prosperity, however, neither tended to enlarge his liberality nor to give him a whit of pride, as the incident recorded proves.

Two farms were in the market, one Sheep Hole, best known as "Two Laws," on the Colne road, three-quarters of a mile below Watersheddles Reservoir, and seen most plainly from the edge of Crow Hill here; the other was named Whorles. William purchased both, and elected to occupy Whorles. In course of time young "Three Laps" fell in love, and the magnet of his affections was one Mary Smith, of Bottoms in Newsholme Dean. After a lengthy courtship the lovers decided to marry. Probably the little stranger which had arrived at Bottoms had a voice in the matter. The author of the pamphlet referred to gives the subsequent history in rhyme:—

> "Three Laps" and Mary were willing to marry,
> And all was prepared for their nuptials with speed,
> When the father of "Three Laps" and father of Mary,
> At this critical moment o'er gold disagreed.
>
> The father of Mary was ready with pride,
> To settle a dowry upon;
> But vow'd that young "Three Laps" should ne'er call her bride,
> Should the father not equally portion his son.
>
> But the father of "Three Laps" refused to comply,
> For gold was the principal love of his heart,
> And when the young lovers deemed happiness nigh,
> Alas, they were doomed in a moment to part.
>
> But "Three Laps" still thought that his Mary was true,
> And straight to the church at the time did repair,
> Believing that Mary whate'er they might do,
> Would hasten to meet him, and tie the knot there."

"But her father, disapproving of the match, kept her confined at home," says William Keighley in *Keighley Past and Present.* This was in 1807, when young "Three Laps" was 30 years of age.

"This great slip between the cup and the lip preyed heavily on the susceptible mind of the ardent lover," continues Mr. Keighley. "He returned home, consigned himself to a small room measuring about nine feet each way, with the determination to spend the rest of his existence between the blankets; and the infatuated man kept his resolution. The floor was covered with stone flags; in one corner was a fireplace which could only be used when the wind blew from one or two points; the window was well fastened down, and where some squares had been broken, was carefully patched with wood. This window was not opened for 38 years. The furniture comprised an old oak clock, minus weights and pendulum, almost thick with cobwebs, a small round table of dark oak, and a plain unvarnished four-post bed, without hangings. In this dreary cell, whose only inlet for fresh air during 38 years was the

doorway, occasionally left open, this strange being immured himself. He refused to speak to anyone, and never answered even those who were his constant attendants. His father, by will, made provision for his temporal wants, and he seemed unconscious of any other. He ate his meals latterly in a curious way, for in process of time his legs became contracted and drawn towards his body; when about to eat he used to roll himself over, and take his meals in a kneeling posture, and to prevent crumbs getting into the blanket on which he lay, he turned the under blanket over and ate them from the bed-tick. In a physical sense he did great credit to his food, for his flesh was firm, fair, and unwrinkled save with fat, and the estimate of his weight was about 240 lbs. During this self-imposed confinement he never had any serious illness till the last week of his life, when his appetite failed and his limbs became partially benumbed, and death terminated his morbid existence on Monday, March 3, 1856. Just before he expired he was heard to exclaim, 'Poor Bill, poor Bill, poor Bill Sharp,' the most sensible and connected sentence he had been known to utter during many years. His usual efforts at speech were only inarticulate grunts like a pig."

A large concourse of people thronged Keighley Parish Churchyard when he was buried. The coffin excited attention because of its extraordinary size. It was 2 feet 4 inches in depth, and so heavy that it required eight men with strong ropes to lower it into the grave. The weight of coffin and corpse was estimated at 480 lbs.

We visit Keighley periodically, and on one occasion we sought the place where "Three Laps" is buried. Acting upon instructions given us by a friend, who remembers as a very little girl elbowing her way through the crowd to the grave side, we found the grave at the foot of the only table-tomb between the churchyard path and church, on the south side. The last of seven names recorded on the horizontal stone reads :—

Also of William, Son of the above named
William and Mary Sharp, who died
March 3$^{rd.}$ 1856, in the 79th Year of his
Age.

Once, too, we strolled up to Whorles and found the place in perfect keeping with all we had heard or read of "Old Three Laps"—a weird-looking, isolated spot. First we were taken into a mistal which, we were told, was "Three Laps'" house, and traces of a dwelling seemed to confirm the information. Out of here we were led through a doorway

on the same floor into a small, dark place occupied by fowls. This was "Three Laps'" bedroom. The farmer eyed us wistfully as we produced a rule to measure the dungeon—9 feet 6 inches by 6 feet. There, in one corner, was the identical fireplace mentioned by William Keighley, and there, 3 feet 4 inches square, the mullion window—now walled up save for an aperture where the fowls entered a field at the back. Through this window the curious sometimes peeped and caught "Three Laps" shooting imaginary pewits with his fore-finger, thus indulging in visions of his youthful sporting days.

* * * * * *

Turning away "fra t' edge" we pass by the "Lad," bid "him" adieu, and leave "him" to:—

> "Calmly lie in heat and cold,
> In the new year, in the old."

Now we skirt "t' owd delph tippins" on our left, and shortly the shooting covers. The amalgamating tributaries rising on Red Mires flat and Stanbury Bog presently confront us, but no great feat is necessary to enable us to land dry-shod on the other side, thanks again to the present drought. The rivulet, partly hidden between isles of green, meanders as if making the most of life ere it tumbles into an abyss, where the waters and those of Middle Moor Clough, rising up in Alcomden Stones, Withens Flat (1,450 feet), are arrested by a sluice and conducted underground to Watersheddles Reservoir. In times of flood the sluices are opened and the water continues down through Ponden Wood (Halliwell Sutcliffe's "Cringle Wood"), Ponden Kirk Valley (Sutcliffe's "Lonely Valley"), to Ponden compensation reservoir (Sutcliffe's "Sorrowful Water"), three-quarters of a mile below. The floods abated, the sluices are closed, and the water is again captured and turned into the artificial course.

Did time permit we would visit Alcomden Stones, away up on our right yonder, and see the rocks described in Lewis's *Topographical Dictionary* as "a Cromlech, an evident Druidical remain, consisting of one flat-stone, weighing about six tons, placed horizontally upon two huge upright blocks now half embedded in the heather." But:—

> "Time speeds on his relentless track,
> And though we beg on bended knees,
> No prophet's hand for us puts back
> The shadow, ten degrees."

Cromlech : Alcomden Stones.

CROW HILL BOG-BURST.

Twenty minutes' saunter from the "Lad" and we stand on the "roof" of Ponden Kirk—Emily Brontë's "Penistone Cragg," and Sutcliffe's "Wyngates Kirk"—where we command a birds-eye view of Ponden Valley, the first recipient of the great bog-slide (now put to use in *Rycroft of Withens*) which occurred September 2, 1824, and is locally referred to as a "Phenomenon," "Crow Hill Earthquake," "Crow Hill Bogburst," and "Crow Hill Flood." Here we will rest a few minutes, and the while refresh memory by an extract from a sermon by the Rev. Patrick Brontë. Preaching from the text (Psalm xcvii., 4-5), "His lightnings enlightened the world; the earth saw, and trembled. The hills melted like wax at the presence of the Lord, at the presence of the Lord of the whole earth," he introduced his discourse by lines from Cowper :—

"When were the winds
Let slip with a warrant to destroy?
When did the waves so haughtily o'erleap
Their ancient barriers, deluging the dry?
Fires from beneath, and meteors from above,
Portentious, unexampled, unexplained,
Have kindled beacons in the skies, and the old
And crazy earth has had her shaking fits
More frequent, and foregone her usual rest."

"I would avail myself," Mr. Brontë proceeded, "of the advantages now offered for moral and religious improvement by the late earthquake and extraordinary eruption which took place lately about four miles* from this very church in which we are now assembled. You all know that on the second day of this month of September, and in this present year of our Lord, one thousand, eight hundred and twenty-four, at about six o'clock in the afternoon, two portions of the moors in the neighbourhood sank several yards during a heavy storm of thunder, lightning, and rain, and there issued forth a mighty volume of mud and water, which spread alarm, astonishment and danger along its course of many miles. Previous to the issuing forth of this flood, as I have learnt from someone who resides near to the place, there was a very considerable tremor of the neighbouring parts, and I was able myself to perceive something of the kind, though at a distance of four miles. This circumstance, which was not noticed by many who live much nearer, requires some explanation, which I shall give you in a few words. As the day was

* The distance from Haworth Church to Ponden Kirk, the place referred to, is just over three miles.

exceedingly fine, I had sent my little children,† who were indisposed, accompanied by the servants, to take an airing on the common, and as they stayed out rather longer than I expected, I went to an upper chamber to look for their return. The heavens over the moors were blackening fast. I heard the muttering of distant thunder, and saw the frequent flashing of the lightning, though ten minutes before there was scarcely a breath of air stirring. The gale freshened rapidly, and carried along with it clouds of dust and stubble; and by this time some large drops of rain clearly announced an approaching heavy shower. My little family had escaped to a place of safety, but I did not know it. I consequently watched every movement of the coming tempest with a painful degree of interest. The house was perfectly still. Under these circumstances, I heard a deep, distant explosion, something resembling, and yet something differing from thunder, and I perceived a gentle tremor in the chamber in which I was standing, and in the glass of the window just before me, which, at the time, made an extraordinary impression on my mind, and which, I have no manner of doubt now, was the effect of the earthquake at the place of the eruption.

This shaking and opening of the earth, and eruption of mud and water, was preceded by a profound calm, and accompanied by a very high wind and much lightning and thunder, and both before and after the air was strongly electrified, as was manifest from the sultry heat, the frequent and vivid lightning and loud thunder, and the apparent mingling of the clouds, and their copper-coloured and hazy, luring gloom. The ground is sunk to a great extent, and risen and shaken for a considerable distance. The operating cause, whatever it was, must have been very powerful, as two cavities were formed, one of which was not less than four or five yards deep in some places, and six or seven hundred yards in circumference, and a rapid torrent of mud and water issued forth, varying from twenty to thirty yards in width, and from four to five in depth, which in its course for six or seven miles entirely threw down or made breaches in several stone or wooden bridges, uprooted trees, laid prostrate walls, and gave many other awful proofs that, in the hand of Omnipotence, it was an irresistible instrument to execute His judgment."

The preacher sums up:—

"We have just seen something of the mighty power of God. He has

†The little ones were Charlotte, in her ninth year; Patrick Branwell, one year younger; Emily Jane, another year younger; and Anne, the youngest, in her fifth year. The eldest sisters, Maria and Elizabeth, two months prior to the "Earthquake," had been sent to Cowan Bridge School.

unsheathed His sword and brandished it over our heads, but still the blow is suspended in mercy—it has not fallen upon us. As well might He have shaken and sunk all Haworth, as those parts of the uninhabited moors on which the bolts of His vengeance have fallen. Be thankful that you are spared. Despise not this merciful but monitory voice of Divine wisdom. Hear, and learn to be spiritually wise. Happy are they, and they only, who attend to the voice of the Holy Spirit ; who deny themselves and take up their cross and follow Christ. They shall have faith, which is the victory that overcometh this world ; they shall come off more than conquerors over death ; and, in perfect security on the last day, they shall fearlessly and triumphantly survey the wreck of universal nature, when the sun shall be turned into darkness and the moon into blood ; when the stars shall fall from their orbits and the heavens and earth shall dissolve in flames and pass away."

The *Leeds Mercury* thus referred to the occurrence :—

" At the distance of about 500 yards from the top of the glen the principal discharge seems to have taken place. Here a very large area of about 1,200 yards in circumference is excavated to the depth of from four to six yards, and at a short distance from this chasm there is a similar excavation, but much less in extent. The concavities have been emptied, not only of their water, but also of their solid contents. A channel of about twelve yards in width and seven or eight in depth has been formed quite to the mouth of the gill, down which a most amazing quantity of water was precipitated with a violence and noise of which it is difficult to form an adequate conception, and which was heard to a considerable distance. Stones of an immense size and weight were hurried by the torrent more than a mile. It is impossible to form any computation of the quantity of earthy matter which has been carried down into the valley, but that it was enormous is evident by the vast quantities deposited by the torrent in every part of its course, and from the great quantity which the river still contains. This destructive torrent was confined within narrow bounds by the high glen through which it passed until it reached the hamlet of Ponden, where it expanded over some corn-fields, covering them to the depth of several feet ; it also filled up the mill pond, choking up the watercourse, and thereby putting an entire stop to the works. A stone bridge was also nearly swept away at this place, and several other bridges in its course were materially damaged. We feel happy, however, in being able to state that it was not fatal to life in a single instance. The torrent was seen coming down the glen before it reached the hamlet by a person who gave the alarm, and thereby saved the lives of several children who would otherwise have been swept away. The torrent at this time presented a breast of seven feet high. It would evidently require a power acting with a great degree of momentum to move and break in pieces the large and almost solid masses of peat and turf which were forced down the hills, to say nothing of the detached rocks which were moved

With all deference to the opinions of the Rev. P. Brontë and Mr. E. Baines, we think the cause of the disruption is to be ascribed neither to an earthquake nor to a waterspout, but simply to the pressure of the accumulated and pent-up waters having become too great for the stability of their mossy embankment."

PONDEN KIRK: NOTE FIGURE, IN CLEFT OF ROCK, EMERGING FROM THE HOLE.

Ponden Kirk.

The brink immediately beneath us, wholly carpeted with bracken-fronds, seems almost perpendicular, and we descend very gingerly to the foot of the Kirk—a stupendous "upright rock, which some have connected with the worship of Druids." Through it there is an opening seemingly partly artificial, two feet high, but not so wide. According to tradition, maidens (some say bachelors, too) who successfully creep through the aperture will be married within the year. Thousands have wriggled their way through the passage, judging by the greasy appearance of the "floor," and on hands and knees we do likewise, though not with the motive of subjecting ourselves to the kirk's charms, since, years ago, we tied the knot we cannot loose.

> "We could not if we would,
> We would not if we could."

It is something of a sensation to feel the props may fall or the foundations give way, and that several tons may fall and crush us flat as a fluke. Besides, we acutely realise bulky figures may stick fast midway. By dint of push, however, we at last emerge safely. Farmer Griffe, in *Through Sorrow's Gate*, says "Once when he was a raw lad, he came here with a lass and she had crept through the hole, ... yet she did not marry him."

* * * * * *

3-30! Since leaving Boulsworth, two-and-a-half hours have rolled away. Our map indicates a line of half-a-dozen springs near here, and O! we should enjoy a drink, but time will not admit of our making their acquaintance; so we continue the descent of the brink, very, very carefully, setting heels firm to break momentum, and presently we gain footing on a path leading to the sluices. We have dropped from 1,200 feet to 1,050 feet—150 feet, in probably less than half the number of yards.

An illustrated guide to Haworth, published there by Mr. Hall, conducting its readers the opposite direction to that we are going, says on reaching here, "On each side of the steep bank is a wild stream tumbling into the hollow, and when we come to the first of these, and cross its rocky bed, with wild, bleak moors around, we feel, if anywhere, the spirit of the moorland. We need seek no more characteristic spot."

"It is said," continues the author, "that coming here, to see these mountain torrents swollen with rain, Charlotte Brontë caught the cold

which hastened her end." We are inclined to the belief that it was not, but rather her visit with her husband to the Fall, as implied by herself and her biographers.

Near the southern sluice a path—the "Scholar's walk," we believe, in Halliwell Sutcliffe's *By Moor and Fell*—strikes across the moor. We presume it leads to Buckley Green; it looks difficult to negotiate, especially for ladies. It is obvious we are again nearing the land of the living, for, though mid-week, a few visitors are here enjoying the solitude. Not since leaving Widdop at nearly nine this morning—six and a half hours ago—have we seen a fellow-subject until now. Sauntering on, we go through the very heart of the bog-burst, the effect of which is very clear.

CHAPTER XIX.

PONDEN HALL—THE HEATONS—PONDEN RESERVOIR—SCAR TOP CHAPEL "CHARITY"—STANBURY SCHOOLMASTER—THE QUAKERS—OLD DAY-SCHOOL—STANBURY PLACES OF WORSHIP—HAWORTH—NEW FRIENDS—HAWORTH CHURCH SCHOOL-HOUSE—PLEASING INTRODUCTION.

SHORTLY we pass a couple of farm-houses, thence bungle down a rough cart-track. Uphill, this road would lead us to Crow Hill delph and the "Lad." Moorland has now given place to cultivation. Presently we turn to the right and stay beneath a line of exceedingly fine mountain ash, while lowing cattle, with udders ruddy and plump, are being driven into a quaint barn from which swallows dart as the kine enter.

Tall trees hem in Ponden Hall—Emily Brontë's "Thrushcross Grange" and Halliwell Sutcliffe's "Wyngates"—opposite which we now stand.

In the Haworth edition of Mrs. Gaskell's *Life of Charlotte Brontë,* edited by Mr. Clement K. Shorter, there is a foot-note which reads :—

> "It is clear . . . . that Ponden House (Ponden Hall), near Haworth, did duty for at least the interior of Wuthering Heights, and that Oldfield, in the same district, was Thrushcross Grange."

The association of Thrushcross Grange with Oldfield (formerly "t'owd gentleman's" residence) is news to us, though our ignorance may be equally startling to those better versed in place-names round Haworth.

A tablet let into the wall over the entrance of the building before us records that:—

THE
Old houfe
(now Standing) was
built by Robert Heaton
for his Son Michael,
Anno Domini 1634.
The old Porch and Peat
houfe was built by his
Grandfon Robert
Heaton A.D. 1680.
The prefent Building
was Rebuilt by his
defcendant R.H. 1801.

The building referred to lies behind us and "look across at its successor with something of a greybeard's mild beneficence who

PONDEN HALL.

sees his eldest-born carrying bravely on the sure traditions; was built when the Heaton race was young, and abandoned, as their fortunes grew, in favour of a roomier dwelling," says Halliwell Sutcliffe.

A magnificent Spanish chestnut, now advancing in leaf, overshadows and leans a great ugly limb on the back of "greybeard," as if resolved on crushing out of "him" the last spark.

TABLET, PONDEN HALL.
(Photo by J. Bradley).

Some have associated Ponden Hall with "Thornfield" in *Jane Eyre*; indeed, we have it in print, though we know that the Ridings, Birstall, partly answers the description. Certain interior features at Ponden Hall tally with Mr. Rochester's dwelling, we are told. And there is also a certain resemblance externally; leastwise, as Mr. Fairfax observed to the new governess at Thornfield, we think "it a very pretty place," but

"OLD HOUSE," PONDEN HALL.

"fear it will be getting out of order unless Mr. Rochester should take it into his head to come and reside here permanently; or at least visit it oftener; great houses and fine grounds require the presence of the proprietor."

A broad strip of garden fenced by a low wall with square wooden railings, dilapidated and pining for a fresh coat of paint, and strengthened at intervals by high pillars, run parallel two-thirds of the facade. Another narrow strip separates this and the road. But what gardens! Nettles predominate. A number of ash and sycamore saplings have established a hold, and raspberry runners have overspread the flower beds. A yew, a variegated holly, rhododendrons, and lilac remind us of Ponden's past glory, when the five Heaton bachelor brothers were "known among the maidens of the district as the five brethren." "It was on the hillside opposite, I remember," says Halliwell Sutcliffe, "that I stood one winter's day—a raw day, with sorrow in the wind, and a thin winding sheet of snow on field and heath—and looked across the steep dip of the valley, and saw a burial party wind slowly down the road. They were carrying John Heaton, of Ponden House, the last of a fine breed of yeomen, to the moorside graveyard."

We have made diligent search and find that Robert was the last survivor, he dying March 3, 1898, aged 76. Only eight days before, his brother, Thomas Midgley, had passed away at the age of 62, while John had died Jan. 17, 1889. All are buried in Stanbury Cemetery.

John married and had two daughters, who died of consumption; they were 16 and 17 years old. Another brother, Michael, married and had children. He died May 29, 1888, aged 52. The last to account for is William. He died first, but the date we are unable to state; nor can an old Stanburyite who knew him well; but he affirms that "it wer' abaart t' time when Stanbury coil mines* wer' shut daahn," adding, "an' that's abune forty yeear sin'." This old man, when a youth, worked at the mines. The last two brothers were buried in Haworth churchyard, where are also recorded the deaths of three Robert Heatons; in 1714, 1794, and 1817. Ponden Hall is still (1905) owned by the Heatons—a Miss Heaton—cousin, we believe, to the "five brethren."

Supporting weary forms against an old horse-mount, we take a last survey of "Thrushcross Grange" and surroundings. The road winds round the gable-end of the "Old House," now used as a store for farm implements, carts, and general rubbish, whilst poultry and a coop of pigeons keep "bluebeard" alive.

* Stanbury "old coal pits," as indicated on our map, lie about 160 yards south of Upper Height, above "Owd Timmy's."

We now dip sharply several feet, to where the road is banked up and tunnelled. A bountiful and tempting run of clear water empties itself into an elevated trough by the road at the foot of the hill, and we eagerly sample its quality. Shouldn't we have smacked our lips at this on Boulsworth!

Ponden Reservoir.

Now we border Ponden Compensation Reservoir—Halliwell Sutcliffe's "Sorrowful Water" or "Scartop Water." The patch of blue on our map, assumes the shape of a lady's high-heeled boot laid on its side. We are at the "heel," where the waters of Ponden Clough enter the "boot"; the river Worth, first arrested at the Watersheddles, a mile further up, enters the "toe" away to our left. Here, then, is the foot of Sutcliffe's "Lonely Valley," in the immediate foreground his "Cringle Wood," the whole shut in at the top yonder by Kirk brink, which we descended less than half-an-hour ago. Rounding the "heel" of the "boot" we skirt, "stitch by stitch" the back of the "upper," to where the reservoir's embankment stretches across the "ankle." A footpath evidently traversed daily leads over the embankment; also a cart track; but this appears very occasionally used. Whether it is public or private we do not know, but the gates bearing the letters K.W.W. (Keighley Water Works) are under lock and key. An open wicket and the absence of any notice against trespassing help to dispel qualms of conscience. An aged man sets us at ease. He assures us we may proceed over the embankment without fear of being "turned back," and that the small gate at each end is always open to the public, but vehicular traffic is restricted to tenants provided with keys, which are for the larger gates. The privilege avoids the going round by Ponden Bridge, and a rise of some 76 feet.

"Ya seea yond narrow piece raaichin' fra t'reservoy awaa up ta Ponden Hall?" continues our friend pointing his crutch over the water.

"Ya meean yond length o' green wi' trees fra t' tup ta t' buttom?" we ask in dialect we are becoming quite versed in.

"Eaah! 'E can tell o' crows mackin ther haam i' them plaans en ashes. But as 'E wer' gaain to saa, that's a bit o' t'owd raad et used ta strike in et Scar Top yonder, an' cut across t' valley alaangside sum mill-ponds; an' this raad whear ya an' maa stond wer' maade i' t' plaace on't."

Bred and born in the locality, our friend, like "owd Timmy" on the moor's border above there, could tell many interesting happenings "sin' 'E wer' a lad," did time permit.

Immediately we are within the gates of the embankment we are challenged ; but a gentle swerve of our umbrella causes a babbling crowd of geese to turn tail. How calm the reservoir and peaceful the vale up towards Watersheddles. Over the embankment we step on the turnpike road (/\ 774-4) from Haworth to Colne, We turn to our right towards Haworth. Across the way is a ruined building, formerly a brewery, we learn.

Scar Top Chapel : "Charity" Day.

To our right are a few cottages and adjoining is Scar Top Wesleyan Chapel, which has really drawn us aside. Though there is nothing striking about it ; it is merely a plain little Bethel. There appears to be no date on the building, but information we possess shows it was built in 1818, as an undenominational chapel, and in 1869 was re-built, a gallery and choir-loft being added. The setting sun lights up the gallery, and we note the time of the clock in front thereof—4-15. A little way past the chapel and at a junction of roads we observe a finger-post indicating: "To Colne, 7 miles ; to Keighley, 5 miles ; to Haworth, 2 miles." We wish ourselves comfortably arrived at the latter place. To our right is Ponden Mill, ten miniature windows long and in two storeys. Close by is a pond (/\ 728.2), rush-grown and bordered with marsh marigolds. This water, in the days of the Heatons, ground corn in premises long since laid waste. Here, Scar Top "Charity" is held, which "Charity," like Blake Dean, is exceedingly popular. Providing the weather is favourable the scene has a most animated appearance. It was an ideal day when (since our saunter) we paid a visit to this widely-noted Sunday School Anniversary.

We left home early, to permit our attending morning service in Haworth Church. After dinner we resumed. It was 2 o'clock as we descended Hob Lane and approached the scene. Here we caught sight of the stage cloaked in red against the old mill. Only very few people had arrived, and were strolling aimlessly about. Some fifty planks, narrow, thin, and apparently uncomfortably slender, placed on trestles, lined the open space. A few rows of chairs were arranged in front of the stage. We elected a seat at the rear with a wall for support and the hot sun at our backs, but the instant we were seated there was a slight creak and a perceptible yielding of timber, we remember, which decided us to move a little further on, where the trestles were not quite so far apart.

At 2-15, a man with white flowing beard appeared, and sat nearest us in a

Scar Top "Charity" Day. Hare Hill in background.

corner of the bottom row of the stage. This was the preacher, Mr. Nathan Moore, farmer, of Luddenden Dean, who, the day before, drove over the hills to be in readiness for the event. He at once recognised us and smiled a surprised salutation. We had hoped for crowds to hear him, but up to now—fifteen minutes before the advertised time of starting—his audience was extremely thin. There was no trace of uneasiness on the preacher's countenance, however ; his composure seemed to say, all is well. Presently some thirty girl-scholars in white appeared suddenly, as angels descended from the sky, filed past, and took up positions on the stage. These were followed by musicians and male singers, who were apparently old hands, knowing their places. A couple of violins flanked the harmonium in the centre. First and second cornet, clarionet, piccolo, tenor and bass trombones and a *bb* (*brass*) formed the highest tier. When the service commenced the congregation was lamentably small. The harmoniumist sounded the key-note, whereat there was a general blowing of instruments. The preacher, now hemmed in by the scholars, stood and announced the first hymn on the sheet, and read aloud the first verse. The conductor, seated in the middle of the front row, rose and faced the stage. An upward movement of the baton and all were attention. The lighter instruments lead off, the heavier ones taking up the strain at the last line, which was the scholars' signal to rise. Now, as Halliwell Sutcliffe says " the voices rise as one, and lift themselves clear, strong and sweet," till the vale re-echoed with the music. Prayer was offered, another hymn sung, the lesson read, a third hymn, then the sermon, " hot and impassioned, a sermon that is hale and lusty with the old, uncompromising dogma," observes Sutcliffe. While the discourse lasted, a number of farmers' traps brought friends from a distance. An occasional wagonette also pulled up with visitors, who helped to swell the listening congregation ; for not all present were " hearers of the Word." Scores of people, unheedful of the preacher's message, paraded the road and bridge near to. Parasols of varied hue were lightly tossed and twirled by fashionably-dressed owners. Couples sat on walls and lolled on the grass, laughing and making merry within audible sound of the preacher's voice. But no matter ! The fete-like spectacle was highly gratifying. At the conclusion of the service the preacher hinted he had done his little part ; the choir had finished theirs, apart from an anthem about to be sung, and now it was our turn. The collection was announced, upon which those appointed to take up the offering appeared, suddenly, as the "angels" in white, from a roofless

" vestry." The young men collectors spread themselves out to present the box in the " outer courts "—no light task. We of the real congregation were waited upon by a stalwart elder with beaming face—a typical-looking Methodist. While the offertory was being taken, the anthem was sung. "They both preach and sing with a will at Scar Top charity, and the service is good as a north-west wind, full of tonic, tingling and alive," declares Halliwell Sutcliffe. The Benediction pronounced, the preacher is besieged by friends wishful to shake hands with him.

There must have been close on 2,000 people present during the day, for the collection realised £30 15s. 1d., and comprised four sovereigns, 12 half sovereigns, one Postal Order for 10s., 26 half-crowns, 18 florins, 83 shillings, 136 sixpences, 339 threepenny-pieces, 693 pennies, and 254 half-pennies.

Scar Top folks never worry about procuring a minister who will prove a draw. Nathan is the acknowledged preacher. For over thirty years he and his brother John conducted the services, preaching alternately. Since John's death (April 19, 1897, aged 76) Nathan has preached on every occasion. More than once he has tried to " back out," he tells us, but the officials won't hear of it ; and little wonder. They take pride in honouring one of their kith and kin, who seems as a father amongst them, though his looks belie his age. He points them to Cold Knoll End on the hill above as the place where he was born, and often takes them back in memory to the days when he attended Scar Top as a lad. For more than the fifty summers gone that he has taken part in the Anniversary, he has only once been absent, when sent as a local preacher delegate to Hull. Long may he still lead this popular service.

* * * * * *

Moving on, we go over Ponden Bridge and up Hob Lane, passing midway the Eagle Inn—Halliwell Sutcliffe's " Silent Inn "—on whose walls we observe a sun-dial dated 1834. " Children coming home from school " stop at a trough above the inn and dip their faces into the water. Did we but wear pinafores as they, we believe we too should make towels of them. Forsooth, we feel the need of a cleansing !

Here we are, again back at Hob Lane top, where the kindly woman at our request supplied the wily customer, who pleaded hunger, with a buttered tea-cake, and where we branched off to Timmy's, up past Withens (" Wuthering Heights "), and over the moor to Walshaw Dean and our haven of rest—Ridge Nook. Since then we have followed a

very circuitous route. When at the weaver's we noted a photo of himself and a girl, say of ten summers, standing beside him and looking down upon him so pleasantly as he sits erect in his high-backed old arm-chair with his legs akimbo, puffing away at his pipe. The photograph was taken, we remember, by Mr. Jonas Bradley, schoolmaster, Stanbury, who entitled the picture "Cum 'ere, Mary, an' set ma orf a bit," a request of Timmy's to the girl during the "sitting." It would give us great delight to possess a copy. Here is the Council School (⩚ 844-6), the doors are closed and, as we are aware, the scholars dismissed. An opportune time, we think, for an interview.

"Say, my dear girl, can you tell us where Mr. Brad—"

"There!" says the bright little miss we appeal to, pointing to an open door almost within reach of our umbrella.

"Mr. Bradley, did I hear you say," inquires a likely gentleman, appearing in the doorway.

"Yes."

"That is my name, sir," says the schoolmaster; then, turning and addressing a Scotch terrier whose welcome (?) reception painfully reminds us of our experience at Widdop reservoir-house, he tenderly scolds, "Hush, Nellie, we cannot hear ourselves speak for you. Shame! you shouldn't be so very noisy. It's very naughty, you know, *very* naughty! Go inside, please, that's a good girl."

And Nellie understands and obeys, on which we introduce ourselves, make known our mission, and are cordially invited in. We had not reckoned on this, and feel somewhat abashed, conscious the figures we cut are anything but presentable; and especially before ladies, to whom our request is stated. The very picture we hanker after hangs on the wall, and our covetousness is barely manifest. Timmy is taken down, divested of his frame, placed in an envelope and presented to us. Payment is resented; we are very welcome to "t'owd chap."

Really, it was not our intention to beg, but there! and "t'owd weeaver" is carefully stowed away inside our crowded notebook.

We at once feel at home in the company of the schoolmaster, his good wife and Miss Marchbank; nobody could help it. A nice garden, enough to consume all the leisure moments of a busy man's life, is attached, and we are taken round, accompanied by "Nellie," their faithful friend, 12½ years old. The day scholars refer to and address the pet as "Ellen Bradley," we are told.

To the casual passer-by the roadside garden appears nothing more

than one ordinarily cared for, but close inspection reveals character in collection of treasures. Almost every stone in the little rockeries has an interesting history. We are not only conducted round, but are given lessons in botany, ornithology, geology, and mineralogy. We sit only a minute or two in the summer-house, with its woodbine matted porch, but we learn the vicinity of Ponden Kirk is a rare hunting-ground for the naturalist; that a pair of dippers rear their young there every year. It is pleasing to hear not one of Mr. Bradley's scholars would rob a bird's nest, nor even disturb a parent bird in hatching time. We express astonishment and hope the scholars will ever maintain the reputation.

Sheltering the garden from the north-east wind is a joiner's shop and timber yard. These sites from about 1653 till after the Revolution, 1688, formed a Quakers' burial ground. No trace of it is visible, but a register in the possession of Mr. J. Horsfall Turner, of Idle, records the burial of 40 odd members. The Rev. T. W. Story, culling from the old Haworth Registers, mentions names of persons interred "in the Quakers' Burial Place at Stanbury," in the years 1659, 1662, and 1681. The Quakers held their meetings in an upper room of Mr. Bradley's dwelling, approached by steps on the outer face of the eastern wall; they were cut away a few years ago, and the doorway was walled in, as we observe.

* * * * * *

After much appreciated kindness we saunter on, escorted by the soldierly figure of the schoolmaster, who volunteers to point out the principle features of the village; we were not so favoured on our outward journey.

Here, on our left, is the old day-school, easily recognised, with master's house attached. They were built in 1805—exactly a century ago. As we listen to stories thereof we are reminded of "Old Eben's," Sammy and Betty Rothery's schools, save at none of these was discipline taught by sticks kept at the desk ready to shy at talkative scholars, as when Abraham Sunderland, the first master, had charge here. More sticks were thrown during prayers, we are told, than at any other time, and after devotions delinquents filed to the master's three-legged table to be "ruled." Mr. Bradley never taught in this school, his career here beginning in the Council school in 1890—fifteen years since. Farther on, set back from the highway, peacefully and picturesquely among trees, is a stone Mission Church, a branch from Haworth, erected in 1848, that year of tribulation for Mr. Brontë, when first Branwell, the shadow of the home, then Emily, its light, were put under the church

pavement. One hundred yards or so on the right is a Wesleyan Methodist Chapel, erected A.D. 1832, enlarged 1845.

Methodism was a force in those days, as Halliwell Sutcliffe in *Man of the Moors* vividly reminds us. Mentioning this we are shown the Manor House, "Gabriel Hirst's," whose strip of garden with round-topped wall "gives it an air that narrowly escapes haughtiness by the contrast with other dwellings in the hamlet." "There is another thing worthy of note which you must see," observes our obliging friend, and he darts towards a farm already known to us. We guess his errand, and beckon him stay. He is taken aback when we tell him we have already seen Grimshaw's pulpit.* In passing we give the relic a kindly thought, sadly deploring its being anchored in this old barn where spiders spin their webs and rats probably race round.

A stiff breeze blows across Haworth Moor, making thereon the windmill-like contraptions which supply power to water-pumps in the quarries above, revolve terrifically. Stanbury is now at our heels, and our guide returning briskly home; so briskly that we could not now keep pace with him for any long distance. So we soliloquize as we stroll languidly down the brow towards Haworth, seen at the top of the hill; but lo, the valley between! At no distant date we hope to re-visit "Ling Cragg," renew our acquaintance with the schoolmaster, and have an introduction to his pupils.

The seat at the Cemetery corner, where lounged the poor soul with besmeared features, is vacant, but we cannot afford a rest. With a special effort we accomplish the sharp rise from Sladen Bridge, and a minute later are interested in people leisurely descending the road leading to Haworth Cemetery, the Moor, and the Fall. Stealing an hour's airing are mothers, with children who romp on the greensward; others wheel their little ones in prams. Invalids, too, have been attracted by the bracing air. Very, very acutely we feel the need of a rest, a wash, and a cup of tea, all which will do much towards renewing vigour required for the last stage homewards.

Old Sol, still beaming, but with diminished power, will soon hide his face behind "Ling Cragg," which "gets a sight of the sun long after the shelter-seeking 'Marshcotes' houses are graying in the twilight."

"The radiant morn hath passed away,
And spent too soon her golden store;
The shadows of departing day
Creep on once more."

* Since our saunter, the pulpit has been restored and placed in Stanbury Mission Church.

HAWORTH, NEW FRIENDS.

Complying with the request of a Halifax friend we presently halt opposite a house whose number corresponds with the pencilled and crumpled paper we fish from an inner pocket.

" Aw've a cousin livin' i' Haworth ! " said this friend on our intimating our intention of touring Brontë-land, " yo'm bi sure ta luck her up ; shoo's o' th' reight sooart, aw con tell yo', an' yo' con reck'n on a hearty Yorkshire welcom' ; yo'll nooan get ta com' away nauther, baht a bite o' sommat t' eyt, aw'll be bun for 't."

Really, we ought to have called when outward bound, but time so pressed. We are scrutinising the little garden patch when a woman appears at the window, but only for a moment. Lace curtains are both cosy-looking, ornamental and *useful*. At the click of the gate, the cottage door, before ajar, is now thrown open, and we are met on the threshold by a motherly body with a countenance reflecting goodness itself. We are sure of it. Undoubtedly this is she whom we desire to see ; the description faithfully tallies. Immediately we introduce ourselves we are accorded the heartiest of receptions.

" 'Av ya had yar teah ? " is the very first query.

As at the schoolmaster's at Stanbury we must needs tell once more how that we hope to have tea at the Church School-house, only a short distance further, which excuse, though plausible, is scarcely deemed satisfactory. We are forgiven on promising not to make similar arrangements if ever this way again.

" Can you tell us anything of interest relating to the Brontë family ? " we ask.

" Na, ya kno' *we* (turning to her husband) can't remember t' Brontës, but iv heeard mi muther tell abaat when my father en her used ta be sizin' en stretchin' the'r warps et t' bottom o' t' moor, near Wattery-loin top—ya kno' yar fooaks wer' 'andloom weeavers—theease Brontë lasses used to cum past when art fer a walk. They'd a bein eeather readin' a bouk, er dooin sum mak o' fancy wark. They wod walk on just es if ther' worn't a soul i' t' rooad, en never lift the'r eyes nor speeak a word tiv yar fooaks, nor tiv onybody they met ; but 'E suppooase it wer' the'r waa ! "

This little information bears testimony to that of Charlotte in her *Biographical Notice of Ellis and Acton Bell*, where she says " In externals they were two unobstrusive women ; a perfectly secluded life gave them retiring manners and habits."

This is all our newly-found friend is able to tell us concerning the Brontës. Plenty of tales she has heard old people relate "at time en time," but she cannot recall them. Many old folks live in and around Haworth who knew the Brontës personally; we are given the names and addresses of a few.

"Likely ya may fynd time ta luke 'em up," observes our friend; but we seriously doubt it. We would fain spend an hour here, as invited, but we must away, for the church clock strikes six. "Nae man can tether time nor tide," else how very often we should desire to arrest the fleeting moments.

Back at Haworth Church School-house.

We pass the Brontë Museum, purposing to pay a visit later. Our present business is to present our unpresentable figures at the Church School-house, and apologise for being so much overdue; and we find we have worried most. Tea is set before us, and to say the least of it, we play havoc with the wholesome victuals. A knock is heard, footsteps approach along the passage, and we are introduced to a Mrs. W———, one of Charlotte Brontë's Sunday School scholars.

Good! this is indeed interesting.

"Are there any more of her scholars living?" we inquire.

"Three more, and all reside in the village."

O that we could converse with them all! Truly, here is an opportunity which, now lost, may never return. We wish the evening was available. Why not stay? Surely we can procure lodgings for the night. Perhaps the sexton can accommodate us. The prospect of interviewing the whole of these scholars of Charlotte's, the mere thought of sleeping under the roof which housed the curates of Brontë times, where Mr. Nicholls lived when married, where Martha Brown (Tabby's assistant) was cradled and reared, beneath the shadow of the old Church Tower and within the sound of its bells, excites us no little, and we blunder out the suggestion. Being strangers, we cannot hope for ready consent, and our joy overflows on receiving a favourable answer. But the concession is conditional. Under no circumstances must they be regarded as having apartments to let, and we promise to make this known in print, assuming our wanderings are published. We are a specially-privileged party, and we hasten to acknowledge our gratitude. Twice now impromptu moves have caused us to vary our original programme. It was our intention to-night, first to visit Brontë Museum, then

catch at Cullingworth—a comfortable hour's walk—the last train from Keighley to Halifax, hence the feeling, all day, of being pressed for time. After despatching a beautiful picture post card of Brontë Waterfall, by Mr. F. Shuttleworth, Haworth, to those at home "looking this way," explaining our prolonged stay at Ridge and our now further sojourning, we settle down to spend the evening in Haworth.

To-morrow, we follow on. We know not the kind of reception which will then await us, but we have surmisings. Albeit, we have breasted storms before, and survived them. Courage!

CHAPTER XX.

CHATS WITH CHARLOTTE BRONTË'S SUNDAY SCHOOL SCHOLARS. AUTHORSHIP OF "WUTHERING HEIGHTS."

OUR minds at ease, now that lodgings are vouchsafed us, we engage the old lady before us in conversation respecting her Sunday School teacher, Charlotte Brontë. At the outset she intimates her aversion to figuring in print, but concedes to being questioned on our promising to refer to her simply as Mrs. W——. She fears she was too young to remember much about her teacher or the class. She was born in September, 1835, which fact she doesn't mind telling us.

At Charlotte's death in 1855 she would be twenty. She says fifty years is a long time to remember scenes and events, though she can recall things which occurred then much better than more recent happenings. In all, she thinks there would be 16 or 18 scholars, and she would be amongst the youngest. She can see her teacher now, as then, dressed so plainly, yet neatly, noiselessly tripping into school in hailstone-pattern cloth boots with square toes, place her muff at the end of a form, adjust her gold glasses, which dangled on a delicate gold chain worn round the neck, and stand facing the scholars as they in turn read verses of Scripture. When Charlotte herself read, she held the Bible rather close to her eyes.

Her teacher wore both eye-glass and spectacles, for in a letter penned July 18th, 1841, to a friend, she says "We waited long and anxiously for you on the Thursday that you promised to come. I quite wearied my eyes with watching from the window, eye-glass in hand, and sometimes spectacles on nose."

"She was very sharp spoken" says Mrs. W——. Promotion was by merit, but it was never her lot to occupy the premier position, an honour which nearly always went to a Miss M—, now Mrs. T——, and one of the surviving four. But then the exaltation was just, admits Mrs. W——., Miss M—— being far the best scholar; she was also one of the eldest, being Mrs. W——'s senior by three years. As with all she undertook, Charlotte in school was strict to a degree.

CHARLOTTE BRONTË.
(By special permission of Mr. John Grant, Publisher, Edinburgh).

She always commanded attention, no matter who her company.

One Sunday morning, Mrs. W—— recalls, the school, through some cause she cannot explain, was in uproar. Miss Brontë appeared, and immediately there was peace. Mr. Nicholls, the superintendent, was always punctual, a practice we are ever ready to advocate. After each service and every Sunday, Charlotte would wait at the foot of the pulpit stairs for her father, walk out by the west door of the tower—now walled up—arm-in-arm with him, and so forward through the churchyard, passing close to Tabitha's grave, and enter the Rectory garden by a gateway which also is walled up.

When her teacher married, a feast was provided for ringers, singers and first select classes of scholars, and she was one of the guests "bidden to the wedding." None, she believes, excused themselves. Every detail of that event arises vividly before her. Mr. Nicholls joined them, but Charlotte withheld her presence, electing to spend the time in quietude at home with her father.

After Charlotte's death, a Dr. Cartman (Mrs. W—— thinks this was his name), who was staying at the Vicarage, conducted a memorial service in the church, his text being "And all wept and bewailed her," (Luke viii, 52). Mrs. W—— remembers also the text of the last sermon Mr. Brontë preached, "Let us hear the conclusion of the whole matter: Fear God and keep His Commandments, for this is the whole duty of man (Ecclesiastes xii, 13).

"Not so bad a memory, after all, Mrs. W——," we remark as she dons her shawl and bids us a cheery "Good night."

* * * * * *

The night is yet young, and to make the most of it we decide to seek interviews with the other surviving scholars, upon which mission we forthwith set out. After a good tea, wash and rest, we feel spick and span—equal to another long trudge.

Wednesday, and the village wears a normal aspect; no one, save ourselves, is in holiday attire, and it is obvious we are recognised as visitors. Men assembled "o' th' top o' Wuthering Street," as apparently is their wont, "to tell or hear some new thing," eye us askance as we pass by, making us feel a trifle uncomfortable. And the company of a barber's shop in which we seek refuge is just as keen in its scrutiny.

How strange that the topic of debate as we enter should be the distance from Upper Withens ("Wuthering Heights") to Walshaw Dean! Why,

we are the very ones to settle the argument, for it is only two days since we covered the ground and timed ourselves. Much sooner than we anticipated we are called upon to " take the chair," the remaining customers requiring hair-cut, it appears. The discussion goes on, all having a voice in the matter save a young man, if anything more smartly dressed than the rest, who seems fidgety to be off ; it is midweek, we remember. A slim youth waxes warm and maintains he " could do t' whoal gaat, fra t' Tup Withens ta t' middle dam i' fifteen minutes." We are sorely tempted to check the braggart, but on second thoughts decide to keep passive, for the lather is being laid on. The operation through, we speak. Eyes are fixed on us and every tongue lies still while we tell of our walking " t' whoal gaat " so recently ; that it took forty minutes, gently going, and that measured it will work out at 1½ miles or more. We agree it may be possible to accomplish the distance in fifteen minutes, but not at walking pace, even when, as now, the moor is in ideal condition. Whispers pass round as we pay and depart.

* * * * * *

The scene is changed. The curtain rises and we are seated in the front room of Mrs. T——, Charlotte Brontë's eldest surviving scholar, doing our best to abstract from her all she remembers of her teacher of half-a-century ago. She is afraid the little she can call to mind will not help in any great measure to the story we purpose printing. Like Mrs. W——, she reminds us it is difficult recalling things which occurred fifty years ago or more. With preliminary notice of our visit, she might have jogged her memory.

Apologetically we remark upon a photo of Charlotte's on the mantelpiece. Mrs. T—— does not consider the picture a good likeness of her teacher ; she always wore her hair as the photo depicts, Victorian style, parted in the middle and combed down over the ears.

" After fifty years, the fashion is revived," we waveringly observe, wondering whether really our observation coincides with the present vogue of hair-dress. We have trod on delicate ground and forthwith change the subject.

To describe Charlotte, Mrs. T—— says, is beyond her power, save that she was very small-built (" stunted," we remember, was Charlotte's description of herself). She was so much out of the ordinary from other women, adds Mrs. T——. Though hasty, she was a good teacher and kind in the extreme ; one of the best of sick visitors, but rarely seen in the street except on errands of mercy or beneficence. Mrs. T——

best recalls the "marriage feast," and she brightens up wonderfully on our naming it; the pleasant evening spent in the school will never be erased from her memory.

The chilly air of the fireless room, we see, is telling on Mrs. T——, who is only recovering from an annual winter's attack of bronchitis, and we feel we must release her earlier than we had hoped to. At 73, she says she does not expect perfect health; her strength is but labour and sorry, and days have come wherein she has little pleasure. We express sympathy and remind her summer is at hand, and brighter days, we trust, are in store.

"Of course you do not mind us associating your name with these reminiscences?" we ask, as we prepare to take leave. But she also begs that we will refrain. We are at a loss to know why, because we ourselves feel we should deem it such an honour to have been one of Charlotte's scholars. Certainly, as Mrs. T——points out, there is the danger of her peaceful dwelling being stormed by such pilgrims as her present visitors.

* * * * * *

In five minutes we find ourselves with our feet on another rug, having a quiet chat with Miss L——, the youngest living member of Charlotte's class. She will be 68 next birthday. The most vivid recollection she has of Miss Brontë is once, in the day school, being helped by her out of a difficulty. She was busy with sampler work, trying to depict the Nativity, and could not weave the arm of Joseph in the proper shade. She was but ten and appealed to her teacher, who, to her delight, surmounted the difficulty. The needlework, which is produced for our inspection, cannot be had for love or money.

A photograph of the interior of Haworth's church hangs on the wall. The Brontë pew, near the chancel arch, is pointed out, and the corner where Charlotte usually sat; but when she became popular she found it too embarassing, and she repaired to the opposite side of the seat to evade the stare of strangers who took up positions in the north and west galleries.

While we and another sister are examining the sampler and photo, Miss L——'s mind has evidently been at work, for she recalls two incidents, but doubts if they are worth repeating.

One Sunday Charlotte chose for her subject "Jezebel," and took extra pains, Miss L—— believes, to instil into their minds something of the life of that wicked person. At the conclusion of the lesson, their teacher inquired of the class:—

" Have I been speaking about a man or a woman ? "

One of them (Miss L—— cannot say who it was) made answer :

" A man ! "

What was her teacher's exact reply Miss L—— does not remember, but she has an impression it was not of a very complimentary character.

Another time, a younger sister, " a regular chatterer," was being taught by Mrs. Nicholls, and as a punishment for talking was made to stand on a form. Miss L—— immediately left her class, snatched her sister from the bench, and taking her into her class, set her beside her.

" And what then ? " we ask, " was your sister allowed to remain with you ? "

" Yes, but I got such a reprimand from my teacher as I never forgot. She was rather hasty tempered ; but then, as I saw afterwards, I ought not to have interfered."

" You could not tolerate your sister being exposed in that fashion ? "

" No ! she was on view of the whole school. There were no such things as class rooms then, you know. The day school was the Sunday school, and the forms used during the week were re-arranged for classes on the Sabbath."

We may pocket our note-book now, Miss L—— says, for further remembrance of her teacher is a blank. We bid her adieu and set out to find the last scholar on our list—a Mrs. Ratcliffe.

* * * * * *

Children together, neighbours yet, are these old scholars of Charlotte Brontë's ; indeed, we doubt if any one of the four has ever moved from the village. It will be interesting to know, and we will make it our business to inquire of the prim old lady with beautiful silvery hair now holding out her hand, shyly, we think, yet courteously, to receive us.

No, neither she nor any of the three surviving scholars has, to her knowledge, lived outside Haworth. She, Mrs. W——, and Mrs. T——, were married in the old church, and have been widows a number of years. Unlike the others, Mrs. Ratcliffe does not mind our publishing her name. Her maiden name was Tabitha Brown.

" Any relation of Tabitha Aykroyd, Brontë's old servant ? " we ask.

No, nor was she christened after her. She is the namesake of an aunt. Mentioning that we come from near Halifax, and Tabitha being on the carpet, a smile steals over the countenance of Mrs. Ratcliffe. She is thinking of an amusing incident which occurred only a short time ago, and she goes on to relate the story.

A party of Halifax ladies were visiting Haworth and staying with friends of Mrs. Ratcliffe's. In conversation Tabitha was mentioned, and the visitors said they would dearly like to see her. Tabitha's address was secured, and shortly the hand of Mrs. Ratcliffe received a shaking she does not remember being equalled during her 71 years. She stood astounded; she could not comprehend. There was some mistake; of this she was convinced, as she watched the strangers round the curve in the street.

"Why, she looks quite young," remarked the visitors on their return.

"Who?" asked their hostess.

"Old Tabitha, Brontë's servant," said they.

Explanations followed, and many a hearty laugh Mrs. Ratcliffe and her friends had. And small wonder, since Tabby, Brontë's servant, was 84 at her death in 1855.

* * * * * *

We had hoped to reap a harvest of interesting things from Mrs. Ratcliffe's lips concerning her Sunday School teacher, but she is afraid she cannot think of anything just now; we have taken her "so sudden." There are, however, two things she will never forget—Charlotte's marriage feast, and her death-bed scene, nine months later. Accompanied by her sister Martha, Mrs. Ratcliffe was permitted to look on the frail form of her teacher as she lay awaiting her Master's call, and she tells us it was heartrending to witness her last moments; she seems to see her now; every gasp "was like a little throstle gaping."

On the general life of the Brontë family Mrs. Ratcliffe believes she could interest us for hours. She considers herself part and parcel of them since she lived neighbour to them in the Church school-house up to her marriage, in 1861. Her father, who died the year Charlotte passed away (1855), was John Brown, sexton at Haworth Church twenty years, and succeeding in turn his father, who held the position twenty-seven years. Her sister Martha became assistant to Tabby at the parsonage at ten, and at Charlotte's death was promoted to housekeeper, and so remained till the decease of Mr. Brontë. "There were six sisters of us," says Mrs. Ratcliffe, "and I am the only one left."

Their father, besides being sexton, was a monumental mason, and she well remembers him coming home one day, having been to Halifax on business, and making the astounding declaration that he had heard who was the real author of *Jane Eyre*. If that which had reached his

ears was correct, "Currer Bell" was none other, he exclaimed, than the parson's daughter, Charlotte. The news was too good and startling to be confined within the walls of the school-house. First it was told Martha, who, at the earliest opportunity, and with elation, plumped Miss Brontë. But the confession the servant hoped for was not forthcoming. She was quietly and mildly put off with :—

"Hush, Martha, hush, you should not talk so very much."

Some time prior to this, their father had sat up all night, fascinated with the novel, unconscious, of course, that the writer of it was his neighbour.

Before, and at the breaking up of the Brontë home, Martha came in for many mementoes Mrs. Ratcliffe now possesses. Some, we are somewhat astonished to learn, money will buy, if the offer is satisfactory.

A row of brass candlesticks there on the mantel-piece once adorned that of the kitchen at the parsonage. A tiny willow-pattern mug, placed in our hands, Mr. Brontë used to sip wine out of, we are told. An item Mrs. Ratcliffe cannot remember to show every caller interested in the Brontës, she withdraws from a remote corner and hands to us. This is a small hammer, suggestive of one used to "spetch"*

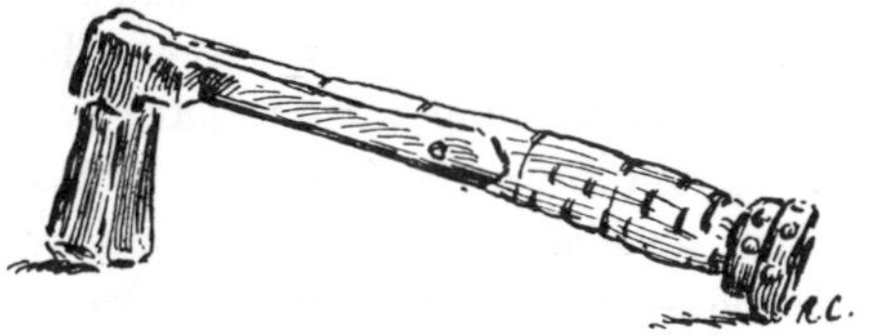

BRONTË HAMMER.

our clogs when children, only more ornamental; a kind of miniature blacksmith's sledge, gripping a well tack-studded wooden shaft. The day it left Haworth Rectory it "retired from active service."

"Pensioned off," we suggest; and its owner smiles acquiescently.

Very kindly we think of Anne when shown her work-box. 'Neath an inner lid are a dozen or so recesses. Here is a faded and moth-eaten needle-case containing an assortment of needles, etc., all rusty and useless.

A plain, delicate and oval-shaped brooch of Anne's, with plaited hair of Charlotte's, and a massive jet necklace which seems to call up visions of Anne's sickness at Scarborough (only 21 miles from Whitby), since it was probably purchased there. These we handle very carefully,

*Repair.

lest an accident should befall them, as has the glass on which we see portrayed original photos of Charlotte, Emily and Anne.

Most of Mrs. Ratcliffe's relics are lent to the Brontë Society for exhibition in the Brontë Museum, which we intend to visit later. She says we shall probably there observe a narrow, striped, shot-silk dress, with scolloped bodice and fringe on scollops. The colour she cannot fairly describe: it appears to be light brown, but at an angle shades to silvery grey. This, lent by a niece of her's, a Miss Binns, she understands, is ticketed "Charlotte's wedding dress" (Mrs. Ratcliffe herself has never visited the Museum), but as a matter of fact it is one she wore on her honeymoon; if her memory serves her, Charlotte was married in cream.

Mrs. Gaskell says "her dress was white embroidered muslin, with a lace mantle, and white bonnet trimmed with green leaves."

We shall also notice a blue delaine skirt which Charlotte wore, and a puce and black figured silk shawl, with fringe, formerly Miss Branwell's. After her death Charlotte wore it, and eventually "she presented it our Martha," says Mrs. Ratcliffe.

"Then you remember the whole Brontë household?"

Yes, she remembers every one, with the exception, of course, the mother and the two eldest children, Maria and Elizabeth, who died years before she was born. They were totally different in natures and temperaments. Charlotte was thoughtful and self-sacrificing, a fact manifested through their bitter bereavements; she was so for others outside the family circle, laying aside reserve when necessity appealed. Notwithstanding these traits, "Miss Brontë was very sharp," Mrs. Ratcliffe hastens to tell us.

"Then patience with Charlotte, it would seem, was scarcely a virtue," we remark, adding "this is the unsolicited testimony of each of your fellow-scholars whom it has been our pleasure to interview."

Emily was exceedingly shy, but in other respects "more like a man than a woman, and very dominant in will."

Anne never seemed to her of this world. She was a most beautiful character; one almost to be adored. Helen Burns in *Jane Eyre* is, she thinks, the prototype of Anne.

[Charlotte writes of her youngest sister, "Always good, mild and patient; long suffering, self denying, reflective and intelligent; a very sincere and practical Christian, but the tinge of religious melancholy communicated a sad shape to her brief, blameless life."]

Branwell was a rough one, Mrs. Ratcliffe recalls, and caused the family no end of trouble. He is, she feels sure, the original of the moral and physical wreck—Arthur Huntingdon, she believes his name is—in Anne's *Tenant of Wildfell Hall.*

Though Mrs. Ratcliffe would be but eight years old when Miss Branwell died, in 1842, she has a vague recollection of her.

Authorship of "Wuthering Heights."

There is one important matter we desire Mrs. Ratcliffe's opinion upon ere we part.

"Did you ever hear your sister Martha say anything respecting the authorship of *Wuthering Heights* ?" we ask.

Mrs. Ratcliffe waxes indignant as she sees our drift.

"Certainly, it was Emily who wrote that book," she declares emphatically, "who else could it be ?"

"Some think Branwell, you know," we reply, a little wincingly, observing we have touched a jarring chord.

"I have heard our Martha tell scores of times," Mrs. Ratcliffe rejoins, unheeding our answer, "how Emily used to take her writing desk and little buffet, now mine—you will see it in the museum—sling it on her arm in this fashion (picking up a four-legged stool and suiting the action to the word), trot into the garden, and in the shade of the trees sit writing for hours together."

* * * * * *

We are deeply indebted to Mrs. Ratcliffe* for favours shown and her reminiscences, and tender her our thanks, which are spurned ; she merits none, she says. If we have enjoyed her company and conversation she has ours, so we have profited equally.

Grasping gently the hand so cordially and enthusiastically shaken by the Halifax ladies in mistake for old Tabby's, we express our wishes for her welfare, hope our meeting will not be the last, and that at some time we may renew the Brontë theme, we bid her and her son "Good night !"

* * * * * *

We were particularly anxious to glean Mrs. Ratcliffe's opinion as to the authorship of *Wuthering Heights,* because we recall an article in February's (1905) issue of *Yorkshire Notes and Queries,* by Mr. J. Long-

*Mrs. Ratcliffe died Nov. 30, 1910, the same day as Timothy Feather ("Owd Timmy") which seems to us singularly coincidental. Both were buried the same day in Haworth Churchyard.

bottom, of Halifax, questioning the genuineness of the name attached to that book. Since then we have studied Mrs. Gaskell's *Life of Charlotte Brontë*, Leyland's *The Brontë Family*, Grundy's *Pictures of the Past*, and others, and are unshaken in our belief that Emily's name is rightly and justly linked to *Wuthering Heights*. Martha Brown, approached on the subject, we read, asks in scornful contempt :—

" Was Mr. Branwell able to do it ? Would Miss Emily, of all people, condescend to such meanness ? Who knew so well as Miss Charlotte ? Haven't I seen Miss Emily at her writing ? "

And here are Charlotte's own words in defence of the alleged fraud—for when the book was published its authorship was disputed.

" What her mind (Emily's) had gathered of the real, concerning them (the natives) was too exclusively confined to those tragic and terrible traits, of which, in listening to the secret annals of every rude vicinage, the memory is sometimes compelled to receive the impress. Her imagination, which was a spirit more sombre than sunny—more powerful than sportive—found in such traits material whence it wrought creations like Heathcliffe, like Earnshaw, like Catherine. Having penned these things, she did not know what she had done. Had she but lived, her mind would of itself have grown like a strong tree—loftier, straiter, wider-spreading—and its matured fruits would have attained mellower ripeness and sunnier bloom.

I am bound to avow that she had scarcely more practical knowledge of the peasantry amongst whom she lived than a nun had of the country people that pass her convent gates. My sister's disposition was not naturally gregarious ; circumstances favoured and fostered her tendency to seclusion ; except to go to church, or to take a walk on the hills, she rarely crossed the threshold of home. Though her feeling for the people round her was benevolent, intercourse with them she never sought, nor, with few exceptions, ever experienced, and yet she knew them, knew their ways, their language, their family histories ; she could hear of them with interest, and talk of them with detail, minute, graphic, and accurate ; but with them she rarely exchanged a word."

Charlotte certainly had a strong regard for the truth. But what tact she had in evading a thing she wished to conceal ; instance those two letters of April 28, and May 3, 1848, to her friend who plumped her with being an author. We much prefer to accept her story, however, to that of Grundy, who avers, " Patrick Brontë declared to me, and what his sister said (which sister, and when, and where and what) bore

out the assertion, that he wrote a great portion of *Wuthering Heights* himself." We favour the opinion, too, of another, that it was unnecessary for Emily to mix with the people, or cross their thresholds to learn their ways and acquire knowledge of the vulgar phrase with which *Wuthering Heights* abounds. Branwell, whose "tone of thought and conversation became gradually coarser" (Charlotte's painful admission), would unconsciously furnish these. Leyland, referring to the latter half of the work only, suggests "he stood to the author as a model for some details of character;" and in a very true sense, we say.

Shirley, too, has been ascribed to Branwell. Truly, some are born great, others have greatness thrust upon them. Eighteen years after William Dearden, author of *Star Seer*, and *Maid of Caldene*, and an acquaintance of Branwell's, wrote to the *Halifax Guardian* that Branwell read to him and Mr. Leyland a fragment of *Wuthering Heights* as his own production, a Mr. D. McB. stated in the *Leeds Times* that Branwell himself read to him the plot of *Shirley*, which statement received the silent sneer it deserved, says Mr. J. Horsfall Turner, who further ridicules the idea. As Leyland points out, "since *Shirley* was not commenced very many months before Branwell's death, and since he had been in his grave a year when it was published, it is obviously impossible that he can ever have desired to draw to himself the praise which was bestowed upon it."

Angus M. Mackay, in the *Bookman*, October, 1904, voices our opinion when he says: "The career of the only son, Branwell, was spoilt by his vices, and in any case it may be doubted whether, either as a painter, or an author, he had talents sufficient to have made him famous. But all the testimony extant concurs in showing that there was about him something bizarre, brilliant, original, which vividly impressed those who came in contact with him. He appears to have belonged to the class of persons who, whether they do or do not achieve great things, possess what may be called the genius of personality." We agree also with Leyland: "his nature was rather to be admired than condemned."

CHAPTER XXI.

A NIGHT AT HAWORTH CHURCH SCHOOL-HOUSE—BRONTË TREASURES.

NINE is being heralded by the church clock as we ascend Main Street back to the school-house. How fortunate that Mrs. W—— should pay that friendly call there just when she did. Had she not, undoubtedly at this moment we should have been making tracks to Cullingworth to catch the 10-7 train to Halifax. On reflection we believe with Shakespeare, that :—

> " There's a divinity that shapes our ends,
> Rough-hew them how we will."

With our feet on the hearth of the school-house what more natural than that thought should again glide towards the Brontës ?

Our hostess, Mrs. Widdop, first tells us that her parents, complying with the suggestion of John Brown, the sexton, christened her Jane Helen, the namesake of " Jane Eyre " and " Helen Burns "—since her advent into the world was shortly after the publication of Charlotte Brontë's first and entrancing novel. She also informs us it was none other than her father, John Greenwood, whom Mrs. Gaskell once interviewed and elicited the following relating to the Brontë sisters :—

" I have known Miss Brontë," said Mr. Greenwood, " as Miss Brontë, a long time, since they came to Haworth in 1819.* But I had not much acquaintance with the family till about 1843, when I began to do a little in the stationery line. Nothing of that kind could be had nearer than Keighley before I began. They used to buy a great deal of writing paper, and I used to wonder whatever they did with so much. I sometimes thought they contributed to the magazines. When I was out of stock I was always afraid of their coming ; they seemed so distressed about it if I had none. I have walked to Halifax (a distance of ten miles), many a time, for half a ream of paper for fear of being without when they came. I could not buy more at a time for want of capital—I was always short of that. I did so like them to come when I had anything for them ; they were so much different to anybody else—so gentle and kind, and

*The Rev. Patrick Brontë and family removed to Haworth February 25, 1820, as stated earlier in these pages.

so very quiet. They never talked much. Charlotte sometimes would sit and inquire about our circumstances so kindly and feelingly. Though I am a poor man (which I never felt to be any degradation), I could talk with her with the greatest freedom. I always felt quite at home with her. Though I never had any school education, I never felt the want of it in her company."

Mr. Greenwood was a painter. Soon after his marriage he had an accident. He fell from a ladder, and was so disabled that he had practically to relinquish his trade, being for a time only able to do such light work as sign-painting.

Highly prized by Mrs. Widdop is a strip of faded paper, containing an injunction from the Parsonage, in an almost illegible hand:—

Feb. 15, 1850.

To Mr. Greenwood, Haworth.

Please order "South's hints on emergencies, or household surgery"—from Charles Cox, 12, King William Street, Strand, London. Price 3s.

P. BRONTË.

Poor Mr. Brontë! Did ever one need *Hints on Emergencies or Household Surgery* more than he? At this time he was 74, and there was but himself and Charlotte left of a family of eight. Well can we understand his anxiety for the health and welfare of the last of the flock; his efforts to turn aside the pale white horse and his rider.

Now is handed us another document, discoloured with age and dated November 14, 1859, the certificate of the christening by "P. Brontë, A.B., Incumbent," of Mrs. Widdop's brother, named Brontë, now in a distant land. She believes the signature the last Mr. Brontë penned. As he feebly grasped the pen, his hand was guided by his housekeeper, Martha Brown. He was now 83, extremely weak and confined to bed.

A warming-pan with long polished handle, in excellent preservation, hangs glittering on the wall. Our hostess well remembers as a girl carrying home this covetable memento from the Brontë sale. More things purchased at the time are placed on the table before us.

Here are the boots Mrs. W—— spoke of Charlotte coming tripping noiselessly to school in. The uppers are of silk rep, hail-stone pattern, and side-laced. Remembering that Mrs. Gaskell affirms, "her hands and feet were the smallest I ever saw," we are curious to learn their measurement. The soles, no thicker than a florin, are 9 in. long and 2¼ in. broad. Is this considered unique in ladies' sizes? we wonder.

A brass-mounted, mahogany writing-desk once bore traces of frequent

usage, but renovation has robbed it of antiqueness, if not of intrinsic value. On it was penned most of the immortal literature that issued from the Parsonage. And cherished exceedingly is an original photo of Charlotte taken on glass, the mode in photography fifty years ago; also a negative of old Haworth Church, School and Parsonage; this latter from a pencil sketch by Mrs. Widdop's brother William. Treasured too, are original copies of *Cottage Poems* and *The Rural Minstrel*, by the Rev. P. Brontë. These we glance through, first noting they were "Printed and sold by P. K. Holden, Halifax," for the author, and dated 1811 and 1813. A few verses in *Epistle to the Labouring Poor* especially appeal to us, and we inscribe them in our note-book.

"You see that lordling glittering ride,
In all the pomp of wealth and pride,
With lady lolling at his side,
And train attendant.
'Tis all, when felt, and fairly tried,
But care resplendent.

As riches grow, his wants increase,
His passions burn, and gnaw his peace,
Ambition foams, like raging seas,
And breaks his reign;
Excess produces pale decease
And racking pain.

Compared with him, thrice happy you;
Though small your stock, your wants are few,
Each wild desire, your toil subdue,
And sweetens rest,
Remove all fancied ills from view
And calms your breast.

Your labour gives the coarsest food
A relish sweet;—cleanses the blood,
Makes cheerful health in spring-tide flood,
Incessant, boil;
And seldom, restless, thoughts obtrude
Our daily toil.

Those relish least who proudly own
Rich groves, and parks familiar grown;
The gazing strangers passing on,
Enjoy them most—
The toy possessed—the treasure flown,
For ever lost."

Mr. Widdop is not ashamed to own that his mother, in her struggling with a family of little ones, used to wash for the Brontës. She could not very well leave the children at home when she was requested at the Rectory, and it was necessary they should accompany her; and at the Rectory they tarried till her duties were completed. An infant

brother of Mr. Widdop's was often fondled by Charlotte while the washing proceeded, but he doubts whether ever he was thus cared for and caressed by her. Plato—a big, brown, curly-haired retriever, successor to Emily's "Keeper"—was one washing-day ranging the kitchen, the while switching his long tail, signifying friendship when, alas! he lashed it with dire results. A terrible howl rent the air. The toiler at the wash-tub was too intent on her work to notice she was twining into the machine the dog's hind appendage.

"Keeper!" We desire to recall his end, but cannot without the aid of Mrs. Gaskell, who tells of Charlotte writing December 8, 1851, "Poor old Keeper died last Monday morning, after being ill one night; he went quietly to sleep; we laid his old faithful head in the garden."

Mrs. Widdop remembers being many a time ridden on the back of Plato along Parson's Fields with Mr. Nicholls as driver.

* * * * * *

Lo! the "wee sma hours" approach. In company so genial, and engrossed in subjects vastly interesting, the night has flown almost imperceptibly. This quick flight we remark upon with regret as we are directed to our sleeping quarters.

And this is the room which, in the Brontë days, served as the curate's sitting-room! How privileged we are! But O! at dead of night how weird the outlook! Though at home we are near neighbours to the dead we never felt so closely allied as now. In the gloom the crowd of oblique tombstones appear like black living figures crouching under motionless trees. Unless haunted by a vision of these we doubt not we shall sleep soundly. The dark column of the old steeple towers like some sturdy fortress, and there, through the foliage and against the streak of lingering twilight, we dimly perceive the Parsonage. Strange as are the surroundings, we hear but twice the church chimes ere we doze off, and old Sol is once more well on his daily course before we again wake to consciousness.

* * * * * *

> "June bursts and torrid summer rules the year,
> The burning heat streams from a cloudless sky."

First of June, and what a lovely morning! How very thankful we are that Dame Fortune condescends to smile upon us. Notwithstanding the brilliant illumination of our room we find it difficult to "shake off

dull sloth and joyful rise," after yesterday's long and breezy moorland tramp.

Our toilet completed we hasten to present ourselves below. A savoury smell greets us, and our boots at the hob-end wear a gloss like a mirror, telling us busy hands have been at work while we have slumbered.

Breakfast over, with our host's permission and guidance we elect to look through the old and new schools, first expressing a wish to see the grave of Mr. Greenwood—Mrs. Widdop's father; and we are taken to the spot, south of the graveyard. The epitaph reads :—

In Loving Remembrance
of
JOHN GREENWOOD,
of Haworth,
WHO DIED MARCH 25, 1863,
AGED 56 YEARS.

Retracing steps, an epitaph catches our eye which asks—and seemingly seriously :—

" Why should our tears in sorrow flow
When God recalls his own,
And bids them leave a world of woe
For an immortal crown ? "

Yes, why? we ask ourselves as we wend our way back through the yard.

Over the porch of the old school is this inscription :—

" This National
Church Sunday School is under the management of trustees, of whom the Incumbent for the time being is one, and was erected A.D. 1832, by voluntary subscription, and by a grant from the National Society in London."

" Train up a child in the way he should go ;
and when he is old, he will not depart from it."
PROV. XXII. 6.

Then it was built during the incumbency of Patrick Brontë, we reflect, twelve years after his removal here from Thornton. The Rectory is opposite, and in fancy we see the fragile figure of Charlotte, on a Sabbath morning, in her silk rep hailstone-pattern boots, gently open the side garden gate, step noiselessly across the road and take up her position at the head of her class of girls.

The thinly-worn boarded floor of the school, with a forest of knots protruding, takes us back in thought to Brontë days. Since the new school was built, this, the old one, we are told, is principally used for functions in which crockery plays a part. Three nights a week it is a gymnasium. Some 1,100 books occupy one end, and there are about 30 borrowers. A round hole in the ceiling speaks of the time when the school was heated by a stove set in the centre of the floor, and the pipe was conducted through the roof. This method of heating was long since dispensed with.

At the present time there are about 450 Sunday scholars, and about 40 teachers. The procession at Whitsuntide, we are assured, is an inspiring sight, which remark calls to our minds the vivid description of that festival by Charlotte in *Shirley*. Hard by is the new school, on the facade of which we read :—

Haworth Parish Church School,
erected 1903.
Rector : T. W. Story, M.A.
Wardens { George Merrall,
Edwin Merrall.

Messrs. Merrall, manufacturers, Haworth, Mr. Widdop tells us, gave £4,000, absolutely defraying its cost. The raising of £500, for the superb furniture of foreign polished oak and pitch pine, was left to the congregation and scholars, and they realized the sum by a sale of work. We do not know a Sunday School so large and well lighted ; but then our knowledge of Sunday Schools generally is decidedly limited. Four hundred and fifty adults can be seated comfortably here. Twelve class-rooms—six for each sex—run the length of the school on each side. A high platform set in a recess at the western end, and equipped with American organ and piano, commands the whole school. This may be screened off by enormous blue curtains draping the arch. These curtains Messrs. Merrall specially wove for the purpose.

CHAPTER XXII.

BRONTË MUSEUM.

We visit next the Brontë Museum, so very conspicuous when ascending Main Street. A sundial on the south wall bears the inscription:—

Mr. Richard Pollard, of Stanbury,
gave it to the church, 1726.

It came into the possession of Mr. Wm. Redman (Mr. Widdop's uncle) when the old church was demolished in 1879. The caretaker of the Brontë relics, in shirt sleeves, awaits us in the street; through a message sent him, he is expecting us. We are introduced to him as a party wishful to look round, and one who most likely will spend more time there than the average visitor, our object, as explained, being to "take notes." "There are no catalogues," he says in answer to our query, and he leaves us to investigate at leisure, the door clanging behind him.

The first case, we find, contains chiefly letters from Charlotte to her dearest of friends, Miss Ellen Nussey. Though age and exposure under glass, in a strong light, have not made the writing any the clearer, we do not need to strain to read it, since beside each epistle there is a type-written duplicate. How exquisitely neat was Anne's writing. Everything in the museum appears to be labelled, and while some things are "on loan," others belong to the "permanent collection." Characters and spots figuring in Brontë writings are pictured on the walls, and a few of Branwell's paintings are hung, but these latter are not very clear. "The colours," as Mr. Francis F. Leyland says, "have vanished; scarcely any tint remains beyond that of the boiled oil with which they appear to have been mixed." One more distinct than the rest depicts a race-horse and rider. This, we fear, only too well serves to illustrate the artist's bent of thought. Another painting shows his three sisters sitting by a table, while Branwell, obviously to hide his diminutive stature,* stands behind it. He is seen grasping with left hand the barrel of a

*Mr. Grundy,—Branwell's companion in youth and "perhaps, his most confidential friend through good and ill until his death,"—says he was "almost insignificantly small—one of his life's trials."

gun, while with the other he points to a brace of lifeless birds on the table. And some would have us believe that the painter, who was much engrossed in sport and other queer propensities, was author of *Wuthering Heights* and *Shirley*. Never!

The best picture in oils by Branwell, we consider, is that of John Brown, the sexton. An excellent half-length portrait of Charlotte, we observe, is "attributed" to him.

Here is an engraving of the Rev. Hammond Roberson, the parson Helstone of *Shirley*, who died 1841, aged 84; another shows the Revs. Wm. Marjetson Heald, father and son, one Vicar of Birstall from 1801 to 1836, the other from 1836 to 1875. They together were the prototypes of the Rev. Cyril Hall in *Shirley*.

Time appears to have made little impression upon the small portrait Mr. Nicholls had taken in Dublin when on his honeymoon. The photo of Martha Brown is of a plain and homely character; beside it are letters she received from Patrick Brontë, Charlotte and Mrs. Gaskell, and a certificate of her baptism by the Rev. P. Brontë, dated June 8, 1828. In another case is a copy of *Shirley* (2nd edition) presented to her by P. Brontë.

Looking down upon us are the Rev. William Carus Wilson—"the black marble clergyman"—and his wife, the Mr. and Mrs. Brocklehurst of *Jane Eyre*. As we endeavour to study the reverend gentleman in his clerical robes, we wonder to what extent injustice was done him by Charlotte in her estimate of his character. Angus M. Mackay says, in effect, not one iota, founding conclusions upon unpublished "Thoughts suggested to the superintendent and ladies of the Clerical Daughters' School," written long after *Jane Eyre*, and upon writings of Mr. Wilson's, which he says, "certainly could not have fallen into Charlotte's hands."

Here, unobserved by visitors as they enter, is Charlotte's most intimate friend, Miss Nussey. What could better testify to their love for each other than this message, addressed from Haworth Parsonage to "Nell," as Charlotte familiarly called her?

"Friday will suit me very well. I *do* trust nothing will now arise to prevent your coming. I shall be anxious about the weather on that day; if it rains, I shall cry. Don't expect me to meet you; where would be the good of it? I neither like to meet nor to be met. Unless, indeed, you have a box or a basket for me to carry; then there would be some sense in it. Come in black, blue, pink or scarlet, if you like.

Come shabby or smart; neither the colour nor the condition signifies; provided only the dress contains E——, all will be right."

Having paid the visit there followed her home these lines:—

"Were I to tell you of the impression you have made on everyone here, you would accuse me of flattery. Papa and aunt are continually adducing you as an example for me to shape my actions and behaviour by. Emily and Anne say they never saw anyone they liked as well as you; and Tabby, whom you have absolutely fascinated, talks a great deal more nonsense about your ladyship than I care to repeat."

Mr. Clement K. Shorter tells us that "Ellen Nussey was a girl of 14 when she first met Charlotte Brontë, who was her senior one year, and that she received in all about 500 letters from her (also two from Emily), all of which were addressed in the most affectionate terms such as "My own dear Ellen," or "Nellie." A postscript of one concludes "Farewell, my *dear, dear, dear* Ellen."

Charlotte's death-bed letters to her dearest friend are preserved in a bound volume. A face-profile, done in chalk by Charlotte in both skill and taste, affords a striking contrast to a weird sketch pencilled by her brother. A number of water colours by Charlotte evoke our admiration. Even on minute detail the greatest care has been bestowed. Flowers appear as if freshly cut. Great dexterity too is manifest in sampler and needle-work wrought by the same skilled fingers.

* * * * * *

But the cynosure of the collection is without doubt the item Mrs. Ratcliffe spoke of, Charlotte's wedding dress.* Near it we see the blue delaine skirt and the puce-and-black silk shawl she also mentioned, a print dress and cape, lace undersleeves and collar, and other portions of the authoress's wardrobe.

Someone has said:—

> "In this abundant earth, no doubt,
> Is little room for things worn out,"

but we would gladly find room for the pair of hide-bound and paper-lined wooden trunks, the ricketty writing-desk, and the irreparable case for stationery from the Brontë homestead which lie near the fireless grate. Naturally we associate the trunks with *Jane Eyre,* when she "bade adieu to Gateshead and left by coach for Lowood." "My trunk," she says, "which had been carried down the evening before, stood corded by the door." When about to leave Lowood for Thornfield,

*See page 213.

she tells us, " the last day sufficed to pack my trunk—the same I brought with me eight years ago from Gateshead. The box was corded, the card nailed on." There, on the lids of the boxes are the imprints of nails. Perhaps one of these was taken by Lucy Snowe to London, thence to Villette per the "Vivid." We think we see her on the landing stage, eagerly watching the unloading of the baggage.

" One by one," she sighs, " I saw these removed, lowered and seized on. I was sure mine ought to be by this time visible ; it was not. I had tied on the direction-card with a piece of green ribbon, that I might know it at a glance ; not a fringe or fragment of green was perceptible. Every package was removed ; every tin-case and brown-paper parcel ; the oilcloth cover was lifted ; I saw with distinct vision that not an umbrella, cloak, cane, hat-box, or band-box remained.

And my portmanteau, with my few clothes and my little pocket-book, enclasping the remnant of my fifteen pounds, where were they ? "

Sharing the company of the trunks is a leather bag of irregular shape. To what purpose could the family put this ? Possibly it was Mr. Brontë's saddle-bag when he hired a horse to take him to distant parts of the diocese ; we do not remember hearing or reading that he ever owned a horse.

A water-colour drawing of the forequarters of Emily's dog " Keeper," the ferocious " Tartar " in *Shirley*, bears this fast fading inscription in imitation print (characteristic of Charlotte and Branwell particularly):—

" 'Keeper,' from life, April 24, 1838 ; Emily Jane Brontë."

" Keeper " was then in his youth. His breed seems difficult to determine. We think we see in the brute, wearing a scowl, with ears set and huge head and neck laid between its paws, some semblance to a wolf. Others, with more knowledge of the canine race than we, have been equally puzzled.

" A Mr. John Stores Smith visited Haworth in 1850, called upon the Brontës and described his experiences in the *Free Lance* of March 14, 1868," says Mr. Clement K. Shorter in the Haworth edition of Mrs. Gaskell's *Life of Charlotte Brontë.*

" In those days I possessed a dog," wrote Mr. Smith, " which had become a loved companion of my rambles. This dog arrived at the garden wicket simultaneously with myself. Now it so chanced that the dog of the Parsonage was taking his siesta in the sun at that very

moment, and lay curled into a huge ball on the doorstep. He was very old, almost toothless, and I believe wholly blind. His breed was conglomerate, combining every species of English caninity from the turnspit to the sheepdog, with a strain of Haworth originality superadded. In the exuberance of his youth, with wagging tail and ears cocked, my dog trotted gaily up to this poor old memento of the past, and in a second there was such an uproar as Haworth churchyard had seldom or never heard. With an angry roar the old dog by sheer weight rolled the younger one over, and commenced a painless worrying with toothless gums ; and the other, smarting under the first rebuff he had encountered, howled from vexation rather than from pain. In a minute or less I had nipped up my animal and held him under my arm, barking furiously, while the old one rolled to and fro among the mandrakes, blindly seeking his vanquished enemy. At this instant the door opened and the servant appeared, and behind her on the stairs was the authoress of *Jane Eyre*."

* * * * * *

Continuing round the room we observe on the wall a small frame containing the autographs of Currer, Ellis, and Acton Bell, and beneath the fac-simile of a letter from Patrick Brontë, to his brother Hugh in Ireland. After an effort we decipher the epistle :—

"This is the first work published by my daughter, under the fictitious name of 'Currer Bell,' which is the usual way at first by authors, but her real name is everywhere known. She sold the copyright of this and her other two works for fifteen hundred pounds, so that she has to pay for the books she gets the same as others. Her other two books are in six volumes, and would cost nearly four pounds. This was formerly in three volumes. In two years hence, when all shall be published in a cheaper form, if all be well, I may send them. You can let my brothers and sisters read this.

P. Brontë, A.B.,
Incumbent of Haworth,
Nr. Keighley."

Jan. 20 (?), 1853.

What a contrast is this autograph, when Mr. Brontë had impaired eyesight, to that written in 1806 ; the last is in a careful and steady hand with some of Anne's characteristics. A photo depicts Patrick Brontë's birthplace, a tumble-down, thatched cottage, typical of Irish peasantry, situated at Emdale, in the parish of Drumballyrony, County Down. He was born on St. Patrick's day, March 17, 1777. A painting of the rev. gentleman hangs on the wall. A critic might call it a daub. Certainly distance enhances the picture. We should like him better, we think, in his heavy, slide-frame spectacles, two pairs of which—one with blue glasses—we observe a little later.

On the floor is the four-legged buffet, associated with Emily.

A very common-place piece of furniture it is. Square, 8⅝ inches high, to be precise, of red deal, painted brown, and with one of four rails broken away. Presumably it was originally a child's chair. A card tacked on the seat (which is evidently "home-made"), reads: "Small wooden stool, used by Emily Brontë on the moors. Lent by Mrs. Robert Ratcliffe, Haworth." We notice that recently it has suffered chipping, and should advise Mrs. Ratcliffe to withdraw it from loan, or urge the Brontë Society to house it under cover. Unless this is done we fear it will continue to lose weight. Most of the articles on loan are owned by Mrs. Ratcliffe or her niece, Miss Binns. Occupying an end window-sill is a plaster cast, after Bochin, of Thackeray, Charlotte's favourite novelist, her "great and strong man," a "Titian of mind." He stands conning the narrow street outside, as if looking for visitors to this building. Like Emily's buffet, this figure has not escaped mauling, for, apparently with something sharp, a piece has been chipped from the base.

"And there came up a lion out of Judah," Charlotte remarked in London after lengthy study of Lawrence's portrait of Thackeray. "His presence and powers impress one deeply, in an intellectual sense," she says, but she "did not always coincide with the sentiments" he expressed. He once stung her to the quick. She thought of her brother as she sat and heard him lecture on *Fielding*. "The hour spent in listening to it was a painful hour. That he was wrong in his way of treating Fielding's character and vices, my conscience told me. Had he owned a son, grown or growing up, and a son brilliant but reckless, would he have spoken in that light way of courses that lead to disgrace and the grave? Had I a brother yet living, I should tremble to let him read Thackeray's lecture on *Fielding*. I should hide it away from him. If, in spite of precaution, it should fall into his hands, I should earnestly pray him not to be misled by the voice of the charmer, let him charm never so wisely."

At Thackeray's feet, near unpublished poems of Branwell's, are specimens of Charlotte's writing, resembling print. Its minuteness we realized a short while ago, when reading in a newspaper column one of her letters which was about to be, or had been, offered for sale. It was addressed to Thackeray, and supposed to have reference to a review of *Shirley*. The entire message, which only covered a space of two inches by three, is here set in newspaper column form and spreads over a larger area:—

RELICS IN BRONTË MUSEUM.

TRUNKS.

SADDLE-BAG.

P. BRONTË'S SPECTACLES AND HEEL SPIKES.

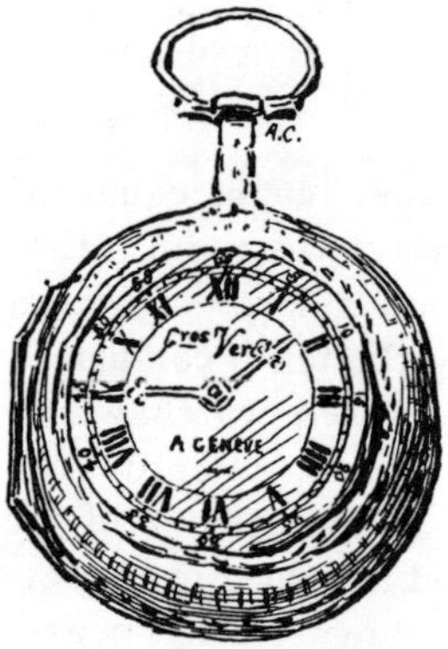

C. BRONTË'S WATCH.

TOY SMOOTHING IRON AND READING LAMP.

C. BRONTË'S BOOTS.

"Dear Mr. Thackeray,—It is with heartfelt pleasure I greet you on the production of my poor book, and with heartfelt gratitude for your generous kindness in passing that review, and eulogising so heartily the humble offering of a brain that can lay no claim to cope with the power and strength of your own. I have long yearned to address you, and the present is a fitting opportunity to express to you the admiration with which your works and characters have inspired me. The prototype of Dobbin is truly in yourself as far as goodness lies. It is a great thing for the poor seeker Renomme to have gained the esteem and friendship of one who, like yourself, has secured a lofty position in the Temple of Fame, but you have secured it by the possession of that which you so flatteringly attribute to me—genius, and the works of W. M. Thackeray will live and be thought more of in future times even than they are now. Many and many thanks from my humble home, and from those who turn to me for the daily necessaries of life. The words you have written will live for ever in my heart, and the advice you have given me will, I trust, be followed in any future production that may emanate from the pen and brain of your devoted servant,

CHARLOTTE BRONTË.

* * * * * *

Lesser relics, but of equal intrinsic value, are stored in cases ranged on two sides of the room; they are too numerous to particularise, but we will name a few. More than once as we pass round we confess to breaking the tenth commandment. One precious item is the peculiar silver and chased watch which is said to have been Charlotte's, and another is a glass, miniature lamp.

Here is an assortment of crockery, and we picture Tabby, the old servant, and Martha Brown, her assistant, in the kitchen at the Parsonage using the things. Tiny plaits of Anne's silvery hair and Charlotte's medium brown we are sure more than we would cherish. "Silvery" and "medium brown!"

Mr. Grundy in *Pictures of the Past* endeavours to "whitewash" the memory of his friend Branwell, and says of the Brontë family, "I knew them all The daughters—distant and distrait, large of nose, small of figure, red of hair," etc.

We are inclined to think it pleased Mr. Grundy to be cynical on this occasion.

Here are two pamphlets on the Crow Hill "Earthquake," by the

THE OLD RECTOR'S DOOR KNOCKER.
The crowning figure, a lion sejant and guardant (minus its head).

MINIATURE CHEST OF MAHOGANY DRAWERS.

Rev. P. Brontë; one, a sermon (from which we have quoted some extracts*), the price, we observe, was 6d.; the other, in verse, was "published as a prize book for higher classes in Sunday Schools, price 2d."

One case is wholly devoted to Brontë editions; one of *Jane Eyre* is in Russian.

More entrancing to us than all we have seen is a miniature chest of mahogany drawers, allotted a place on the floor with the trunks, writing desk, stationery case, and saddle-bag.

A Gomersal guinea bank-note, dated July 10, 1813, and signed by Joshua Taylor, the Squire Hiram York, of *Shirley*, is an interesting item; as is also the circular announcing the Brontë Sisters' School project, the particulars of which we transfer to our note-book:—

The Misses Brontë's Establishment

FOR

THE BOARD AND EDUCATION

OF A LIMITED NUMBER OF

YOUNG LADIES,

THE PARSONAGE, HAWORTH,

NEAR BRADFORD.

Terms:

Board and Education, including writing, arithmetic, history, grammar, and needlework, per annum	£35	0	0
French, German, Latin — each per quarter	1	0	0
Music, Drawing — each per quarter	1	0	0
Use of Pianoforte, per quarter		5	0
Washing, per quarter		15	0

Each young lady to be provided with one pair of sheets, pillow cases, four towels, a dessert and tea-spoon.

A Quarter's Notice, or a Quarter's Board, is required previous to the removal of a pupil.

What a pity the project never came to a successful issue, since it was Charlotte's desire it should "above all things;" indeed, it was the sisters' "pole star."

*Page 184.

Here are cards commemorating the deaths of the Rev. Patrick Brontë, Charlotte Nicholls and the curate, William Weightman, that of the latter being merely thin paper with deep black border.

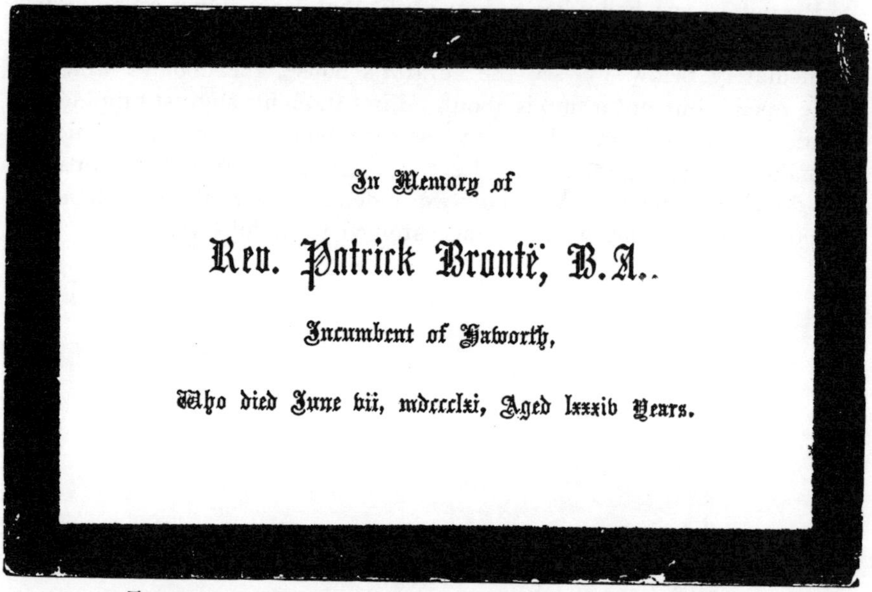
In Memory of

Rev. Patrick Brontë, B.A.,

Incumbent of Haworth,

Who died June vii, mdccclxi, Aged lxxxiv Years.

FACSIMILE OF THE REV. PATRICK BRONTË'S FUNERAL CARD.

Another case contains a jumble of things, each telling a story. A pair of Charlotte's boots, with plain black cloth uppers of similar design to those of silk rep. Beside these is a photograph of a "Bag worked by C. B. at Brussels in 1842,"* Patrick Brontë's spectacles, his snuff box, two walking sticks, "Keeper's" collar with "P. Brontë, Haworth" engraved upon it, a toy smoothing iron, scissors, the Rectory's old door-knocker, and a pair of Mr. Brontë's heel-spikes, most sensible contrivances to ensure safety when the roads are slippery, and especially in and around hilly Haworth.

* * * * * *

There ! the church clock booms eleven. We had no idea the forenoon was so far advanced. We doubt whether we have heard the chimes more than once during our stay of two-and-a-half hours, so intent have we been on our "notes."

* This bag, we afterwards ascertain, was worked for Miss Lætitia Wheelwright, of Kensington, an intimate schoolfellow and friend of Charlotte Brontë's—1842-55. The bag is in the possession of Mr. Joseph J. Green, Godwyn Lodge, Clive Vale, Hastings, to whose courtesy we are indebted for our illustration. The first owner became the wife of Dr. Thomas Wheelwright, of London, and was grandmother of the wife of our kind Hastings friend.

We are about to leave when, to our chagrin, the door refuses to yield. The fear comes over us that the curator may have forgotten our presence in the Museum. And if we have to wait till the usual time of opening to the public, two hours hence, how about that early dinner we requested at the School-house ? We re-ascend to the top of the stairs, from where, immediately below we see the curator's house, the door of which is wide open ; but not a soul is about. First thoughts suggest tapping the window, but we refrain, lest we rouse the street ; for we have no desire to make our plight public. We descend again, and more closely scrutinise the door's fastenings. Ah ! now we understand why the door banged. In our country home we are unaccustomed to artful latches.

HAND BAG, WORKED BY CHARLOTTE BRONTË.
(By kind permission of Mr. Joseph J. Green, Hastings).

CHAPTER XXIII.

A DAY-SCHOLAR OF CHARLOTTE BRONTË'S—CHARLOTTE'S BED AND COLLARET—SOME STATISTICS OF HAWORTH PRESENT CHURCH—LAST SERVICE IN HAWORTH OLD CHURCH—HOMEWARD BOUND—"THE BALCONY"—GRIMSHAW'S HOME AND TABLE—MARSHLANDS.

BELIEVING we have seen all there is in Haworth appertaining to the Brontës, we turn our thoughts homewards; but another important item is yet to be revealed to us, and here in the School-house too. To another room we adjourn, a cover is removed, and we see a plain, firmly-made chest of common deal, say 3 ft. 6 in. long, 2 ft. 3 in. broad, and deep as broad. Originally the lid—uplifted and displaying two compartments—was secured with lock and clasps, remnants of which only remain "to show that they have been." This is the box which accompanied Charlotte and Emily to Brussels. Then our friends remember there is yet someone else, a Mrs. Tempest living on the outskirts of Haworth at a place called Rough Nook, who would probably be one of Charlotte's scholars; if so, perhaps we may count on still more reminiscences of the Brontës. In any case we must seek an interview. Our host, desiring to leave no stone unturned in our pursuit, pilots the way.

Mrs. Tempest! Rough Nook! "Rather odd," we remark to the sexton as we saunter through Parson's Fields.

On so lovely a day "Rough Nook" seems inappropriate; but it will be bleak enough when the north winds of winter tear over Hare Hill with a velocity boding ruin to roof and chimney stack; or when blustering gusts from the west rush off the point of Crow Hill.

Introduced, and our mission explained, Mrs. Tempest at first resents the thought of our publishing her name, but two daughters change her mind (she has three daughters and five sons). Without hesitation she confides that she is 63. She remembers Charlotte Brontë very well, when she herself was quite a little girl. She was not in Charlotte's Sunday School class, being too young, but as a day scholar she recalls

her very vividly. She came into the school twice a week to inspect work done by girls. She would request, say, a stocking a scholar was knitting, insert her delicate hand, raise it near her large luminous eyes—she was very short-sighted—slowly draw it up her arm, the while twisting it and exposing every round and stitch over her hidden fingers, then, apparently satisfied, she would turn to the knitter and in a somewhat mistrustful yet kindly tone would quietly inquire—" O, so quietly," says Mrs. Tempest:—

" And have you knit it all yourself, my dear ? "

Mrs. Tempest—then Ann Hopkinson—considered herself greatly exalted when she was asked to knit Mr. Nicholls a pair of socks. We would extract more from her respecting the Brontës, but she cannot think of anything further just now; as with other scholars interviewed, we have come upon her unawares, else she might have recalled a few stories in relation to the family which might have interested the readers of our " Saunter." At her sister's, Mrs. Tempest casually intimates, is the bed on which Charlotte died. Our hearts leap at the disclosure. We determine, if at all possible, to see it.

" Is your sister's far from here ? " we ask.

" Perhaps ten minutes' walk."

" And is there a possibility of our being permitted to see the bed ? "

Of this we are assured, if we but state who has commissioned us. Our guide not only volunteers to accompany us to the dwelling, but to undertake the introductory part. And who more likely to be successful in the quest than the verger, known to every inhabitant, everyone known to him? Presently we are being received by a lady displaying the courtesy shown by all our newly-formed Haworth acquaintances. We perforce contrast these kindly words and pleasing smiles with Mrs. Gaskell's statement on Yorkshire in general, but Haworth in particular: " A stranger can hardly ask a question without receiving some crusty reply, if, indeed, he receive one at all. Sometimes the sour rudeness amounts to positive insult." And people of Haworth feel the sting. " Mrs. Gaskell must have thought us little better than barbarians," one remarked to us only last night. But Charlotte's biographer said kindlier things than these of Haworth people, part of which reference seems to us a little inconsistent: " The attachments, the antipathies, and the hospitalities of the district are ardent, hearty, and homely. As a people, these mountaineers have ever been accessible to gentleness and truth, so far as I have known them; but excite suspicion or resentment,

and they give emphatic and impotent resistance. Compulsion they defy."

Yes, with pleasure, we may see the bed, if it will so interest us, and we are invited to "step this way please." We follow with feelings akin to Charlotte's when she ascended to the boxes to see an opera in London. "You know I am not accustomed to this sort of thing," she remarked to Mr. Williams, so bewildered was she "with the architectural effect of the splendid decorations."

How stupid of us! Mrs. Tempest made no mention of a bedstead, yet this is what we pictured; the bedding only is here.

"Is it a feather bed?" we ask, as the coverlet is turned down.

"No, common flocks."

"And is this the original tick?" we further make bold to inquire.

"No, this is an outer covering, which keeps clean and protects the original tick."

Our attention is drawn to a most plain wash-stand with one drawer, beside the bed. This was Charlotte's. It seems fitting they together should share the same home, and somehow we feel glad their lines have fallen in so pleasant a place.

Yet another treasured article here of Charlotte's is placed in our hands.

"And what in print might we term this?" we falteringly ask, as we lightly finger the quarter-moon-shaped delicate fabric.

"It is what we ladies call an embroidered collaret."

"Thank you!"

"We value it, not particularly because it was Charlotte's, but in remembrance and for the sake of those since passed away, who prized it very, very dearly; the embroidery is the work of Charlotte's youngest sister, Anne."

* * * * * *

We are profuse in appreciation of so great a privilege, and depart for the School-house. Back thither, our host tells us he has stored away a newspaper report of the stone-laying of the church, and forthwith produces the copy for our perusal. It states that "in the presence of upwards of a thousand persons the corner-stone of the new church of St. Michael and All Angels, Haworth, was laid by Michael Merrall, who said, 'that if spared, and he continued to have means, he would be glad to make the edifice a beautiful place of worship. You must remember, however,' he added, 'that, through unforeseen circumstances sometimes money slips through our fingers, and we are reduced and not able to do that which under other circumstances we should be only too glad to."

No mention is made of the £50 given by him at the time, but this is an insignificant sum compared with the £6,000 he had already provided towards the £8,000 or £10,000, the estimated cost. Whilst the opportunity affords, we will jot down statistics given of the new church; we may find them useful. The contractors were Messrs. Crabtree Bros. and Sugden, Oxenhope, and the architects Messrs. T. H. Healy, Bradford. The measurements are: Nave 77 ft. by 22 ft., 42 ft. to the ridge; side aisles 63 ft. by 13 ft. each; chancel 30 ft. by 21 ft. and 37 ft. high; and north and south chapels 21 ft. by 14 ft. The pews, of oak, and modern construction, will accommodate about 700.

Another cutting from a paper of September 19, 1879, tells the story of the closing services in the old church. By five o'clock the churchyard and porch were filled with people desirous to be present at the last service. The doors at that hour were opened, and directly there was not even standing room left. The Rev. J. Wade, rector, preaching from Psalm lxxviii, 67, said:

"They might think that was an occasion not without solemn interest to him, notable for the fact that, by accident and not design, it so chanced that that night he finished eighteen years' ministry in the parish. For 125 years that church had resounded with prayer and praise. Upon its site at least two or three churches stood before it, so that for 500 or 600 years that soil had been consecrated to God."

* * * * * *

Now we must up and away, for the church clock, a few minutes ago, chimed a quarter after three.

How shall we repay our host and hostess, whose bill is a mere acknowledgment?

Happy thought! why not extend to them an invitation to the breezy heights of Tabor? Yes, why not? Poor return, certainly. Moreover, why not invite the whole of Charlotte's surviving scholars whom we have interviewed, to join them? What an interesting party! What pleasure would be ours to be sure; never before have we been honoured by such distinguished guests. The idea is not absurd, we hope. Such thoughts flash across our minds, and we think of our friend Betty o' th' Fly, who often avers "wer thowts wer quick":—

"How fleet is a glance of the mind!
  Compared with the speed of its flight;
The tempest itself lags behind,
  And the swift-winged arrows of flight."

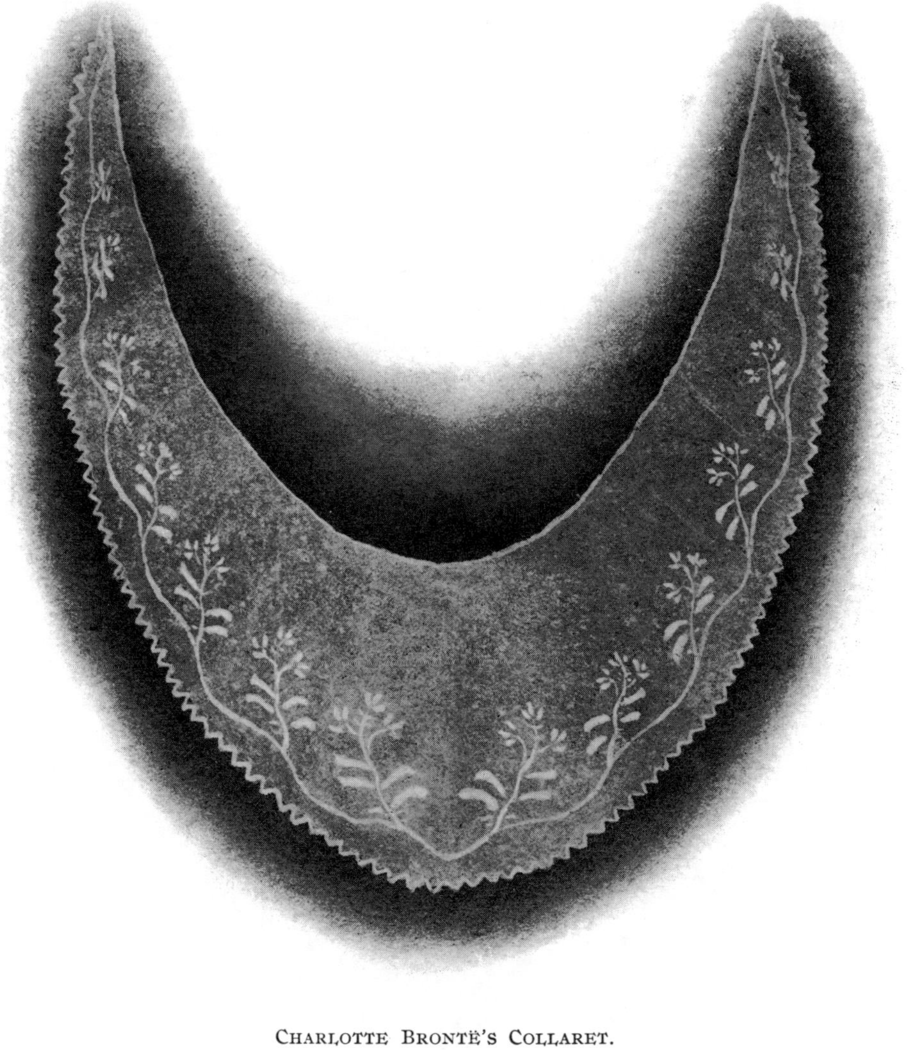

Charlotte Brontë's Collaret.
(*Drawn by A. Comfort*).

Nothing would give them more pleasure, the sexton and his wife assure us, than to take a trip over, and we may count on such a picnic being organised if the outing but depends upon them. Our invitation shall be conveyed to each scholar.

"Since Mount Tabor is inaccessible by train or tram, if we hire a wagonette, which way shall we go; over Cock Hill?" we are asked.

"You had better not," we advise, "or on reaching Midgley the driver may be alarmed to find the wide and deep Luddenden valley separates that old-time village from ours. He probably would request his fares to walk from Luddenden to Mount Tabor—a mile, and a rise of more than 700 ft. So that it will be well to study the route for the scholars' sake," we point out. "No, on the outward journey travel via Cross Roads, Many-wells Heights (locally pronounced "Manuel 'Eights"), Denholme, Causeway Foot, and through the villages of Mixenden and Moor-End. You may venture back over Cock Hill, thus forming a circular route, in which case you would encounter only one short rise of moment—Booth Hill—and even this may be avoided by paying a toll of 3d. per horse to Messrs. Bracken, at Dean Paper Mills." A memorandum is made of these particulars.

Our host promises to see us well on our way to Oxenhope, and suggests taking us the higher of three routes, which suggestion we readily approve; it will add variety to our saunter. We proceed along the churchyard path west of the church, and enter a field-path leading to a lonely lane, skirted with ash and sycamore, which Mr. Widdop tells us is called "The Balcony," because of the view. Though not extensive it is worth a moment's stay. Two sides only of the world are presented to us—south and east. Old Haworth fills the Worth aspect northwards, and rising pastures at our backs block the prospect westwards. Across the valley eastward is the road mounting over Brow or Flappit Moor, the same we should have taken last night to Cullingworth, according to our original programme. To the left is Brow estate—New Haworth in reality. A little distance away are Lees and Cross Roads, prosperous villages; and beyond, in a hollow, is Keighley, which cannot be seen, but we locate it, as from Crow Hill, by the pall of smoke. In the foreground we look down on what we term the southern tail-end of Old Haworth, through which runs Sun Street, whereby we entered Haworth four days ago. Four miles south, Nab Hill rises sharply; we recognise it with the ruined cottage—Nab End—midway up the slope, outlined like a black box against the sky. Thitherward we are making.

A by-lane, up on our right, leads to a farm (which on consulting our map we note is called " Balcony "), seen amid trees, and forward on to Haworth Moor. This, we assure ourselves, would be the chosen favourite walk of the Brontë sisters when out "to meditate," since the road leads more direct on to the moor proper than the path through Parson's Fields, and is very quiet and secluded. And this, we surmise, is probably the way Miss Brontë used to bring Tabby when she had become very deaf, that she might impart to her information which she desired to keep secret from " whoever might be in or about the house."

At the end of " The Balcony," an obtuse angle turns us upwards, which is somewhat vexatious, for it is obvious we are already above our ultimate level. When we become land-owners, we soliloquize, it shall be ours to study the common weal ; yea, we will open out footpaths across lands wherever they are likely to give pleasure and prove a blessing—*when* we are lords of the manors. But then we agreed to our being led this way, so cannot justly murmur.

Grimshaw's Home.

Two minutes later we are intensely glad we were obliged to rise to still higher ground, for here is Sowdens, we are told, where the Rev. William Grimshaw lived prior to the erection of Haworth Church Parsonage. We turn to examine the place. In the old farm-house, still standing, we learn, is an oaken table of some significance ; it belonged to the enthusiastic divine. Perhaps we can get to see it. We will ascertain.

Grimshaw's homestead in his day commanded an extensive view eastward, but now the prospect is shut out by a villa embraced in the folds of tall trees, like a bird in a cage, as it were. On the wall of the villa is a sundial, fixed corner-cupboard-wise. Where is the use (as Charlotte Brontë would put it) of a sundial in so shaded a spot, except as an ornament ?

As we enter the farmyard we find a modern-looking barn, but we presently observe it was built in 1860, apparently on the site of another, since over one door on a crumbling sandstone are undecipherable letters and the date 1657. We linger on the threshold of the porch of Grimshaw's house, admiring the heavily-studded oak door, with antique hinges. Representatives of three generations, presumably, greet us in answer to our knock. Two receive us courteously, but baby-in-arms eyes us mysteriously and resents our presence. Later, however, we part friends. " It's cappin, sometimes what a haw'penny can do," though the coin fails to evoke in children nowadays the rapture it did when Hartley sang its power to soothe.

Invited in, we are shown the table—Cromwellian, profusely carved and bearing the date 1688. What an unwieldy piece! The top, 7ft. 8 in. by 2 ft. 10 in., is supported on six lathe-turned legs, strengthened by stout rails a few inches from the floor. Curiosity once more appeased, we tender thanks for the privilege and again saunter on.

GRIMSHAW'S TABLE.

Now we are conducted through fields from which we see, clearly silouhetted on the sky-line, two miles south-west, the keeper's lodge on Cock Hill, near which is the grave of two pointer dogs. On the head-stone are these *dog*gerel lines :—

"Here lieth a faithful old dog, called Don—
A better, stone was ne'er laid upon;
He was true to his game, and true to his master;
Reader, his equal, I doubt, will not be after."

Died on Cockhill, May, 1845, aged 13 years. Shot over by James Walton, Halifax, 12 years.

Also Betty, sister to the above, who died Nov., 1846, aged 12 years.

Below the keeper's, at the foot of Cock Hill, we locate Dike Nook (Λ 1153-0), a convenient baiting house, and offering welcome refreshment also for man. Shortly we gain the road near Old Oxenhope Mill, whose iron-hooped chimney stack and pear-shaped dam are notable features. Here, between forty and fifty hands are employed in the worsted industry; so the masters tell us in conversation with them.

MARSHLANDS.

Further down we pass a residence which, in size and shape, reminds us of Haworth Rectory, prior to the adding of the wing. This is Marshlands. One would never suspect the place had any history of note. Abutting the northern end is what might be regarded as an out-kitchen, though its ivy front and leaded panes between mullions give it a church-like appearance. We hunger for a better view than is obtained from the road, but are loth to trouble the occupant; to clamber the wall and trample the grass in the adjoining field might rouse the ire of the farmer and bring us to book. We are therefore circumspect and remain law-abiding.

Once this apparently disused one-storey building was a free Grammar School. The writer of *The Wild Moor* gives its history in brief. He tells us "it was founded for the education of the youths of the district," and that "it was established by the kind liberality and generous munificence of Charles (another writer says Christopher) Scott, Esq., in 1638. This worthy gentleman built the School-house and endowed it with lands. The laudable object of the founder of this institution was to instruct children in the Greek and Latin classics. The trustees in 1818 enlarged the school, and built a house for the master." Here the Rev. J. B. Grant taught for some time prior to the building of Oxenhope Church.

The endowment is now devoted to scholarships which bear the founder's name. These give three years' education, valued at £16 a year at some secondary school to the two boys and two girls who are successful in examinations held at Haworth schools every year.

* * * * * *

At Marshlands we and our friend the sexton* part company. Words fail us to express our thanks for the manifold kindnesses and time devoted to us whilst guests at the school-house. We are exceedingly welcome, he assures us, to any little service he may have rendered,

*John Heaton Widdop died suddenly, January 22, 1912. He is buried in Haworth Churchyard beside the wall in front of the old school. His tombstone tells of him being 17 years verger at the church.

and he will be pleased to see us at Haworth again whenever we can make it convenient to come.

" Don't forget that little wagonette jaunt to Tabor," we answer.

Three hundred yards, perhaps, separate us when, in taking a sharp turn down to our left, near a cycle danger-post, we signal a last salute by waving our caps.

CHAPTER XXIV.

KIND FRIENDS—SAM AND BETTY'S—
MOUNT TABOR.

Now we saunter beneath trees under whose shade we observe, on our right, an old hall and farm, and a quaint row of low-roomed, deserted cottages. Further down on our left are two modern villas, and on our right a rich, well-wooded pasture. A somewhat sudden yet short dip in the road lands us on an arched stone bridge, which spans the now tame and insipid brook—Bridgehouse Beck. In our one-and-a-half miles saunter from Haworth Church to Oxenhope Station here, we have descended 171 feet.

Leaving the peaceful terminus of the Worth Valley Line on our left, we proceed up past Oxenhope Board School, erected, we observe, in 1883. Here the clang of an anvil falls on our ears. The village smithy, unshaded by a "spreading chestnut tree," affords a striking illustration of the scene depicted in Longfellow's "Village Blacksmith," for indeed :—

> "Children coming home from school
> Look in at the open door ;
> They love to see the flaming forge,
> And hear the bellows roar,
> And catch the burning sparks that fly
> Like chaff from a threshing floor."

A child of about three lay sprawling across the causeway having a real happy time, and we wonder if he is the little chap who was being lulled to sleep by "That will be glory for me," when we passed the door opposite four days ago.

* * * * * *

We have friends in Oxenhope and purpose calling, though our conscience accuses us of passing them by on our outward journey. We will admit the omission and seek pardon ; "an honest confession is good for the soul." We *do* hope they are not at tea. Some folks, we believe, have

a knack of dropping in upon friends about this time, but the accusation cannot truthfully ever be laid to *our* charge. No, this is an exception and not the rule.

Our cordial reception and the exceedingly genial hospitality extended are indeed coals of fire upon our heads. Lo, the cloth is already spread and tea, to which we are heartily invited. We beg to be excused, explaining that we are due at our friends 'at Fly in the next hour.

"Betty will be down to-morrow," our friends put in, unmindful of our plea, "and she will likely give us a call, when we will make all serene."

It is clear that to refuse to bite or sup will cause offence, so we submit to the inevitable and accept the vacant chairs set beside the good things. While viands are disappearing we relate our wanderings over moor and fell, and promise to forward the *Halifax Courier* as each instalment appears—assuming the editor will accord space for our notes.

Soon, too soon, we grasp hands—and O, what warmness in the grip!—now set faces to climb "th' Hill 'ous Edge," and Nab Hill, down which it seems but a few minutes since we came. We feel decidedly more equal to the task than an hour ago, now the gnawing internally—which in truth we really suffered, the results of an early dinner—is appeased.

The off lane leading past St. Mary's—so very, very peaceful—we discard, and by way of variation keep to the highway, past a policeman's house. Surely there is no necessity for the services of a vigilant in this quiet place; and beside the church and vicarage, too! We stay a moment and view the latter, situated at an elbow in the road. Higher up, we note some forty stone posts in two rows, running parallel with each other across a meadow. These, we are told, define the track of a conduit conveying water from the moors into Leeming reservoir. Another elbow rounded, and presently we read on an iron mile-post, "Hebden Bridge 6 miles; Keighley, 5 miles." This evidently serves in lieu of the original mile-post at the bottom of Hill House Edge, 150 yards or so further up.

Interested in the country before us and eager to be on our way, on the outward journey we ignored the rural seat at the top of "th' Hill 'ous Edge," where now we rest a few minutes. Oxenhope, some 500 feet below, is being gripped in the "scog"* of the dale. Marshlands, Old Oxenhope Mill, and Haworth's Church roof and tower are still visible. Absorbed in tracing the track we have recently covered, we fail to notice, until quite near, a man coming up the steep. Slow in gait and with bent form, he carries a small bucket three-parts filled

*Mist.

with a yellowish mass. We guess both his errand and his ailment, as, gasping for breath, he takes a seat beside us. Poor fellow! Acute asthma and bronchitis apparently make it a struggle for him to live. His hopeless condition awakes our souls to thankfulness; we "count our many blessings," and realize the health and strength which is ours, enabling us to enjoy, in so high degree, the outing which soon will be a vision of the past.

"It's sich a claam froo Loower Toon up here," the man remarks in vernacular remote from Stanbury dialect, as he regains breath.

Immediately we arrived here we wondered who could own the multitude of poultry ranging the waste behind us, since no dwelling is near. The 200 or so hens and chickens, the sufferer tells us, find him employment, and it is practically all he can do. The tribe know feeding-time instinctively, and are now collected over the fence, petulantly chuckling for supper.

"Are eggs plentiful with you?" we ask, moving off.

"Not wery," our stranger friend replies, adding as he clambers over the wall, "yoo see the waather kapes desperate cood, 'ticular on these 'ill tups. Besaades, ivrything, as yoo knoo, is soo wery parched. If it wood ony raan an' cum a bit warmer it'd maa a graat diff'rence ta tha'r layan."

We linger a moment and watch the man, whose progress to the coops is made tardy by the family about his feet; the marvel is none get their corns, or rather, claws trod on.

* * * * * *

Sauntering on, we keep to the road, discarding the shorter cut alongside Thornton conduit* across the moor, the path traversed on our outward journey. Presently we hear footsteps, and the next moment recognise our friend Stan'orth returning after the day's toil. True, as we remark, he is somewhat late, and he proceeds to explain.

"Eah! Aw been workin' ower a bit. Aw'd a tooathry slate-st'ns aw whanted ta finish afooar aw ligg'd away. Ther's plenty dayleet naah, en we'st 'av ta mak' 'ay whol th' sun shines."

"Quarrymen especially," we rejoin.

But our revered friend has news of another character to impart, which we are very pleased to hear; someone awaits us at Samson's.

"Oh, did she seem good humoured?" we jocularly inquire.

"Well, aw seed nought na different wi' her; shoo's allus vaary quiet,

*See illustration, page 81, and note conduit, left of ruin and 110 feet below, winding across the moor.

Aw think shoo expected yo' back tho' o' Tuesday ; but shoo'd 'ad a pooast card fra Haworth, if aw understood Betty reight, ta say yo' wodn't be back whol ta-day, en at shoo'd ta meet yo' et th' Fly. Aw think yo've bin away longer ner yo' thowt on ? "

" Rayther."

" But yo've 'ad grand weather."

" It's bin splendid ; cudn't o' made better es seln. Well, good neet, William ! "

" Gooid neet ! "

* * * * * *

Then our missive carried safely, we muse, as we again tradge on.

Rounding the next bend come Stan'orth's work-mates and they, like he, are particularly interested in our outing.

" Yo'r just returnin' then, like, um, whaah ! Aw reck'n yo'v 'ad a fair aght, um, ah, whaah ! " shouts the more talkative of the two, while yet some distance away. There is no mistaking this voice, so clear, shrill and familiar to our ears

" Aw'r dahn on't o' Monday tho', after yo'd called at th' Samson's. Just turned dinner, it luck'd varry black i' th' direcshun yo'd set aght for ; ha'ever, it breetened, en it's kept op ever sin' ; but a drop o' rain 'ell'd do gooid ; it 'll'd do gooid, yo' kno', um, whaah ! "

" Aye, aye, yo'r reight ; we'r raather latter hooam ner uzal," says the quarryman in tones up in the top staves, characteristic of him.

" We've bin o' mak o' foorced ta work ower a bit," Sam goes on to tell us, while Fred is nearly home, " Yo see, it's a bit awk'ard when ther's a demenshun order com's in, es ther did this mornin', en it's whanted th' furst thing. Th' cart 'ell be at th' delph bi seven i' th' mornin', sooa the'r nooa way for't nobbut stickin' tul't wol we'd finished. The'r waaitin' on't yo' kno' ; the'r waaitin' on't, d'yo' see, um, ah, whaah ! "

We shout " Good afternoon ! " to Fred, but Sam sharply retorts :

" Nay, it's whaat yo' ma call neet ; it'll be hauf-past six or turned ? "

" Twenty minutes to seven."

" They've bin expectin' yo' op at Betty's a fair while nah, aw believe. Well, goo-id neet ! goo-i-d neet ! ! g-o-o-i-d neet to yo' ! ! ! "

" Good neet, Sam ! "

* * * * * *

As our friend's last wish dies away on the still air another voice salutes our ears. But we heed not " Laddie " of Nab Water farm, loud and fierce as is his bark, for we proved him friend and not foe when last we met.

Now we pass the house in ruins so clearly seen from "The Balcony" at Haworth, and whose four square walls remain intact but are fast succumbing to buffeting storms.

Collar work is now over, save Sandy Fore Hill—a short gentle gradient close to home—and we welcome the ease.

Fly Flat reservoir, down on our right, has perceptibly shrunk since we passed four days ago. Immediately we pass the stone-post dividing Haworth Parish and Warley, we feel a sense of homeland.

* * * * * *

It pleases us to sight again our friends' at Fly. In waiting, as foretold us, is the recipient of our message from Haworth. Betty's greeting is almost verbally what we expected. "Thankful it's pleeased th' Hand o' Providence to land yo' safe back," dropping for the moment the thread of the story she has been pouring into the ears of her visitor. Presently we are "raked over th' coils," as we foreshadowed, for having had "wer teas," but we are forgiven on promising to stay supper, and the time, alas, is too soon here and gone.

Darkness is setting in and we are anxious to lessen the $3\frac{1}{2}$ miles or so 'twixt here and Mount Tabor, since there are no friendly lamps up in this region to light travellers on their way. We tender thanks, have hearty hand-shakes, now grope our way through the wicket, still answering remarks of our friends, whose forms we see against the lamp-lit window.

"Come op ageean when yo've a day to spare," they call, and we pledge our word we will, shouting our reply through the gloom as we steal away, at first, somewhat gingerly, remembering the treacherous nature of the road near Old Fly ruins. But this and wild unfenced Fill Belly we safely negotiate. The night now is considerably lighter, due to the illumination over Halifax and its suburbs, four or five miles ahead. Quite discernible is the path leading to Slade and over the embankments of Cold Edge Dams—whose waters we see shimmering in a black setting. But it is a path we dare not attempt to travel now; discretion advises us to keep to the road.

The "scog" investing the Worth valley is conspicuous for its absence this side of the hill; the atmosphere is remarkably clear, affording us a grand panorama of lights practically all the way in our descent of Cold Edge. We watch two trams, fifteen minutes apart, leave Booth Town, rise to Catherine Slack, and burrow out of sight at Stocks Gate—some four miles away across space—on their way to Queensbury. Another

appears at top of Wrigley, Illingworth, proceeds along Illingworth Moor—now on both sides of the road, rich, cultivated land—to Bradshaw Lane top, thence forward to Causeway Foot. This car is the last outwards, leaving Halifax at 10-30, we muse, as with increased lights by an extra draught at our pipes we obtain the time of night.

Now we are passing close by, and on the east side of Sampson's Hut* at the top of Cold Edge Hill, now Cold Edge Bottom and Lumb Lane end where we deviated from this, the main road, on our outward journey in making towards Cold Edge Dams.

In exactly an hour and ten minutes after leaving our friends at Fly we arrive back home ; no need consult our watches, for we have sauntered the ground innumerable times, and know precisely the time involved.

* * * * * *

We have jogged along together most amicably, dear readers, but now we must part. How far your humble servant's ideal of pleasure attains to that set forth by the following authorities I leave you to judge.

John Ruskin says "The greatest thing a human soul does in this world is to see something, and tell what it saw in a plain way."

Richard Kearton, the naturalist, says "To learn to appreciate the beauties of the world in which we live is a great victory. It establishes within us a never-failing source of pleasure, and enhances the value of existence a thousand fold. I would not exchange the every-day joys of a healthy observant ploughman for the worrying wealth and cares of a millionaire. The idea that to be rich in gold is to be happy is a dying, vulgar fallacy. Men are coming to know that there are greater possessions than those which can be measured by the surveyor's chain or locked in iron safes. A love of nature is one of them, and it has the unspeakable good quality of endurance."

And someone with kindred nature to the "Saunterer's" hath said :—

"You take the crowded city street
With life and shop galore ;
I'll take the little woodland path
Down by the river shore,
You take the public garden, where
All is arranged by plan ;
I'll take the scenes laid out by God
And undisturbed by man.

*See illustration, page 29, and note building on the horizon at extreme left of the picture.

You take the fountain on the lawn
  And listen to its tale ;
I'll listen to the little brook
  That murmurs in the vale.
You live the artificial life
  And I will live the real ;
And joy will come to me in mine
  That yours can ne'er reveal."

THE END.

DETAILS OF THE HALIFAX WATERWORKS AND LOCAL & COUNTY ALTITUDES.

HALIFAX CORPORATION WATERWORKS.

STORAGE AND SERVICE RESERVOIRS.

Name of Reservoir.	Depth.	Capacity.	Feet above the sea.
STORAGE.	Feet.	Gallons.	
Widdop	65	640,511,000	1,050
Walshaw Dean—			
Upper	67	204,945,000	1,100
Middle	69½	244,354,000	1,043
Lower	66½	159,971,000	965
Warley Moor	30¼	193,251,000	1,350
Dean Head (Upper)	54½	59,143,000	1,050
Dean Head (Lower)	60	63,012,000	1,000
Castle Carr	18	2,629,000	900
Ogden	66	221,806,000	990
Mixenden	30	106,122,000	875
SERVICE			
Ramsden Wood	21½	11,295,000	810
Albert	14½	27,341,000	795
Victoria	14½	12,209,000	790
Royles Head	22	6,013,000	1,050
Hanson Lane	9	2,594,000	700
Gibbet	6	26,000	568
*Ogden Kirk	16	500,000	1,250
	Total	1,955,722,000	

*This Reservoir was constructed solely for the supply to Bradshaw.

YORKSHIRE HILLS, &c.: HEIGHTS ABOVE SEA LEVEL (including the chief altitudes in the County and near its borders. The heights of Halifax are followed by altitudes in townships round that borough, then by Huddersfield and Keighley figures, and finally a general list).

HALIFAX.

	Feet above sea level.
Akroydon—All Souls' Church	548
Albert Promenade	640
Beacon Hill	850
Chevin Edge, Exley	375
Claremount—St. Thomas's Church	658
Copley—St. Stephen's Church	250
Copley Station	310
General Post Office	483
Godley Bridge	610
Highroad Well	855
Holmfield Station	630
Horton Street Station (Booking Office)	404
King Cross Street (opposite Old St. Paul's)	660
Navigation Road	353
North Bridge	454
Norton Tower	1030
Old Racecourse	1000
Ovenden Station	550
Lee Bridge (Dean Clough)	423
Parish Church	382
Pellon—Christ Church	750
Pellon Station	720
People's Park—Terrace	635
Piece Hall	438
Queen's Road	700
Salterhebble—All Saints' Church	460
Savile Park—Fountain	600
Shibden Hall	350
Shroggs Park—Fountain	640
Siddal—St. Mark's Church	375
Southowram Bank End—300 yards south of tram terminus	850

HALIFAX.—*Continued.*

	Feet above sea level.
Stoney Royd Hospital	408
Stump Cross	447
Town Hall—Street	475
West View Park—Lodge	830

BARKISLAND.

Barkisland Cross	742
Barkisland—Christ Church	764
Dean Head—St. Bartholomew's Church	1000
Firth House Mills	500
Gallows Pole Hill	950
Krumlin	925
Ringstone Reservoir	980
Ripponden	441

ELLAND-CUM-GREETLAND.

Calder at Elland Weir	210
Elland—Lower Edge	520
,, Park Nook	575
,, St. Mary's Church	300
,, Town Hall	294
,, Upper Edge	600
Greetland—St. Thomas's Church	535

ERRINGDEN.

Edge Moor End	1025
Law Hill	1250
Rake Head	1080
Withens Clough Reservoir	950

HEPTONSTALL.

Black Hambledon	1521
Black Moor	1535
Broadstone Baptist Church	1025
Cross Lane U.M. Church	550
Colden Clough Dam	1275
Gainley Hill	1300

HEPTONSTALL.—*Continued.*

	Feet above sea level.
Heptonstall—St. Thomas's Church	850
Heptonstall Slack	912
Highgate Wesleyan Chapel	1075
Hoof Stones	1574
Moorcock Hill	1400
New Bridge (near entrance to Hardcastle Craggs)	442
Widdop Gate	894
White Hill Nook	825

HIPPERHOLME-CUM-BRIGHOUSE.

Brighouse—Briggate	188
,, Station	250
Calder at Anchor Pits, Rastrick	175
Coley—St. Matthew's Church	689
Hipperholme—White Hall	516
,, Station	421
Lightcliffe—St. Matthew's Church	450
,, Station	425
Rastrick—St. John's Church	371
Round Hill (Rastrick)	600

LANGFIELD.

Coldwell Hill	1300
Gaddings Dam	1200
Stoney Edge	1312
Stoodley Pike	1307
Whirlaw Stones	1224

LUDDENDEN FOOT.

Calder Bridge	295

MIDGLEY.

Brearley	329
Castle Carr—House	990
Castle Carr—Low Lodge	765
Crow Hill	1251
Dean Head Reservoir...	1001
Ewood Hall	500

MIDGLEY.—*Continued.*

	Feet above sea level
High Brown Knoll	1450
Holme House Bridge	450
Luddenden—St. Mary's Church	350
Midgley Village (Scout Head)	725
Oats Royd Mills	560

NORLAND.

Clough Moor Bridge	735
Ladstone (Norland Moor)	925
Norland—St. Luke's Church	750
Triangle Station	400

NORTHOWRAM.

Catherine Slack	1023
Coley—St. Matthew's Church	689
Ringby	1075
Westercroft Lane End, Northowram	733

OVENDEN.

Bob Hall (Ogden Golf House)	900
Causeway Foot	1034
Denfield, Wheatley	699
Gibb Lane (top)	975
Gibb Lane (bottom)	675
Hambleton Hill	1175
Holmfield Station	650
Illingworth—St. Mary's Church	890
Mixenden Bridge	775
Mixenden Reservoir	875
Moor End Congregational Church	1025
Mount Tabor Wesleyan Chapel	1047
Mount Zion U.M. Church	1025
Ovenden Cross	625
Ogden Reservoir	990
Ramsden Wood Reservoir	810
Round Hill, Ogden Moor	1321
Soil (or Swilling) Hill	1320

Rishworth.

	Feet above sea level.
Blackstone Edge Moor	1553
Derby Inn	850
Dog Hill	1428
Green Withens Reservoir	1150
Pike End	1080
Ripponden	441
Rishworth	479
Way Stone Edge	1550

Southowram.

Southowram	739
,, Law Hill	825
,, St. Anne's Church	596

Sowerby.

Bank Top, Cragg Vale	925
Boulder Clough U.M. Church	550
Cotton Stones—St. Mary's Church	685
Cragg Vale—St. John's in the Wilderness, ...	564
Crow Hill	1257
Hathershelf Scout	775
Junction of Cragg Vale and Sowerby Roads	961
Mill Bank Wesleyan Chapel, ...	600
Moor End	1086
Mytholmroyd—St. Michael's Church	302
Nab End	1069
Sowerby Church—St. Peter's	667
Steep Lane Baptist Church	850
Triangle—St. John's Church	378
White Holme Reservoir	1250

Sowerby Bridge.

Calder Bridge	259

Soyland.

Blackstone Edge	1220
Byron Edge	1360
Flints Reservoir	1100

SOYLAND.—*Continued.*

	Feet above sea level.
Gt. Manshead	1316
Lightazles U.M. Church	801
Manshead End	1368

STAINLAND.

Holywell Green Station	400
Sowood	800
Stainland Moor	1140
Stainland—St. Andrew's Church	664

STANSFIELD.

Blackshawhead Wesleyan Chapel	1100
Bride Stones	1434
Cross Stone—St. Paul's Church	740
Eastwood—Wood Mill	374
Greenland Hill	1405
Hoof Stones Height	1574
Keb Cote	1338
Mytholm—St. James's Church	362
Pole Hill	1408
Redmires Dam	1390
Stansfield Hall Station	501
Winters—Old Ruin Mill	775

TODMORDEN AND WALSDEN.

Black Edge	1360
Calder, at York Street, Todmorden	405
Carr and Craggs Moor	1425
Clough Foot	785
Clough Head	1256
Dobroyd Castle	635
Fielden Hospital	640
Higher Hanging Shaw	1214
Holden Gate	1151
Lower Hanging Shaw	1000
Lower Moor	1200
Lumb Foot	861
Maden Pasture	1353
Main Road (Todmorden and Bacup Boundary)	1260

TODMORDEN AND WALSDEN.—*Continued.*

	Feet above sea level.
Mankinholes	725
Midgelen Bank	1251
Oatley Hill	1250
Portsmouth (County Boundary)	702
Slate Hill	1400
Sourhall Hospital	605
Spa Hill	1275
Three Nooks	1350
Todmorden Moor	1425
Todmorden Town Hall	423
Trough Edge End	1475
Walsden (County Boundary, at Steanor Bottom)	605
Walsden Station	496
White Edge	1300

WADSWORTH.

Alcomden Bridge	800
Birchcliffe Baptist Church	563
Black Moor, Widdop	1535
Blake Dean Baptist Church	844
Blake Dean—Stepping Stones	750
Bog Eggs Edge	1250
Cock Hill Road—summit	1424
Dove Stones	1573
Flaight Hill	1350
Fox Hole Hill	1500
Greave Height	1344
Grey Stone Hill	1516
Hardcastle Craggs—summit	750
Heather Hill	1521
Hebden Bridge—Old Bridge	327
Hoar Nib	1172
Jackson's Ridge	1501
Lumb Bridge (Crimsworth Dean)	800
Mount Skip	950
Pecket Well—shed	969
Round Hill	1350

WADSWORTH.—*Continued.*

	Feet above sea level.
Shackleton Knoll	1300
Tom Tittiman	1350
Wadsworth Moor	1310
Wainsgate Baptist Church	970
Walshaw—Shooting Lodge	941
Walshaw Dean—Upper Reservoir	1100
Wesley's Rock (Widdop)	1050
White Stone Hill	1450
Widdop (County Boundary)	1202
Widdop Reservoir	1050
Withens Height	1505

WARLEY.

Butts Green Baptist Church	700
Camp End	1050
Castle Carr—Height Lodge	1100
Cat i' th' Well (Wainstalls)	764
Cold Edge Dam—Upper	1225
,, ,, Lower	1200
Cote Hill	650
Cromwell Mount	1025
Cross Roads	1019
Fly Flat Reservoir	1350
Fly Flat Road	1418
Fly Flat	1450
Holme House Bridge	450
Knoll Hill	1425
Luddenden Bridge	350
Luddenden Dean Wesleyan Chapel	760
Mount Pleasant U.M. Church (Wainstalls)	1025
Rocking Stone	1350
Royles Head Reservoir	1050
Sentry Edge	1100
Warley Town	750
Withins—summit of New Road, Ogden Moor	1393

Oxenhope, Haworth and Stanbury Districts.

	Feea above sea level.
Alcomden Stones	1450
Bleak House	960
Brearley House Farm	1124
Bodkin Top	1175
Brontë Waterfall—top	1084
,, ,, at Brontë Bridge	950
Brow Top	850
Buckley Green—Timmy's Cottage	925
Cross Roads	710
Crow Hill—Trawden	1500
Cullingworth Gate	666
Cullingworth—Station	675
Dike Nook	1153
Flappit	850
Griffe Mill	650
Harbour Hill	1250
Harbour Lodge	1180
Harehill	1000
Haworth—St. Michael's Church	796
Height Farm (Upper)	1161
Hawking Stone Baptist Church	964
Laneshaw Bridge	606
Lees Board School	693
Master Stones	1200
Manywells Heights	890
Mill Hey Bridge (near Haworth Station)	556
Nab Hill	1473
Nab Water	1264
Oldfield School	925
Oxenhope—St. Mary's Church	850
Oxenhope—Station	650
Oxenhope Stoop Hill	1462
Ponden Bridge	698
Ponden Hall ("Thrushcross Grange")	850
Ponden Kirk—top	1200
Rough Nook	772
Sawood Moss (footpath, between Ogden and Oxenhope)	1400

OXENHOPE, HAWORTH AND STANBURY DISTRICTS.—*Continued.*

	Feet above sea level.
Scar Top Wesleyan Chapel	744
Sladen Bridge	640
Stake Hill	1413
Stanbury	850
Sun Hill	1398
Tewit Hall	1000
Thornton Moor Reservoir	1200
Top of Stairs	1397
Two Laws	1000
Watersheddles Reservoir	1100
West End Quarry	1025
Withens—Upper (" Wuthering Heights ")	1376
Wycoller	700

KEIGHLEY DISTRICT.

Bingley Altar	750
Branshaw Moor	925
Cliffe Castle (Keighley)	425
Cottage Hospital (Keighley)	525
Devonshire Park—Promenade (Keighley)	440
Double Stones	1000
Gill Grange Farm	875
Greensyke, or Whorle's End	1150
Harden Moor—highest point	975
Hitching Stones	1175
Ingrow Church (St. John's)	420
Jubilee Tower (Steeton)	650
Keighley Gas Works	275
Keighley Gate—Rombalds Moor	1247
Keighley or Peat Moor Dam	1222
Kildwick Church	330
Laycock	775
Lund's Park (Keighley)	450
Lund's Pinnacle (Cowling)	1125
Newsholme Church	900
Oakworth House	715
Parish Church (Keighley)	365

KEIGHLEY DISTRICT.—*Continued.*

	Feet above sea level.
Redcar Tarn (Keighley)	952
Robin Hood's Stone	950
Rombalds Moor—highest point	1323
Rivock End	1175
Slippery Ford	862
Station Bridge (Keighley)	325
Stockbridge (Keighley)	282
Sutton Stoop	1125
Turkey Mill (Goose Eye)	596
Thwaites Brow (St. Barnabas' Church)	640
Victoria Park (Keighley)	315
Wainman's Monument (Cowling)	1150
Whorles	1000
Windgate Nick ("Winny o't' nick")	1200

ROUND ABOUT HUDDERSFIELD.

Black Hill (Saddleworth)	1909
Buckstones Road (Scammonden, Huddersfield)	1485
Castle Hill	900
Cook's Study (Bretland Edge, Dunford Bridge)	1477
Dean Head Moss (Meltham)	1662
Featherbed Moss (Crowden)	1762
Fixby Hall	690
Fixby Ridge	850
Goat Hill (Scammonden)	1156
Greenfield	700
Holme Moss (Woodhead)	1888
Isle of Skye (Meltham)	1298
Lindley Moor	875
Marsden	625
March Hill (Marsden)	1250
Meltham	544
Mill Stone Edge (Scammonden)	1466
Moss Moor Edge (Buckstones)	1500
Nont Sarah's (Scammonden)	1150
Pickenage Moor	1218
Pole Moor (Outlane, Huddersfield)	1120

ROUND ABOUT HUDDERSFIELD.—*Continued.*

	Feet above sea level.
Slaithwaite	534
Slaithwaite Hill	1089
Snailsden Pike (Dunford Bridge)	1565
Stand Edge (Diggle)	1250
Tinker's Monument (Pike Law, Fulstone Edge, Holmfirth) ...	1250
West Nab (Meltham)	1641
Westend Moss	1729
Wholestone Moor (Outlane)	1245
Windgate Head	1717
Worts Hill (Scammonden)	1283

GENERAL LIST.

Baugh Fell (Sedburgh)	2216
Beamsley Beacon (Bolton Abbey)	1314
Blackstone Edge (highest point, Littleboro' or Ripponden) ...	1553
Blackstone Edge (Reservoir)...	1270
Blackstone Edge (White House)	1238
Blackstone Edge (division of Yorkshire and Lancashire)... ...	1280
Booth Dean Road (Rishworth, division of do., do.)... ...	1277
Boulsworth (Widdop, Colne or Hebden Bridge)	1700
Bradford Town Hall	324
Buckden Pike (Kettlewell)	2304
Buckden Birks (Kettlewell)	1999
Buckstones (Shooting Box)	1421
Burton How (Ingleby)	1419
Byron Edge (North of Blackstone Edge Reservoir)	1360
Cam Fell (Gearstones)	1926
Denholme Gate (Denholme)	1000
Dent Crag (border Yorkshire, Lancashire, Westmorland) ...	2253
Dod (Gearstones)	2189
Fountains Fell (Settle)	1944
Great Shunnor Fell (Hawes)	2351
Great Whernside (Kettlewell)	2310
Hard Flask Malham)...	1746
Hollingworth Lake (Littleboro')	561
Holme Moss (border, Yorkshire and Derbyshire)	1859
Ingleborough (Ingleton)	2373

GENERAL LIST.—*Continued.*

	Feet above Sea level.
Kirklees Hall (Cooper Bridge)	300
Little Whernside	2384
Lovely Seat (Hawes)	2216
Micklefell (Middleton-in-Teesdale—highest point in Yorkshire) ...	2580
Moughton Fell (Malham)	1404
Mountain Mills (near Queensbury)	1207
Nine Standards (Keld, Westmorland border)	2153
Otley Chevin	925
Pendle Hill (Clitheroe)	1831
Penyghent (Horton-in-Ribblesdale)	2273
Pin Seat (Muker, Swaledale)	1914
Queensbury Church	1142
Raisegill Hag (Kettlewell)	1987
Rhosbery Topping (Guisborough)	1022
Rogan's Seat (Muker, Swaledale)	2204
Shelf (Halifax and Bradford Tram Terminus)	825
Simon's Seat (Bolton Abbey)	1593
Stags Fell	2212
Thorag (Settle)	2164
Whernside (Dent)	2414
Widdale Fell (Hawes)	2205
Widdop Cross (Extwistle)	1250
Widdop—summit of Road	1276

LIST OF
FIRST EDITION
SUBSCRIBERS.

FIRST EDITION SUBSCRIBERS.

Thirteen subscribers' names, unwittingly omitted in the first and second editions, have been inserted, making the total number of subscribers 1687, and the number of copies, 2,046.

	VOLS.
Aaron, 39, Woolshops, Halifax	1
Ackroyd, Mrs. J., Hob Lane, Brearley	1
Ackroyd, Mrs., 1, Kiln House, Luddenden	1
Ackroyd, A., Oakley Street, Queensbury	2
Ackroyd, Herbert, Hillside Cottage, Ogden	1
Ackroyd, J. T., Well House, Midgley	2
Ackroyd, P., Lee Mount Road, Halifax	1
Ackroyde, J. T., 10, Rose Place, Luddenden Foot	1
Acrid, J., Little Scout, Luddenden Foot	1
Addison, Martin, Chapel House, Luddenden	1
"A Friend," Lee Mount, Halifax	1
Ainley, E., Gordon Street, Halifax	1
Ainley, W., 35, Corby Street, Birkby, Huddersfield	1
Aked, J., 10, Newstead Heath, Halifax	1
Akroyd, Miss, Bell Hall Mount, Halifax	1
Akroyd, F., 2, Fountain Street, Ripponden	1
Akroyd, J. W., 8, Woodbine Place, Mytholmroyd	1
Aldam, J. W., Union Street, Halifax	1
Alderman, G. C., Copley, Halifax	1
Alderman, Dr. H. C., Ty-Croes, Halifax	1
Alderson, Mrs., Lane Side, Wainstalls	1
Alderson, Miss E., Kirkland, Stow, Midlothian	3
Alderson, J. W., 17, Lord Street, Halifax	1
Alderson, W., Burnley Road, Luddenden Foot	1
Alderson, W., Diamond House, Luddenden	1
Allen, Jas., c/o A. W. Lord, 47, Henderson Street, Levenshulme, Manchester	1
Allott, Miss E. A., 9, Bairstow Lane, Sowerby Bridge	1
Ambler, D., Sowood, Oxenhope	1
Ambler, H., 358, Prospect View, Ovenden Road Halifax	1
Appleyard, E., 1, Mayfield Terrace, Halifax	1
Appleyard, M. E., 24, Thomas Street South, Halifax	1
Appleyard, R E., 58, Essex Street, Halifax	1
Archer, W., 31, Gerrard Street, Halifax	1
Argyle, Mrs., Greenfield, Haworth	3
Armstrong, J. W., 4, Spring Hall Place, Halifax	1
Armitage, J., 185, Claremount Road, Halifax	1
Armitage, R., Post Office, Triangle	1
Arundale, J. H., 31, Audley Street, Halifax	2
Ashworth, E., 2, Clover Hill Terrace, Halifax	1
Ashworth, J., 82, King Cross, Halifax	2
Ashworth, N., 36, Bayswater Terrace, Halifax	1
Ashworth, R., 31, Mount Pellon, Halifax	2
Aspinall, C., 25, Trooper Lane, Halifax	1
Aspinall, F., 17, Bowman Terrace, Halifax	1
Asquith, J., Avonside, London Road, Bath	1
Astin, A., 50, Staups Lane, Stump Cross, Halifax	1
Atkinson, E., 66, Duckworth Lane, Bradford	1
Atkinson, George, 18, Chapel Street, Sowerby Bridge	1
Atkinson, L., 16, New Mill Terrace, Wainstalls	2
Ayrton, Mrs. W., Sykes Farm, Cragg Vale, Mytholmroyd	1
Ayrton, D., 42, Tivoli Place, Little Horton, Bradford	1
Ayrton, L., Rye Croft, Holmfield, Halifax	2
B, E., Trinity Wesleyan Brotherhood, Halifax	1
Backhouse, G H., 4, Irving Street, Halifax	1
Baker, S., 117, Hanson Lane, Halifax	1
Bailey, H., 11, Oates Street, Halifax	1
Bainbridge, 12, Marlborough Avenue, Halifax	2
Baines, Chas. H., 25, Hampden Road, Birkenhead	1
Bairstow, B., Ovenden, Halifax	1
Bairstow, G., 51, Savile Park Street, Halifax	1
Bairstow, W. G., 9, Hyde Park Gardens, Halifax	1
Balme, Wm., 11, Francis Street, Halifax	1
Balmforth, Mrs., T. C., 172, Parkinson Lane, Halifax	1

	VOLS.
Balmforth, Miss R., 20, Wharf Street, Sowerby Bridge	1
Balmforth, Dyson, 40, Green Lane, West Vale	1
Balmforth, E., 137, Bolton Brow, Sowerby Bridge	1
Balmforth, James, 39, Mount Tabor, Halifax	1
Balmforth, J. S., Beech Cottage, Upper Greetland	1
Balmforth, T., Wainstalls Lodge, Wainstalls	1
Bamforth, Wright, 7, Nettleton Hill, Golcar	1
Bancroft, Mrs. S., Dale View, Sowerby Bridge	1
Bancroft, Miss, West View House, Oxenhope	1
Bancroft, Mary H., 1, West View, Boothtown	1
Bancroft H., 8, Cromwell Street, Halifax	2
Bancroft, J., 41, Cobden Street, Halifax	1
Bancroft, J., Darcey Hey, Halifax	2
Bancroft, J. W., Hillcrest, Oxenhope	1
Barber, F. P., Claremont, Horley Green, Halifax	1
Barker, Mrs. J., Albert Road Top, Sowerby Bridge	1
Barker, Miss M. J., 14, Swan Street, Loughbro', Leicestershire	1
Barker, A., 164, Ashley Road, West Harton, South Shields	1
Barker, George, Jubilee Road, Siddal, Halifax	1
Barker, J., Lower Newlands Farm, Keighley Road, Halifax	1
Barker, J. S., 3, Cotton Street, Range Bank, Halifax	1
Barker, J. W., 8, Stoodley Terrace, Halifax	1
Barker, W., Booth Stead, Mount Tabor	1
Barker, W., 103, Shroggs Road, Halifax	1
Barnes, G., 51, Old Lee Bank, Halifax	1
Baron, W., 8, Calder Avenue, King Cross, Halifax	1
Barraclough, A., 32, Industrial Road, Sowerby Bridge	1
Barraclough, Inman, Lumbrook, Northowram	1
Barraclough, J., Thrum Hall Post Office, Halifax	1
Barraclough, S., Carr House, Booth, Luddenden	1
Barraclough, Wm., 11, Summergate Place, Parkinson Lane, Halifax	2
Barraclough, W. D., 124, Warley Road, Halifax	1
Barras, S. S., 15, Herbert Street, Clayton	2
Barrett, Miss Mary, 2, Union Street, Hebden Bridge	1
Barrett, Eliz. C., 7, Heathfield Place, Halifax	1
Barrett, H., Regent Street, Queensbury	2
Barrett, J., Abbey Walk, Halifax	1
Barrett, J., 70, West End, Queensbury, Bradford	1
Barrett, J. W., Swift Place, Soyland	1
Bateman, J., 52, High Street, Queensbury	1
Bateman, R. S., The Gables, Halifax	1
Bates, Mrs., 1, Moorgate Street, King Cross, Halifax	1
Bates, Miss, 10, Swires Terrace, Halifax	1
Bates, F., 15, Clover Hill View, Halifax	1
Bates, F. D., 39, Nimrod Road, Streatham Park, London, S.W.	1
Bates, J., Albert Road, Halifax	1
Bates, Z., Gladstone Place, Ovenden	1
Battye, J., Upper Bell Hall, Halifax	1
Baume, Mrs. H., Duke Street, Luddenden	1
Baume, J. W., 18, Cross Hills, Halifax	2
Baxter, W., 10, Newstead Grove, Halifax	1
Beanland, Sergeant, 35, Park Place, Halifax	1
Beaumont, H., Westroyde, Elland	2
Beaumont, Wm., Roylands Farm, Hipperholme	1
Beaver, Ald. J. H., Gledhow Mount, Oxenhope	1
Beaver, W., 30, Victoria Road, Keighley	1
Bedford, Mrs. J. E., Walt Royd Farm, Wheatley	1
Bedford, J. R., Riding Farm, Ovenden Wood	2
Bedford, M. J., Spring Royd, Brearley	2
B. F., Sparkhouse Lane, Norland	1
Bell, S., Dean Cottage, Luddenden	2
Bell, Rev. W. C., M.A., Vicarage, Norland	2
Bellamy, 32, Warley Street, Halifax	1

	VOLS.
Bentley, H. R., 25, Clare Road, Halifax	1
Bentley, W., 347, Queen's Road, Halifax	1
Bentley, W. H., 30, St. Augustine's Terrace, Halifax	1
Benton, J., Little Wood Lane Cottage, Sowerby	1
Berry, A., 84, Sowerby Green, Sowerby	1
Berry, M., 5, Winter Neb, Luddenden Foot	1
Berry, S., 10, Upper Cross Wells, Soyland	1
Berry, W., 46, Howard Street, Halifax	1
Beverley, Mary E., Tongue End, Wainstalls	1
Beverley, Miss M. H., Sandy Fore, Mount Tabor	1
Bibby, H., West Street, Sowerby Bridge	1
Bilton, E., 26, Booth, Luddenden	1
Bilsbury, Arthur, 20, Beckenham Place, Halifax	1
Binns, Mrs., 72, West Lane, Haworth	1
Binns, Mrs. W. T., 23, Naylor Street, Halifax	1
Binns, Miss, 14, Cobden Street, Halifax	2
Binns, Miss, 37, King Cross Street, Halifax	1
Binns, H., 7, North Street, Haworth	1
Binns, J., 13, Cross Street, Pellon	
Binns, M. Victor, 11, Byron Street, Tuel Lane,	1
Sowerby Bridge	1
Binns, R., 10, Tennyson Street, Lee Mount, Halifax	2
Binns, S., 20, Woodhead Terrace, New Pellon, Halifax	1
Binns, Coun. T., 2, New Street, Haworth	1
Binns, T., Square, Wainstalls	1
Birtwhistle, E., Trinity Wesleyan Brotherhood	1
Birtwhistle, Wm. Denholme, Luddenden Foot	2
Blackburn, Miss D., 10, East Parade, Sowerby Bridge	1
Blackburn, R., Prospect Villas, Holmfield	1
Blackburn, Bobert, Scar Top, Upper Greetland	1
Blackburn, T., 24, Upper Bolton Brow, Sowerby Bridge	1
Blacker, Alice, 27, Blaithroyd Lane, Southowram	1
Blackett, J., 20, Bayswater Terrace, Halifax	1
Blakeley, Mrs., Heckmondwike	1
Blakey, A., 9, Nichol Street	1
Boardall, H., 31, Clough Lane, Mixenden	1
Boardall, J., Mill Hill, Brearley	1
Bolton, J., 23, The Green, Oxenhope	1
Bonner, W., 40, Warley Street, Halifax	1
Boocock, Mrs., Brook Terrace, Luddenden	1
Boocock, 19, Union Street, Halifax	3
Booth, Mrs., Eltam Park, Kent	1
Booth, Mrs., 3, Greenwood's Terrace, Shroggs Road, Wheatley	1
Booth, Hilda, 19, Union Street South, Halifax	1
Booth, A., 15, Chester Road, Akroydon, Halifax	1
Booth, G., 102, Albert View, Albert Road, Halifax	2
Booth, J., 39, Clapton Grove, Halifax	1
Booth, W., 12, Spring View, Luddenden Foot	1
Boothman, Miss, 8, Tuel Street, Sowerby Bridge	1
Bottomley, A., Oak Mount, Oakenshaw, Bradford	2
Bottomley, A., Syke Hill, Ripponden	1
Bottomley, Fred, 14, Westbury Terrace, West End, Halifax	2
Bottomley, G., 57, Albert Road, Beach, Sowerby Bridge	1
Bottomley, I., Ashleigh, Ovenden	1
Bottomley, J. E., 13, Coronation Terrace, Greetland	1
Boulderclough Working Men's Club	1
Boulton, T., 4, Gladstone Building, Mytholmroyd	1
Bracewell, Thomas, 27, Keighley Road, Ovenden	2
Bradford Corporation: Public Libraries	2
Bradley, F., 18, Beech Road, Sowerby Bridge	1
Bradley, F., Catherine House Farm, Luddenden Dean	1
Bradley, J., Horton Croft, Stanbury, Keighley	12
Bradley, J., Maude Street, Ovenden	1
Bradley, J. W., 41, Horley Green Road, Halifax	1
Bradley, W., 8, Delph Street, Halifax	1
Bradley, Wm., Woodland Street, Cowling, Keighley	1
Braithwaite, T. R., 29, Bull Green, Halifax	2
Bray, 24, Lord Street, Heap Bridge, Nr. Bury	1
Brayshaw, Fred, Ashcroft, Greetland	1
Brayshaw, Geo., Hollybank, Stainland	1
Brear, C. E., 36, Stoodley Terrace, Halifax	1
Brearley, Mrs. Lena, 78, Blackwood Grove, Halifax	1
Brearley, H., 11, Lilac Street, Lee Mount, Halifax	1
Brearley, J. H., Gasworks, Longwood	1
Brigg, Tom, Kildwick Hall, Keighley	1
Briggs, Alan, Highfield, Mount Tabor, Halifax	1
Briggs, David, Denholme, Bradford	1
Briggs, D., Upper Highfield, Mount Tabor	1
Briggs, George, Allerton Street, Halifax	1
Briggs, H., 1, Heys Terrace, Pellon, Halifax	1
Briggs, H., Savile Park, Halifax	1
Broadbent, 24, Thomas Street, Halifax	1
Broadbent, G., 7, Hawthorne Terrace, Halifax	1
Broadbent, H., 33, Delph Hill Terrace, King Cross	1
Broadbent, H., Myrtle House, Halifax	1
Broadbent, Joseph, Little Wood Lane Farm, Sowerby	1
Broadbent, W., 31, Clifton Street, Sowerby Bridge	1
Broadbent, W. H., Pear Street, Halifax	1
Broadhurst, Mrs. H., 7, Keighley Road, Ovenden	1
Broadley, A., High Grove Place, Halifax	1
Broadley, E., Bond Street, Halifax	1
Brook, Mrs., Ambry Well, Wadsworth	1
Brook, Miss, 9, Violet Street, Hanson Lane, Halifax	1
Brook, D., 27, Abbey Walk South, Halifax	1
Brook, E., 24, Penn Street, Halifax	1
Brook, H., Ambry Well, Wadsworth	1
Brook, H., 25, Brackenbed Lane, Halifax	1
Brook, J., Height Lodge, Wainstalls	1
Brooke, A. D., Savile Mount, Halifax	1
Brooke, E. P., Gibbet House, Halifax	2
Brooke, W., 36, Knight Street, Halifax	1
Brooks, Miss C. H., 32, Brinton Terrace, Halifax	1
Brooksbank, Mrs., 1, High Street, Luddenden	1
Brotherton, J., Luddenden Dean, Wainstalls	2
Brown, E., Bank Buildings, Luddenden Foot	1
Brown, E., 4, St. Alban's Avenue, Halifax	1
Brown, J. B., Stalheim, Hebden Bridge	1
Buckley, J. W., 16, Woodbine Street, Halifax	1
Buckmaster, Sir Stanley O., K.C., M.P., 1, Porchester Terrace, London, W.	1
Bullock, Wm., 77, Booth Town Road, Halifax	1
Bulmer, P., Union Workhouse, Halifax	1
Bunce, J. W., 23, Parliament Street, Halifax	1
Bunting, 10, Rose Bank, King Cross, Halifax	1
Burke, Gunner A. S., 91st Battery, R.F.A., Chitral Barracks, Nowshera, Punjaub	1
Butler, Rev. A. E., 218, Pershore Road, Birmingham	1
Butler, Hy., 15, St. Ives Road, Halifax	1
Butler, T., 23, West Mount Street, Halifax	1
Butterfield, R., Curator, Museum, Keighley	1
Butterfield, R. H., John Street, Cullingworth	1
Butterfield, T., Moorcock Inn, Wainstalls	1
Butterworth, Miss A., 21, Edward Street, Sowerby Bridge	1
Butterworth, B., 14, Bracken Hill, Pellon, Halifax	1
Butterworth, G., Lee Mount Road, Halifax	1
Butterworth, J. W., 3, Hollins Bank, Sowerby Bdge.	1
Butterworth, Wm., 21, Edward Street, Sowerby Bridge	2
Butterworth, W., 29, St. James's Road, Halifax	1
Byron, A., Moorland House, Ogden	1
Calvert, Mrs. T., Heaton Grove, Frizinghall, Bradford	2
Calvert, Miss Florence, 30, Savile Park, Halifax	1
Calvert, Forest, Ovenden	1
Calvert, Frank, Windy Bank, Holmfield	1
Calvert, Fred, Keighley Road, Ovenden	1
Calvert, J. W., J.P., Beech Wood, Ovenden	2
Calvert, Midgley, The Bungalow, Ovenden	6
Capper, W., 30, Gerrard Street	1
Carnell, T., 48, Brow Lane, Shibden, Halifax	1
Carnell, Wm., 59, Penn Street, Halifax	1
Carr, Mrs. E. A., Lyndall, Park Crescent, Tonbridge	1
Carr, G., Greenfield, Haworth	2
Carter, Ben, 22, Union Street South, Halifax	1
Carter, Geo., 56, Woolshops, Halifax	1
Carter, J. B., Hillend, Norwood Green	1
Carter, W. H., Millbank, Triangle	1
Casson, Henry, 30, Gladstone Road, Halifax	1
Casson, J. E., Whitehall, Hipperholme	1
Catherall, Miss S., 16, Chapel Street, Queensbury	1
Cattell, H. H., Lower Hough House, Halifax	1
Caunt, Miss L., 26, Newstead Grove, Halifax	1

LIST OF SUBSCRIBERS.—*Continued.*

	VOLS.
Cawthra, Miss E. E., 5, Villiers Street, Halifax	2
Chadwick, A., Chapel Street, Ovenden	1
Chadwick, H., 13, Hollins Bank, Sowerby Bridge	1
Chamberlain, J. T., 12, New Bank, Halifax	1
Chambers, Mrs. L., Melrose Cottage, Fenton Place, Halifax	1
Chapman, F., 29, Hyde Park Gardens, Halifax	1
Chapman, H., Blackwall, Halifax	1
Chapman, T., Cold Edge Bottom, Wainstalls	1
Charlton, Arthur, 110, East Parade, Keighley	1
Charnock, Mrs., Wheatley	1
Cheetham, E., 52, Hanson Lane, Halifax	1
Child, Louis H., 39, Harrison Road, Halifax	2
Christie, E. J., F.B.E.A., 30, Chester Road, Halifax	1
Clark, S., Bethel Terrace, Luddenden	1
Clark, T., 35, Eton Street, Halifax	1
Clark, W. N., 15, Knight Street, Halifax	1
Clarke, Stephen, 7, Fox Street, Pimlico Road, Clithero, Lancs.	1
Clarkson, J., Wilton Lodge, Halifax	1
Clayton, Turner Top, Rishworth	1
Clayton, E., 10, Pohlman Street, Halifax	1
Clayton, Jas. Ed., 49, Dyson Road, Pellon, Halifax	1
Clayton, J. W., 4, Carlton Street, Halifax	1
Clayton, P., Lee Mount, Halifax	1
Clegg, Alice, Hall Bank, Mytholmroyd	1
Clegg, Sarah A., Kirby Farm, Cragg Vale	1
Clegg, Chas., 34, Milton Street, Halifax	1
Clegg, F., Traveller's Rest Inn, Luddenden	1
Clegg, J. H., Park View, Stump Cross, Halifax	1
Clegg, J. H., 180, Boothtown Road, Halifax	1
Clewer, J. H., 49, Hyde Park Road, Halifax	1
Cliberon, Mrs., 13, Colbeck Street, Halifax	1
Cochran, Miss Fanny, South 22nd Street, Philadelphia, U.S.A.	1
Cockcroft, Mrs. H., Brink Top, Mytholmroyd	2
Cockcroft, W. H., West End, Hebden Bridge	1
Cockhill, L., Winterburn Hill, Warley	1
Cockroft, Mrs., 19, Baines Street, Halifax	1
Cockroft, Mrs., Springfield, Hipperholme	3
Cockroft, 83, Surrey Street, Halifax	1
Cockroft, Frank, 247, Willow Mount, Bairstow Lane, Sowerby Bridge	1
Cockroft, Joseph, 1, Miry Lane, Sowerby	1
Cockroft, W., 78, St. Augustine's Terrace, Hanson Lane, Halifax	1
Collins, 64, Crossley Hill, Salterhebble	1
Collins, M., 14, New Street, New Pellon, Halifax	1
Collinson, Thos., 17, Heath Mount, Halifax	1
Comfort, A., Palatine Chambers, Halifax	6
Conway, G. H., Abbey Walk South, Halifax	1
Conway, Wm., Homestead, Salterhebble	1
Cooke, Clara A., 43, Savile Park Street, Halifax	1
Copley, J., 30, Martin Street, Boothtown Road, Halifax	1
Corlett, J., Victoria Buildings, Luddenden Foot	1
Coton, E. E., Raven Street, Queen's Road, Halifax	1
Coulston, E., 16, Conway Street, Halifax	1
Cox, Mrs., 10, Tatton Grove, Withington, Manchester	1
Crabtree, F., 4, Heath Park Avenue, Halifax	1
Crabtree, H., 4, Commercial Street, Hebden Bridge	1
Crabtree, J., East Terrace, Lees, Keighley	1
Crabtree, J., 27, Church Street, Keighley	1
Crabtree, K., Highroad Well, Halifax	1
Crabtree, Lewis, Luddenden Foot	1
Crabtree, T., 5, Lower Slack, Wainstalls	1
Crabtree, W., 60, Keighley Road, Ovenden	1
Crabtree, W., 6, Stretchgate Lane, Pellon, Halifax	1
Crabtree, W., West View, Ovenden	1
Crabtree, Walter, Springfield, Oxenhope	1
Crabtree, Wilfred, 4, Rough Bottom, Mytholmroyd	1
Crabtree, Willie, 6, Rough Bottom, Mytholmroyd	1
Crabtree, William, 2, St. George's Square, Lee Mount	1
Cragg, R., "Observer" Office, Bradford	1
Cragg, W., 21, St. Paul's Road, Halifax	1
Crapper, W., 30, Gerrard Street, Halifax	1
Crawshaw, A., 42, Ripon Street, Halifax	1
Crawshaw, C. E., Queen's Road, Halifax	2
Crawshaw, L., Linthwaite, Huddersfield	1
Crossland, Chas., 4, Coleridge Street, Halifax	1
Crossley, Mrs., 8a, Bedford Terrace, Sowerby Bridge	1
Crossley, Mrs., Denton Row, Holywell Brook	1
Crossley, Miss Ada, 5, Thorney Lane, Midgley	1
Crossley, Ellor, 10, Rose Terrace, Halifax	1
Crossley, Emma, 35, Booth Terrace, Luddenden	1
Crossley, Miss L., 7, Butts Green, Luddenden Foot	1
Crossley, Ellis, 10, Rose Terrace, Halifax	1
Crossley, G., 27, Gladstone Buildings, Sowerby Bridge	1
Crossley, J., New Laithe, Luddenden	2
Crossley, W., Lumbrook, Northowram	1
Crossley, W. H., Wood Top, Cragg Vale	1
Crown Works, Boothtown	2
Crowther, A., Margate Street, Sowerby Bridge	1
Crowther, B., 8, Belle Vue Place, Halifax	1
Crowther, John Henry, 52, Chapel Ash, Wolverhampton	1
Crowther, N., 13, Leather Street, Claremount	1
Cukson, F., Village Farm, Northowram, Halifax	1
Culpan, Mrs. D., 54, Penn Street, Halifax	1
Culpan, Miss E., 27, Baines Street, Halifax	1
Culpan, A., 13, Ashbourne Grove, Halifax	1
Culpan, H., 4, Mayfield Street, Halifax	1
Culpan, John T. B., 6, Mile Cross Terrace, Halifax	1
Culpan, W. H., 11, Tyson Street, Halifax	1
Cumming, Miss, Priory Terrace, Dumfermline, Scotland	1
D, E., Halifax	1
Darch, E. J., 27, Cheltenham Place, Halifax	1
Dawson, J. W., 59, New Bank, Halifax	1
Dawson, Smith, 20, Broad Carr, Holywell Green	1
Dealey, W., Grove Cottage, Ovenden	1
Dean, E., 13, Colin Street, Halifax	1
Denison, Mrs. W. E., Rostellan, Halifax	1
Denison, John, Willow Field, Greetland	2
Denison, Egerton, 11, St. Bevan's Road, Halifax	1
Denison, George, Rostellan, Halifax	1
Denison, Percival, Rostellan, Halifax	1
Denison, W. E., Rostellan, Halifax	5
Denley, J., Osborne Terrace, Luddenden Foot	1
Dennis, A. E., 92, Lister Lane, Halifax	1
Dennis, J. R., 26, Clapton Mount, Halifax	1
Denton, H., 14, Baker Street North, Holmfield	1
Dewhirst, Mrs., 22, Bright Street, Halifax	1
Dewhirst, Mrs., 2, Scar Bottom, Mytholmroyd	1
Dewhirst, Mrs. J. A., 90, St. Alban's Road, Skircoat	1
Dewhirst, Miss, 16, Savile Park, Halifax	2
Dewhirst, H., 739, Bellevue Avenue, Detroit, Mich., U.S.A.	1
Dewhirst, Isaac, Elland	2
Dewhirst, J., 3, Glenholme Heath, Newstead, Halifax	1
Dewhirst, W., 19, Hammond Street, Halifax	1
Dilworth, C., 21, Steps Lane, Halifax	1
Dobson, F., High Street, Queensbury	1
Dodds, J. A., 11, Mayfield Mount, Halifax	1
Dodsworth, Mrs., 16, Clay Street, Halifax	1
Downsborough, E., 39, Violet Street, Halifax	1
Drake, Miss, 9, Crown Street, Halifax	1
Drake, F. R., Iona Street, Boothtown	1
Drake, the late J. Armitage, J.P., Heath Lodge, Halifax	4
Drake, P., 1, West Grove Terrace, Halifax	1
Drake, Thos., 25, Summergate Street, Halifax	1
Dransfield, J. W., 93, Stainland Road, West Vale	1
Duckworth, F. P., 5, Bancroft Terrace, Halifax	1
Dugdale, E., Carr Field, Luddenden Foot	1
Duries, J., Co-operation Street, Illingworth	1
Dyson, Mrs., 67, Albert Road, Sowerby Bridge	1
Dyson, Miss E., Abbott's Terrace, Gibbet Lane, Halifax	1
Dyson, Ed., 2, Newstead Place, Halifax	1
Dyson, H., 4, Church Terrace, King Cross Street, Halifax	1
Dyson, Jno., 21, Kingston Street, Halifax	1
Dyson, John H., 73, Clowes Street, West Gorton, Manchester	1
Earnshaw, Mrs. H., 26, Heath Crescent, Halifax	1
Earnshaw, J., Hole Bottom Farm, Square, Wainstalls	1
East, W., Hanson Lane, Halifax	1

VOLS.

Eastabrook, Mark, 75, Smallshaw Lane, Ashton-under Lyne 1
Eastburn, J. W., 1, Milton Place, Halifax . . 1
Easton, Miss Mary, 148, McRoberts Avenue, Toronto, Canada 1
Eastwood, Fred, 245, Quarmby Road, Huddersfield 1
Eastwood, H. H., Regent Street, Halifax . . 1
Eastwood, Harry, 23, Otley Street, Halifax . . 1
Eastwood, J., Edge End, Illingworth 1
Eastwood, J., 8, Haddon Avenue, Halifax . . 1
Eastwood, J., Junr., 32, Whitegate Road, Halifax 1
Eastwood, J., 84, Williamson Street, Halifax . 2
Eastwood, S., 30, May Street, Crosland Moor . 1
Eastwood, S. G., 8, Green Hill Terrace, Halifax . 1
Eccles, 349, Salterhebble Hill, Halifax . . . 1
Edmondson, Miss F., Mill Hey, Haworth . . 1
Edmondson, W., Mill Hey, Haworth . . . 1
Edwards, J. R., 5, Eldroth Road, Halifax . . 1
Eglin, Wm., Widdop, nr. Hebden Bridge . . 1
Eglin, W. Ernest, Laurel Bank, Luddenden . . 1
Elgar, G. H., 221, Queen's Road, Halifax . . . 1
Elliott, Mrs., 80, Williamson Street, Halifax . . 1
Elliott, G., 50, Summergate Place, Halifax . . 1
Elliott, H., 31, Keighley Road, Ovenden . . . 1
Elliott, H., 4, Laura Street, All Souls' Road, Halifax 1
Ellis, Mrs., Queen's Road, Norwood Green . . 1
Ellis, Miss, Warley Road, Halifax 1
Ellis, Dr., Craven House, Hopwood Lane, Halifax 4
Ellis, E., 22, Mount Street, Sowerby Bridge . . 1
Ellis, F. S., 1, Weaste Road, Manchester . . . 1
Ellis, H. H., Irlam's o'th Height, Manchester . 1
Ellwood, W., New Road, Luddenden 1
Emmott, A., Finkle Street, Sowerby 1
Emmott, F., 3, Brook Terrace, Luddenden . . 1

F. B., Spark House Lane, Sowerby Bridge . . 1
F. N. G., 27, West View, Halifax 1
Fahy, Frank, 39, Howard Street, Pellon Lane, Halifax 1
Farrar, Mrs., 88, Blackwood Grove, Pellon, Halifax 1
Farrar, Emily, 21, Beckenham Place, Halifax . 1
Farrar, Albert, Heath Park Avenue, Halifax . . 1
Farrar, A., 13, Ramsgate Street, Halifax . . . 1
Farrar, A., 20, Rochdale Road, Ripponden . . 1
Farrar, D., 19, Fascination Place, Queensbury . 1
Farrar, E., B.A., B.Sc., The Haugh, Todmorden 1
Farrar, F. M., 8, Holbein House, Sloane Square, London, S.W. 1
Farrar, J., 11, Belle Vue Terrace, Southowram . 1
Farrar, J., Dyson Lane, Ripponden 1
Farrar, J., 61, Nelson Street, Lees, Keighley . . 1
Farrar, J. P., Mill House, Luddenden . . . 1
Farrar, J. W., 5, Knight Street, Parkinson Lane, Halifax 1
Farrar, T., The Popples, Holmfield 1
Farrar, Wm., 23, Edward Street, Sowerby Bridge 1
Fawcett, 4, Laurel Bank, Hyde Park, Halifax . 1
Fawcett, A., 37, Dyson Road, Halifax . . . 1
Fearnley, F. E., Ovenden Road, Lee Mount . . 1
Feather, Miss, 27, West View, Halifax . . . 1
Feather, Miss R., 18, Edward Street, Tuel Lane, Sowerby Bridge 1
Feather, F., 21, Walton Street, Halifax . . . 1
Feather, G., 103, Commercial Road, Halifax . . 1
Feather, H., 18, Knight Street, Halifax . . . 1
Feather, Jas., 90, Grasmere Place, Ovenden . . 1
Ferry, J., 24, Paradise Street, Halifax . . . 1
Fielding, Arthur, King Cross, Halifax . . . 1
Fielding, A. W., 13, New Bond Street, Halifax . 1
Fielding, C., Clover Hill, Halifax 1
Fielding, Peter, 195, Gibbet Street, Halifax . . 1
Fielding, S., Scarr Mill, Greetland 2
Fielding, S., 34, Victoria Road, Hanson Lane, Halifax 1
Fielding, W., Mill Bank, Triangle 1
Fielding, W. R., Queen's Road, King Cross, Halifax 1
Finch, T. G., Jerusalem Farm, Luddenden Foot 1
Fingland, 6, Park Place, Halifax 1
Firth, Miss M., Burnley Road, Sowerby Bridge . 1
Firth, Miss M. E., Hipswell, Richmond, Yorks. . 1

VOLS.

Firth, A., 66, St. James's Road, Halifax . . . 1
Firth, Daniel, Hall Green, Dukinfield 1
Firth, J., Lillands Lane, Rastrick 1
Firth Joe, Saw Hill, Triangle, Halifax . . . 1
Firth, L., 13, White Hill, Illingworth 1
Fisher, R. E., 20, Clare Road, Halifax . . . 1
Fitton, A., 10, Clevedon Place, Ovenden Road, Halifax 1
Fleming, C. J., 12, Hope Hall Terrace, Halifax . 1
Fleming, W., Stansfield Street, Halifax . . . 1
Fletcher, A., 2, Buttress, Luddenden 1
Fletcher, J., Fold Farm, Shibden 1
Flockton, J. W., 51, Crossley Terrace, Halifax . 1
Ford, Miss Alice, 12, Willow Drive, Burnley Road, Halifax 1
Fortune, S., 48, Oak Tree Lane, Selly Oak, Birmingham 1
Foster, Mrs. T. H., 48, Victoria Terrace, Mill Bank, Triangle 1
Foster, Mrs. W., White Shaw, Denholme . . . 1
Foster, C., 9, Stead Street, Halifax 1
Foster, E., 7, Hall Street, Milnrow, Rochdale. . 1
Foster, J., 106, Preston Old Road, Blackpool . 1
Foster, J. T., 320, Queen's Road, Halifax . . 1
Foster, P., 11, Cranbourne Road, Bradford . . 1
Foster, T., 3, Clare Street, Halifax 1
Fox, M., Battinson Road, Halifax 1
Frankland, J., 3, Ingram Street, Halifax . . . 1
"Friend," Wheatley 1
Frobisher, T., 7, Wynn Street, Halifax . . . 1

Garforth, Miss H., 127, Gibraltar Road, Halifax . 1
Garside Norman, Co-operative Buildings, Wheatley 1
Garth, M. M., Rosemary Hall, Bradshaw . . . 1
Gartside, Miss, 18, Church Place, Halifax. . . 1
Gaukrodger, Frederick, "Chaseley," 155, St. Anne's Road East, St. Anne's-on-Sea . 1
Gaukroger, 5, Westbourne Grove, Salterhebble . 1
Gaukroger, J. B., Friendly, Sowerby Bridge . . 1
Gaukroger, J. W., Carr Terrace, Luddenden . . 4
Geary, C. W., Washington House, Greetland . 2
Georgeson, J. H., Cairnduna, Halifax Road, Brighouse 1
Gibson, F., 5, Smith Street East, Siddal . . . 1
Gilbert, 4, Westbourne Terrace, Salterhebble . 1
Gledhill, Mrs., 26, Pulman's Place, Skircoat Green 1
Gledhill, J., Lower Edge, Rastrick 1
Gothwaite, Miss, West Croft, Heath Avenue, Halifax 1
Graham, A., Laurel Mount, Luddenden Foot . 1
Granger, P. M., 1, Heath Park Avenue, Halifax . 1
Graydon, H., 38, Baines Street, Halifax . . . 1
Graydon, H., 16, Victoria Buildings, King Cross, 1
Greaves, J., 1, Coleridge Street, Halifax . . . 1
Green, Mrs. C. E., 716, Hawk's Avenue, Vancouver, British Columbia, Canada . 1
Green, C., 8a, Clare Street, Halifax 1
Green, Fred, 16, Trooper Lane, Halifax . . . 1
Green, James, 7, Clapton Avenue, Halifax . . 1
Green, Lewis, 22, Holdsworth Road, Halifax . 1
Green, R., Filey Avenue, Midland Road, Royston 1
Greenwood, Mrs., Fold Farm, Mixenden . . . 1
Greenwood, Mrs., 11, Halifax Lane, Luddenden . 1
Greenwood, Mrs., 10, Lower Saltonstall, Mount Tabor 1
Greenwood, Mrs., 21, Rhodes Street, Halifax . 2
Greenwood, Mrs., Thorn Bank, Mytholmroyd . 1
Greenwood, Miss C., 12, Princess Street, Sowerby Bridge 2
Greenwood, Miss E., Walshaw School, Hebden Bridge 1
Greenwood, Miss M., Chapel House, Booth . . 1
Greenwood, Sarah, 44, Park Place, Halifax . . 1
Greenwood, A., 73, Albert Road, Sowerby Bridge 1
Greenwood, Albert, 34, Carlton House Terrace, Halifax 1
Greenwood, Arthur, 6, Crossley Terrace South, Ovenden 1
Greenwood, Arthur, 2, Lower Brown Hurst, Ovenden Wood, Halifax 1
Greenwood, A., 14, Violet Street, Halifax. . . 1
Greenwood, B., Warley Town Lane, Warley . . 1
Greenwood, C., 34, Beechwood Avenue, Holmfield 1

LIST OF SUBSCRIBERS.—*Continued.*

	VOLS.
Greenwood, E., 5, Chestnut Street, Parkinson Lane, Halifax	1
Greenwood, F., 12, Montague Street, Sowerby Bridge	1
Greenwood, F., Wainstalls Lodge, Wainstalls	1
Greenwood, F. W., 64, Vickerman Street, Halifax	1
Greenwood, G. F., 21, Abbey Walk, Halifax	1
Greenwood, H., 25, Bingley Road, Cross Roads, Keighley	1
Greenwood, H., 34, Bull Green, Halifax	8
Greenwood, Harry, 101, Rochdale Road, Heap Bridge, Bury	1
Greenwood, H., 10, Stephen Street, Hebden Bridge	1
Greenwood, Herbert, 3, Trimmingham Lane, Halifax	1
Greenwood, H. M., High Street, Luddenden	2
Greenwood, H. W., Reservoir Lodge, Ramsden Wood	1
Greenwood, J., 18, Blackwood Hall, Luddenden Foot	1
Greenwood, J., Clunter's Farm, Luddenden Foot	1
Greenwood, J., 81, Crossley Terrace, Halifax	1
Greenwood, J., Hammond Street, Halifax	2
Greenwood, J., Long Riggin, Mount Tabor	1
Greenwood, J., Moor House, Highroad Well, Halifax	1
Greenwood, John, 13, South View Terrace, Queen's Road, Halifax	1
Greenwood, J., 15, St. James's Street, Halifax	1
Greenwood, J., 4, Winter Neb, Luddenden Foot	2
Greenwood, J. A., Whitehouses, Mytholmroyd	1
Greenwood, J. E., Peace Cote, Wainstalls	1
Greenwood, Morris, Souris, Manitoba, Canada	1
Greenwood, R. W., East Height, Mixenden	1
Greenwood, S., Crown Street, Hebden Bridge	1
Greenwood, S., 11, Lodge Gate, Denholme	1
Greenwood, S., 4, Sefton Cottage, South Street, Halifax	1
Greenwood, T., Ambry Well, Wadsworth, Hebden Bridge	1
Greenwood, T., Bethel Terrace, Luddenden	1
Greenwood, T., Buckley Lane, Pellon, Halifax	1
Greenwood, T., 2, Churn Lane, Highroad Well, Halifax	1
Greenwood, T. H., 18, Boston Street, Halifax	1
Greenwood, W., 259, Layauchetiere East, Montreal, Canada	1
Greenwood, W., Post Office, Boothtown	1
Greenwood, W., 18, Woodbine Road, Fartown, Huddersfield	1
Greetland & West Vale Naturalists' Society	1
Gregson, A., 38, Joshua Street, Todmorden	1
Gregson, E., 34, Ashbourne Grove, Halifax	3
Gregson, S., High Street, Queensbury	2
Grundy, Miss, 12, Liverpool Row, Warley Town, Halifax	1
Goggs, Hartley, 1, Clough Lane, Mixenden	1
Gelder, G., The Green, Hipperholme	1
Goodwin, A., 66, Hopwood Lane, Halifax	1
Goodwin, D., 51, Ripon Street, Halifax	1
Gothwaite, Miss, West Croft, Heath Avenue, Halifax	1
H, J., Stainland	1
Haigh, Mrs., Nestleton, Newbold Road, Chesterfield	1
Haigh, Mrs. T. Heywood, Chesterfield	1
Haigh, Gladys A., 5, Central Beach, Blackpool	1
Haigh, A., Spring Field, Mount Tabor	1
Haigh, A., 140, St. Stephen's Street, Copley	1
Haigh, Benj., 17, Rhondda Place, Halifax	1
Haigh, F., 222, Queen's Road, Halifax	1
Haigh, G. E., 19, Ovenden Wood Road, Halifax	1
Haigh, H., 17, Walton Street, King Cross, Halifax	1
Haigh, John, Aked's Road, King Cross Lane, Halifax	1
Haigh, J., Jessamine Terrace, Halifax	1
Haigh, J., 7, Steep Lane, Sowerby	1
Haigh, J., 67, York Crescent, King Cross, Halifax	1
Haigh, J. A., 3, Orion Place, Sowerby Bridge	1
Haigh, L., 3, Montague Street, Sowerby Bridge	2
Haigh, Oscar, 7, The Greens, Sowerby	1
Haigh, S., 29, West View, Halifax	1
Haley, Mrs., 30, Mill Lane, Mixenden	1
Haley, F., 5, Sutcliffe Street, New Pellon, Halifax	1
Halifax Mechanics' Institute	1
Halifax Public Library	3
Hall, Mrs., 6, Albert View, Pellon	1
Hall, F. J., Dudwell Bank, Skircoat, Halifax	1
Hall, G., Cycling Club, Haworth	1
Hall, G. H., Strines Farm, Ambler Thorn, Halifax	1
Hall, J., 24, Otley Street, Skipton	1
Hall, W. H., Ryburn Buildings, Sowerby Bridge	4
Halliday, F., 14, Marlbro' Avenue	1
Halliday, G., 5, Clare Street, Halifax	1
Halliday, H., Fenny Cottage, Hipperholme	1
Halliday, W., Bull Green, Halifax	1
Halliday, W. H., 12, Bank Field View, Halifax	1
Hallowell, E., Public Library, Sowerby Bridge	1
Hamer, S. H., Bleak House, Claremount Road, Halifax	2
Hann, Rev. Adam, 1, Park Terrace, Halifax	1
Hanson, Mrs., Carlton House Terrace, Halifax	1
Hanson, Miss, Manchester	1
Hanson, Akroyd, Heywood Chapel House, Northowram	1
Hanson, F., 3, Pleasant Street, Beech, Sowerby Bridge	1
Hanson, F., Knowles Lane, Gomersal	1
Hanson, F. W., 32, Southgate, Halifax	2
Hanson, J., 14, Hornby Terrace, Halifax	1
Hanson, M., 26, Market Street, Halifax	8
Hanson, S., 14, Cecil Street, King Cross	1
Hanson, T., 266, Gibbet Street, Halifax	1
Hanson, T. W., Southgate, Halifax	2
Hanson, W., 24, Gladstone Buildings, Sowerby Bridge	1
Hardaker, Mrs., Brookhouse, Mixenden	1
Hardaker, Springfield, Holmfield	2
Hardy, Mrs., 11, Ashfield Terrace, Greetland	1
Harris, H., 28, Spring Hall Place, Halifax	1
Harrison, Miss Lily, Black Castle Farm, Bradshaw	1
Harrison, Elizabeth, 10, Westfield Place, Halifax	2
Harrison, A., 147, Claremount Road, Halifax	1
Harrison, C. E., 63, Bath Place, Halifax	1
Hartley, Miss, 226, Hanson Lane, Halifax	1
Hartley, A., 13, Fern Street, Boothtown	1
Hartley, Fk., Prospect Villa, Ovenden	1
Hartley, G. T., Scar Bottom, Mytholmroyd	1
Hartley, John, 11, Sea View Avenue, Liscard	2
Hartley, J. H., "Mayfield," Beechwood Road, Illingworth	1
Hartley, W., 14, Thorn View, Boothtown	1
Harvey, B. N., Grove House, Luddenden Foot	1
Harwood, A., Rose Place, Luddenden Foot	1
Harwood, F. H., Calder Vale, Bedhampton Road, Portsmouth	1
Harwood, H. W., 17, Westbury Place, West End, Halifax	1
Harwood, J., Crown Street, Halifax	2
Harwood, W., 10, Oxford Street, Sowerby Bridge	1
Hawkridge, John, High Lees, Moor End, Mount Tabor	1
Hayhurst, R. H., 36, Clapton Mount, Halifax	2
Hayward, F., Mixenden	1
Heap, Miss Mary, 6, Sutcliffe Street, Pellon	1
Heap, F., 34, All Souls' Road, Halifax	1
Heap, J., Mount Zion Chapel House, Ovenden	2
Heap, J. T., Wangarie, New Zealand	1
Heap, James Thomas, Kamo, Auckland, New Zealand	1
Heap, T., Sowerby	1
Hebden Bridge Co-operative Society, Educational Dept.	1
Hebblethwaite, J., 11, Eldroth Road, Halifax	1
Halliwell, Mrs., 11, Hollins Lane, Sowerby Bridge	1
Halliwell, Mrs., Lower Saltonstall, Mount Tabor	1
Helliwell, Mrs., 36, Wadsworth Street, Halifax	1
Helliwell, Mrs. L., 1a, Buttress, Luddenden	1
Helliwell, Hilda, Church Street, Haworth	1
Helliwell, H., Bent Close, Cragg Vale	1
Helliwell, H. W., Banks-fields Road, Mytholmroyd	1
Helliwell, J. W., Hollin Hey Farm, Mytholmroyd	1
Helliwell, T. N., Laurel Bank, Luddenden	2
Helliwell, W., Holly Grove, Mount Tabor	1

	VOLS.
Hellowell, Miss, Victoria Buildings, Mill Bank, Triangle	1
Hemingway, E., 41a, Crown Street, Halifax	1
Henry, 27, Hall Street, Halifax	1
Hepworth, Miss, 47, Bath Place, Halifax	1
Hesselden, Mrs., 3, Thorney Lane, Midgley	1
Hesselden, J., 281, Queen's Road, Halifax	1
Hesselden, J. W., 3, Thorney Lane, Midgley	1
Hewitt, Miss Edith, Croft Villa, Luddenden	1
Hey, B., Little Haworth Farm, Smallbridge, Rochdale	1
Heydon, A. E., 12, Moor End, Mount Tabor	1
Heydon, C. E., 13, Ovenden Road Terrace, Halifax	1
Higham, J. S., M.P., Birkdale, Southport	12
Hill, Arthur, "Studleigh," Skircoat Green Road, Halifax	1
Hill, R., 28, Birks Hall Terrace, Halifax	1
Hill, Sutcliffe, 2, Bennett Street, Trooper Lane, Halifax	1
Hinchcliffe, A., Rhodes Street, Halifax	1
Hinchliffe, F., Scar Cottage, Stainland	1
Hinchliffe, W. A. Simpson-, J.P., Cragg Hall, Mytholmroyd	1
Hind, J., 28, Stoodley Terrace, Warley Road, Halifax	1
Hindle, Siddal	1
Hindle, H., 25, Kell, Wainstalls	1
Hirst, Mrs. 3, Grandsmere Place, Halifax	1
Hirst, Arnold, 120, South Bank, Lister Lane, Halifax	1
Hirst, C., 9, Gibb Lane, Ovenden Wood	1
Hirst, Herbert, The School House, Wainstalls	2
Hirst, J. E., 38, Baines Street, Halifax	1
Hirst, L., 30, Hopwood Lane	1
Hirst, Rowland R., 116, South Bank, Lister Lane, Halifax	1
Hirst, Vernon, Thornton Street, King Cross	1
Hirst, W., Crossfield, Stainland	1
Hitchen, Mrs., Claypits, Soyland	1
Hitchen, David, 236, Hanson Lane, Halifax	1
Hitchen, H., Bethel Terrace, Sparkhouse Lane, Norland	1
Hitchen, Hartley, 65, Dyson Road, Halifax	1
Hitchen, J. W., Ivy House, Mill Bank	1
Hobson, B., Holly Grove, Mount Tabor	1
Hodgson, Mrs. G. H., Swift Street, Salterhebble	2
Hodgson, Miss E., 1, Maple Street, Fenton Road, Halifax	1
Hodgson, Salterhebble	2
Hodgson, A. B., Auckland, New Zealand	1
Hodgson, C., 23, Bacup Road, Rawtenstall	1
Hodgson, Dr. J. F., Trafalgar House, Halifax	1
Hodgson, J. W., The Hollins, Triangle	1
Holden, M., 294, Pellon Lane, Halifax	2
Holdsworth, Miss, 16, Clay Street, Hanson Lane, Halifax	1
Holdsworth, Black Boy Farm, Shibden	2
Holdsworth, 31, York Crescent, Halifax	1
Holdsworth, J., 20, Alexander Street, Claremount, Halifax	1
Holdsworth, J. L., 15, Diamond Terrace, Halifax	1
Holgate, R., Greenwood Street, Halifax	1
Holland, Ivy House, Ripponden	1
Holland, J. W., 17, Glen Terrace, Halifax	1
Hollas, A., 51, Richardshaw Lane, Pudsey	1
Hollas, F., 22, Market Street, Halifax	1
Hollas, H. A., Parkin Hall, Triangle	1
Hollins, Miss G., 28, Ashwell Road, Heaton	1
Holmes, Mrs., Shepherd's Rest, New Barton, Sowerby	1
Holmes, A., 24, Cromwell Terrace, Halifax	1
Holmes, E., 91, High Utley, Keighley	1
Holmes, Geo., Assistant Overseer, Shaw, Oxenhope	1
Holmes, H., Savile Crescent, Halifax	1
Holmes, L. M., 9, Sladdin Street, Boothtown	1
Holroyd, Mrs., 3, Grandsmere Place, Halifax	1
Holroyd, Mrs. E., Lower Wormald, Rishworth	1
Holroyd, Mrs. J., New Barn, Rishworth	1
Holroyd, Tenterfield House, Northowram	1
Holroyd, 106, West Street, Sowerby Bridge	1
Holroyd, J. W., 6, St. Augustine's Terrace, Halifax	1
Holroyde, B., Ryburn Cottage, Sowerby Bridge	1
Holroyde, W. E., 73, Park View, Tuel Lane, Sowerby Bridge	1
Holt, J., Scarr Head, Sowerby Bridge	1
Hopkinson, J., Bankfield, Ripponden	1
Horner, Miss, Portland Place, Halifax	1
Horner, G., 16, Charles Street, Sowerby Bridge	1
Horner, Willie, Whitehouse, Waltroyd, Wheatley	1
Horobin, J. D., 6, Waterhouse Street, Halifax	1
Horsfall, Miss, E. A., 5, Buttress, Luddenden	1
Horsfall, C., 25, Gladstone Road, Halifax	1
Horsfall, E., Elmfield Terrace, Halifax	1
Horsfall, H., 13, Ovenden Road, Halifax	1
Horsfall, J. E., 4, Harley Street, Todmorden	1
Horsfall, M., 5, Buttress, Luddenden	1
Horsfall, Willie, St. Catherine's, Manor Heath Road, Halifax	1
Horsfield, Miss E., 10, Luddenden Lane, Luddenden Foot	1
Horsfield, H., 1, Lower Slack, Wainstalls	1
Horsfield, J., Luddenden Lane, Luddenden Foot	1
Horsefield, J. S., Wood Bank, Luddenden Foot	1
Houseman, F., 197, Walton Lane, Walton, Liverpool	1
Houseman, H., 30, Malton Street, Boothtown	1
Howard, T., Oakroyd, Manningham, Bradford	1
Howarth, Ethel A., Hodges Street, Park Road, Wigan	1
Howarth, Egbert, Springfield, Midgley	1
Howarth, E., Woodville, Cragg Vale	1
Howarth, G., Laurel Bank, Holmfield	1
Howarth, H., Great House, Midgley	1
Howarth, I., 75, Rochdale Road, Ripponden	1
Howarth, J. L., 3, Trooper Lane, Halifax	1
Howarth, N., Thorney Lane, Midgley	1
Howarth, R. H., 13, Wharf, Sowerby Bridge	1
Howes, A., Crow Wood Cottage, Sowerby Bridge	2
Hoyle, 42, Grosvenor Terrace, Halifax	1
Hoyle, Albert, 5, Bond Street, Denholme	2
Hoyle, C., 29, Gladstone Road, Halifax	1
Hoyle, Ernest, 4, Ashville Street, Lee Mount	1
Hoyle, J., Cross Roads, Wainstalls	1
Hoyle, J., 5, Gibb Lane, Ovenden Wood	1
Hoyle, J. E., Slaney Street, Oakengate, Wellington, Salop	1
Hoyle, J., Rose Villa, Brighouse	1
Hoyle, L., Reign Farm, Mount Tabor	1
Hoyle, M., 6, Commercial Street, Queensbury	1
Hoyle, P., Back Slode, Mount Tabor	1
Hoyle, T., Rushton Hill, Pellon	3
Hoyle, Thos., Savile Royd, Halifax	2
Hoyle, W., 9, Arundel Street, Halifax	1
Hudson, A., Reservoir House, Ogden	1
Hunsworth, Miss, Elmfield Terrace, Halifax	1
Huntriss, Ed., West Field, Halifax	1
Hutley, Rev. G., Settle	1
Hutchinson, G., Bar House, Stanbury	1
Ingham, Miss Daisy,	1
Ingham, Daniel, 44, Arden Road, Halifax	1
Ingham, P. C., Mattematta, Auckland, New Zealand	1
Ingham, W., 34, Booth, Luddenden	1
Ingham, W., Post Office, Stanbury	1
Ingham, W., 6, Tennyson Street, Lee Mount	1
Inman, W. J., 50, Thomas Street South, Halifax	1
Irvine, E., High Lea Green, Luddenden Foot	1
Irvin, T., Clough, Sowerby	1
Jackson, Health Dept., Town Hall, Halifax	1
Jacobs, V., 7, Trafalgar Row, King Cross	1
Jagger, Miss, Ambler Thorn	2
Jagger, M., 18, Belle Vue, Shelf	1
Johnson, Mrs., 17, Ripon Street, Halifax	1
Johnson, E., 346, Gibbet Street, Halifax	1
Johnson, F., 9, Thornton Street, Halifax	1
Johnson, H., 29, Dyson Road, Halifax	1
Johnson, H., Mixenden Lane Ends, Halifax	1
Johnson, H., North View, Stretchgate Lane, Halifax	1
Johnson, T., 29, Dyson Road, Halifax	1
Johnson, T., School House, Sowerby	1
Jones, E. A., 12, Wallace Street, Halifax	1
Jones, T. H., 13, Waterhouse Street, Halifax	1

LIST OF SUBSCRIBERS.—*Continued.*

	VOLS.
Jowett, A., 6, Bath Place, Woodside, Halifax	1
Jowett, A., Withins Clough, Cragg Vale	1
Joy, C., Beatrice Street, Oxenhope	1
Kay, E., Hopwood Lane, Halifax	1
Kay, W., Prospect Terrace, Southowram	1
Keighley, 97, Savile Park Road, Halifax	1
Keighley Public Library	2
Kemp, L. E., 5, Lumb Terrace, Wainstalls	3
Kendall, H. P., 1, Beech Villas, Sowerby Bridge	1
Kendall, T., 88, Gibraltar Road, Halifax	1
Kennedy, E. N., 4, Westfield Place, Halifax	1
Kenyon, Mrs., 43, Park Place, Halifax	1
Kenyon, E., 4, Conway Street, Halifax	1
Kergon, G. C., 57, Hanson Lane, Halifax	1
Kerr, W., Lower Shaw Booth, Mount Tabor	1
Kershaw, F., 32, Town Hall Street, Sowerby Bridge	1
Kershaw, N., Bleak House, Cross Roads, Keighley	1
Kilburn, T. W., 69, Rochdale Road, Ripponden	1
King, H. J., 14, Aspley Terrace, Halifax	1
Kinsley, Albert, R.I., 2, Corinne Road, Tufnell Park, London	1
Kirkbride, J., Field House, Wainstalls	1
Kitching, J., 3, Norfolk Mount, Halifax	1
Kitchen, Miss R., Rhena House, Bridlington	1
Knight, J., 7, Hermon Grove, Halifax	1
Knight, Jno. W., 19, Sefton Terrace, Halifax	2
Knowles, Miss Florence M., 20, Brinton Terrace, Halifax	1
Knowles, W., 74a, Wakefield Road, Sowerby Bridge	1
Lant, G., 189, Gibbet Street, Halifax	1
Lassey, Mrs., Ivy House, Norton, Doncaster	3
Lassey, M., 1, Dowker's Street, King Cross	2
Lawrence, J. & Sons, 67, St. James's Road, Halifax	3
Lawson, H., The Lodge, Bermerside	1
Laycock, John, Box 91, North Tonawanda, N.Y., U.S.A.	2
Laycock, J. W., 87, Waverley Road, Bradford	1
Laycock, Wm., Braithwaite, Keighley	1
Leach, Mrs., Eton Street, Halifax	1
Lee, Mr. A., West End, Queensbury	1
Lees, E., Carlton Terrace, Halifax	1
Lees, F., 1, Ripley Terrace, Luddenden Foot	1
Lees, J., 3, Cliffe Terrace, Friendly	1
Lees, J. W., 14, Colin Street, Halifax	1
Lees, Maurice, Meadow Dairy Co., Ltd., Commercial Street, Rothwell, nr. Leeds	1
Lees, W., 9, Bolton Brow, Sowerby Bridge	1
Leviston, Mrs., Waggon & Horses, Moorside, Oldham	1
Leviston, S., Waggon & Horses, Moorside, Oldham	1
Levitt, G. H., 37, East View, Lee Mount	1
Lightazles Mutual Class, Ripponden	1
Lingard, W. B., 194, Pellon Lane, Halifax	3
Lister, Mrs., 1, St. John Street, Halifax	1
Lister, D., 5, Carlisle Street, Pellon	1
Lister, J. Norman, First Avenue, Halifax	1
Lister, W., 31, New Road, Halifax	1
Lockwood, H., 90, Hartley Street, Halifax	1
Lofthouse, B., Moorfield Lodge, Wainstalls	1
Lomas, John, 83, Salterhebble Hill	1
Longbottom, Mrs. W., Gibb Farm, Ovenden Wood	2
Longbottom, 20, Town Hall Street, Sowerby Bridge	1
Longbottom, A., 98, Haigh Street, Halifax	1
Longbottom, H., 17, Handel Street, Hopwood Lane, Halifax	2
Longbottom, J., 11, Midgley Road, Mytholmroyd	1
Longbottom, J. H., 25, Springfield Terrace, Somerset Road, Huddersfield	1
Longbottom, J. W., Pellon Farm, Halifax	1
Longbottom, Tom, Savile Heath, Meadowfield Road, Bridlington	1
Lonsdale, Miss L., 13, Gladstone Road, Halifax	1
Lonsdale, Henry, 5, Swires Road, Halifax	1
Lord, A., 222, Pellon Lane, Halifax	1
Lord, A. E., Brighton Grove, Pellon Lane, Halifax	1
Lord, F., 29, Wharf Street, Sowerby Bridge	1
Lord, H., 42, Kliffen Place, Halifax	1

	VOLS.
Lord, Wm., 29, New Bank, Halifax	1
Loryman, Miss, 13, Mayfield Grove, Halifax	1
Lumb, Mrs., Duke Street North, Charlestown, Halifax	1
Lumb, Mrs., 7, Greenwood's Cottages, Turvin, Mytholmroyd	1
Lumb, Mrs., 25, Moor End, Mount Tabor	1
Lumb, Mrs. D., Mirey Lane, Sowerby	1
Lumb, Mrs. R. T., 203, Gibbet Street, Halifax	1
Lumb, Miss E., Chapel House, Moor End	1
Lumb, Francis L., 7, Chestnut Street, Parkinson Lane	1
Lumb, Miss L., 16, Abbott's Terrace, Halifax	1
Lumb, Miss N., Dowry Farm, Ripponden	4
Lumb, A., 6, Bethel Street, Lee Mount	1
Lumb, A., 9, Willow Terrace, Sowerby Bridge	1
Lumb, A., 24, Boy Lane, Wheatley	1
Lumb, Carl Johnson, 203, Gibbet Street, Halifax	1
Lumb, Edwin, 34, Mitchell Street, Sowerby Bridge	1
Lumb, F., 24, Mayfield Grove, Halifax	1
Lumb, H., Slough, Bucks.	1
Lumb, J. H., 32, Undercliffe Terrace, Scar Bottom	1
Lumb, L., B.A., 34, Wallace Street, Halifax	1
Lumb, R., 85, Rochdale Road, Ripponden	1
Lumb, W., Essex Street, Halifax	1
Lumb, Wm., 10, Thompson Terrace, King Cross	1
Lunn, B., 24, South Darley Street, Halifax	1
Lyon, M., St. Luke's Hospital, Halifax	1
Macaulay, Dr., Benbecula, Queen's Road, Halifax	1
Mackie, W., 23, Waterhouse Street, Halifax	1
Magson, W., Waterhouse Street, Halifax	1
Mallinson, J. E., Marton Street, Lytham	1
Mallinson, M. H., 121, Wheler Street, Higher Openshaw, Manchester	1
Mann, Miss H., 24, Moor End, Mount Tabor	1
Mann, L., Chapel House, Mount Tabor	2
Mann, S., 55, King's Road, Prestwich, Manchester	1
Mann, W., 22, Charlesworth Grove, Pellon	2
Mann, W., 9, Osborne Terrace, Luddenden Foot	1
Mansfield, Warley View, Highroad Well, Halifax	1
Mansfield, G., 55, Wheatley Lane, Lee Mount	1
Mansley, E. J., 14, Nelson Street, Old Causeway, Halifax	1
Marchbank, Miss E., Horton Croft, Stanbury	1
Marriott, R. W., Shibden, Halifax	1
Marsden, A., 13, All Souls' Terrace, Halifax	1
Marsden, Fk., 38, St. Mary's Street, Halifax	1
Marsden, W., 43, Horley Green Road, Halifax	1
Marshall, M. G., 23, West Street, Sowerby Bridge	1
Marshall, T., 28, Cobden Street, Halifax	1
Marshall, W., Westcroft Farm, Northowram	3
Marsland, E., Heather Bank, Mount Tabor	1
Marsland, F., Kiln House Lodge, Luddenden	1
Marsland, F. W., 7, Delph Mount, Leeds	1
Marsland, John, New Bank, Halifax	1
Marsland, J., 12, Berry's Court, New Bank	1
Marsland, V., 194, Queen's Road, Halifax	1
Marsland, W., 19, Rhondda Place, Gibraltar Road, Halifax	1
Martin, Mrs., Springfield, Oxenhope	1
Maude, H., 6, Rosebery Terrace, Pellon Lane, Halifax	1
Maude, Walter, 12, Cheapside, Halifax	1
Maude, W., 18, Victoria Terrace, Halifax	1
Maudsley, Mrs., 17, Mixenden Stones, Mixenden	1
Mawson, T., Commercial Buildings, Oakenshaw	1
McGowan, Miss E., 26, Heath Crescent, Halifax	1
McIntosh, Miss, Winter Neb, Luddenden Foot	1
McManus, W., 4, Newland Gate, Warley	1
Meadowcroft, Wm. H., 94, Crowford Street, Newton Heath, Manchester	1
Meadowcroft, W., 12, Gladstone Building, Mytholmroyd	1
Mellor, Amelia A, 142, Horsedge Street, Oldham	1
Mellor, H., Manchester and Liverpool District Bank, Manchester	1
Mellor, J., Ripponden	2
Mellor, Robert C., 89, Killinghall Road, Bradford	1
Merritt, M. A., 44, Emscote Avenue, Halifax	1
Metcalfe, G., 13, Salisbury Place, Akroydon	1
Metcalfe, J., 45, Savile Park Street, Halifax	1
Middleton, E., Cross Roads, Keighley	1

	VOLS.
Midgley, Mrs., 310, Hopwood Lane, Halifax	1
Midgley, Mrs. G. M., Albert Road, Pellon	1
Midgley, Mrs. H., 4, Grove Street, Ovenden	1
Midgley, Miss I., 12, Regent Road, Blackpool	2
Midgley, Miss R., 16, Thorney Lane, Midgley	1
Midgley, A., 329, Queen's Road, Halifax	1
Midgley, Albert, 37, Holly Grove, Parkinson Lane, Halifax	1
Midgley, E., 17, First Avenue, Halifax	1
Midgley, J. W., 442, Silver Grove, Utley, Keighley	1
Midgley, M., Booth Farm, Luddenden	1
Midgley, Walter, Fern Cottage, Halifax	1
Mill Bank Working Men's Club, Triangle	1
Miller, Fair View Terrace, Lee Mount	1
Milligan, J., 2, Hanson Lane, Halifax	1
Milner, Mrs. J., 256, Crescent Street, Jamestown, New York, U.S.A.	1
Milnes, J., 164, Gibbet Street, Halifax	1
Mitchell, 9, Mayfield Mount, Halifax	1
Mitchell, Mrs., 22, Baines Street, Halifax	1
Mitchell, Miss, Ainley House, Illingworth	1
Mitchell, A., Beech Royd, Illingworth	1
Mitchell, A. H., 10, Corporation Street, Halifax	1
Mitchell, C. H., Ivy House, Triangle	1
Mitchell, D., Bell Hall, Halifax	1
Mitchell, D. H., Hairini, Te Awamutu, New Zealand	1
Mitchell, E., Bradshaw, Halifax	1
Mitchell, J., 11, Ladywood Terrace, Pellon Lane, Halifax	2
Mitchell, J., 3, Walton Buildings, Foundry Street, Ovenden	1
Mitchell, John, Fountain Street, Halifax	1
Mitchell, J. W., 20, Wallace Street, Kingston, Halifax	1
Mitchell, W. H. Gordon Bank, Midgley	1
Moorcroft, Lee Mount	1
Moore, A., Peel Buildings, Gildersome	1
Moore, B., Forest Cottage Farm, Wheatley	2
Moore, F., Arrow-Butt Lee, Luddenden Dean	2
Moore, G. H., Pellon Lane, Halifax	1
Moore, J., 78, King Cross Street, Halifax	1
Moore, J., Hob Hill, Stanbury	1
Moore, Nathan, Ferncy Lee, Luddenden Dean	1
Moore, Wm., 15, Cross Hills, Greetland	1
Moore, W., Prospect View, Ovenden	1
Moorhouse, Louisa, 10, Osborne Terrace, Luddenden Foot	1
Moorhouse, J., 18, Hope Hall Terrace, Halifax	2
Moorhouse, W. A., 9, Kingston Street, Halifax	1
Morecroft, 5, Tennyson Street, Lee Mount	1
Morley, W. H., The Wells, Halifax	1
Mortimer, E., Silver Street, Halifax	3
Morton, A. E., 1, Coronation Street, Greetland	1
Morton, H., 9, Byron Street, Sowerby Bridge	1
Moss, Rich. A., Dicconson Street, Wigan	1
Mozley, J., Portland Street, Haworth	1
Murgatroyd, Mrs., 4, Holme House, Mount Tabor	1
Murgatroyd, Bloomergate, Midgley	1
Murgatroyd, E., Horne Street, Halifax	1
Murgatroyd, F. W., Clermont, Greenroyd, Halifax	1
Murgatroyd, H., 26, Warley Grove, Halifax	1
Murgatroyd, J., 412, Graves Street, Bridgeland, Calgary, Canada	2
Murgatroyd, L., 3, Stocks Lane, Luddenden	1
Murgatroyd, S., Dick Ing, Old Town, Hebden Bridge	1
Murgatroyd, T., 63 Market Street, Watford, Herts.	3
Murgatroyd, T., Wave Crest, Bispham, Blackpool	1
Murgatroyd, W., 15, Haydn Street, Halifax	1
Murgatroyd, W. H., Rough Hall, Wainstalls	1
Mulvannah, J. E., Box 193, Greystone, R.I., U.S.A.	2
Naylor, Woodside Terrace, Halifax	1
Naylor, A., 37, Cavendish Terrace, Gibbet Street, Halifax	2
Naylor, A. E., Northowram	1
Naylor, H., 4, Stoney Lane, Ovenden Road, Halifax	1
Naylor, J. W., 26, Third Avenue, Halifax	1
Naylor, R. S., Lane Side, Luddenden Foot	1
Naylor, T., Stanningley Green, Mixenden	1
Nelson, T., 54, Baines Street, Halifax	1
Nettleship, W., Clapton Avenue, Halifax	1
Nettleton, Miss B., Jessamine Terrace, King Cross,	1
Newell, J. A., 88, Mytholmes Lane, Haworth	1
Newton, L., 9, Luddenden Lane, Luddenden Foot	1
Nicholl, Mrs., Commercial Street, Halifax	1
Nicholl, Mrs. W. H., 1, Shelf Moor Road, nr. Halifax	1
Nichol, 25, Harrow Street, Halifax	1
Nicholl, A., 52, Douglas Street, Boothtown	1
Nicholl, C., 7, Rose Street, Hopwood Lane, Halifax	1
Nicholl, James, Post Office, Sowerby	1
Nicholl, J. B., 2, Woodside Crescent, Halifax	2
Nixon, Wm., 31, Trinity Crescent, Edinbro'.	1
No name (per M. Hanson, 26, Market Street, Halifax)	2
No name (per Maiden, Hebden Bridge)	1
No name (per E. Park & Son, Stainland)	2
No name (per Pickard, 18, Lee Bridge, Halifax)	1
No name (per C. H. Pickles, Huddersfield)	1
No name (per Walton, Cragg Vale)	1
Noble, J. W., 24, Woodside Terrace, Halifax	1
Noble, M., 30, Victoria Terrace, West Vale	1
Normanton, 16, Emscote Place, Halifax	1
Normington, Miss E., 152, Boothtown Road, Halifax	2
Normington, E., 15, Lowfield Street, Manchester Road, Bradford	1
Nutter, A. C., 11, Hammond Street, Halifax	1
Nutton, J. H., 84, Pear Street, Halifax	1
Oates, J. H., Royd House, Lightcliffe	1
Oddy, C., New Bank, Halifax	1
Ogden, Mabel, 35, High Street, Luddenden	2
Ogden, Bentley, 200, Browroot Gate, Cote Hill	1
Ogden, H., 4, Lombard Street, King Cross	1
Oldfield, Miss, Greenwood Cottage, Turvin, Cragg Vale	1
Oldfield, H., Ford Hill, Ambler Thorn	1
Oswin, Trinity House, Blackwall, Halifax	1
Ovenden Naturalists' Society	1
Oyston, Miss, Gomersal	1
Palfreyman, Miss, Rose Villa, Kilnhurst, Nr. Rotherham	1
Park, J. T., Stainland	1
Park, T., Victoria Road, Elland	1
Park, W., Beestones, Stainland	1
Parker, Miss, Hoyle House, Sowerby Bridge	1
Parker, Jas., M.P., 22, Salisbury Place, Halifax	1
Parker, John, Widdop Gate, Nr. Hebden Bridge	1
Parker, J. W., Wainsgate, Hebden Bridge	1
Parker, T., Lyndene, Halifax	2
Parker, W., Holderness Farm, Cragg Vale	1
Parkinson, B., Lee Mount, Halifax	1
Patchett, A., 26, Eldon Place, Halifax	1
Patchett, R., 24, High Street, Luddenden	1
Patchett, S., Bank House, Mount Tabor	1
Patchett, T., Winn Street, Halifax	1
Patrick, E., 4, Goit Side, Luddenden	1
Pawson, Arthur, Oxenhope	1
Payne, J., 17, Melville Place, Halifax	1
Pearson, A., 4, Naylor Street, Halifax	1
Peel, J. D., Church Street, Elland	1
Perry, A., 19, Savile Park, Halifax	1
Pickles, Pecket Well, Hebden Bridge	1
Pickles, 38, Edward Street, Sowerby Bridge	1
Pickles, F., 9, White Houses, Mytholmroyd	1
Pickles, G., 5, Devon Street, Halifax	1
Pickles, G. E., 51, Wheatley Lane, Halifax	1
Pickles, G., Nursery Lane, Ovenden	1
Pickles, J., Crimsworth	1
Pickles, J., West Lane, Haworth	1
Pickles, J. W., 40, Bromham Road, Bedford	2
Pickles, P., 74, Rochdale Road, Halifax	3
Pickles, Thos., Turn Lee, Luddenden Foot	2
Pickles, T. H., Nutclough, Hebden Bridge	1
Pickles, W., Gad's Hill, Sowerby	1
Pickles, W. H., 29, Regent Street, New Scarbro', Wakefield	1
Pighills, John Henry, Post Office, Oxenhope	1
Plat, G., Jack Royd, Wheatley	1

	VOLS.
Pogson, M., Ambler Thorn, nr. Halifax	1
Pollard, B., Broad Street, Halifax	1
Pollard, L., 2, Goit Side, Luddenden	1
Pollick, W. H., 1, Unity Terrace, Halifax	1
Potterton, Mrs. E., Coggeshall, Essex	1
Pratley, G., 6, Cross Rhodes Street, Halifax	1
Priestley, Mrs., 15, S. Larchmont, Greystone, R.I., U.S.A.	1
Priestley, Miss, 75, Crossley Terrace, Halifax	1
Priestley, F., 53, Orange Terrace, Greetland	1
Priestley, Hy., 96, Industrial Road, Sowerby Bridge	1
Priestley, J., Dean House, Luddenden	1
Priestley, J., Edward Street, Sowerby Bridge	1
Priestley, J. W., 9, Mapperley Street, Sherwood, Nottingham	1
Priestley, L. E., 5, Park Road, Halifax	3
Priestley, T. H., 43, Clapton Avenue, Halifax	1
Priestley, W. H., 8, Batley Street, Lee Mount, Halifax	1
Prior, Miss Elizabeth A., 4, Ripley Terrace, Luddenden Foot	1
Proctor, Mrs., 7, Westfield Lane, Idle	1
Prudence, W. J., 143, Huddersfield Road, Halifax	1
Pulman, A., 40, Hopwood Lane, Halifax	1
Quarmby, J., Summerfield, Stainland	1
Radcliffe, E., 8a, King Street, Halifax	1
Radcliffe, J., 11, Bell Hall Terrace, Halifax	2
Radcliffe, M. E., 21, West Street, Sowerby Bridge	1
Raistrick, S., The Tannery, Lister Mill, Haworth	1
Ramsden, Mrs. Alfred, Holmwood, Greenroyd, Halifax	1
Ramsden, Mrs. T., 19, Spring Grove, Newstead, Halifax	1
Ramsden, Miss, 1, Lee Mount Road, Halifax	1
Ramsden, C., The Gables, Halifax	2
Ramsden, D., 9, Handel Street, Hopwood Lane, Halifax	1
Ramsden, J. W., 19, Hermon Avenue, Halifax	1
Ramsden, S., Hightown Heights, Liversedge	3
Rankin, W. M., M.Sc., B.Sc., Technical College, Bournemouth	1
Raper, Rev. J. W., The Manse, Oakworth	1
Ratcliffe, Miss, West View, Oxenhope	1
Ratcliffe, Mary, Green Houses, Midgley, Luddenden Foot	1
Ratcliffe, A., 35, Kell Fold, Wainstalls	1
Ratcliffe, H., South View, Mount Tabor	1
Ratcliffe, J., 38, Clifby, Pellon	1
Ratcliffe, T., 36, Clifby, Pellon	1
Raw, G., 44, Changegate, Haworth	1
Rawbon, Mrs., 31, Emscote Grove, Halifax	1
Rawbon, A. E., 119, Parkinson Lane, Halifax	1
Rawson, Mrs. E., 42, Wharf Street, Sowerby Bridge	1
Rawnsley, F., 31, Eton Street, Halifax	1
Rawnsley, Fk., 44, West End, Queensbury	1
Rawnsley, Howarth, Prior Terrace, Stainland	1
Rawnsley, J., 4, Stanley Street, Queen's Road, Halifax	1
Rawnsley, T., 31, Violet Street, Halifax	1
Raynor, Mrs., Birdcage, Halifax	1
Readyhough, J., 13, Perseverance Terrace, Halifax	1
Redman, Mrs. Percy, Withens, Arnside	1
Redman, John, Lower Baiting House, Alcomden, Wadsworth	3
Redman, T., Well Royd, Halifax	1
Redman, W., 12, Minnie Street, Haworth	1
Redman, W., 18, St. Stephen's Road, Bradford	1
Rhodes, C. T., 3, Commercial Street, Halifax	1
Rhodes, C., 49, New Crown Street, Halifax	1
Riddlesden, W., 20, New Delight, Boothtown	1
Rigg, E., West End, Queensbury	1
Rigg, H., 11, West End, Queensbury	1
Rigg, J. R., West End, Queensbury	1
Riley, Mrs., 28, New Lane, Siddal	1
Riley, Mrs., 5, Spring View, Luddenden Foot	1
Riley, Hey House, Ripponden	1
Riley, B., Ploughcroft Lane, Halifax	1
Riley, C., 33, Clapton Avenue, Halifax	1
Riley, F., Threadneedle Street, King Cross	1
Riley, Hervey, 40, Hollins Street, Triangle	1
Riley, J., 55, Stainland Road, West Vale	1
Riley, Coun. J. H., Elizabeth Street, Elland	1
Riley, J. H., 14, Willow Drive, Halifax	1
Riley, T. B., 4, Strawberry Gardens, Ogden	1
Ritchie, A., Bank Terrace, Luddenden	1
Roberts, Miss M., 61, Mount Tabor	1
Roberts, The Wells, Burnley Road, Halifax	1
Roberts, E., 33, St. Albans Avenue, Halifax	1
Roberts, G., 7, Woodside Terrace, Halifax	1
Roberts, Geo. Hy., The Wells, Burnley Road, Halifax	1
Roberts, P., Greystones, R.I., U.S.A.	1
Robertshaw, Mrs., 1, Cragg Road, Mytholmroyd	1
Robertshaw, Edwin, 1, St. Peter Street, Boothtown	1
Robertshaw, J. H., Lee Mount	1
Robertshaw, O., 37, Highfield Lane, Keighley	1
Robertshaw, W., 15, Hill Crest, Burnley Road, Sowerby Bridge	1
Robinson, Mrs., 23, West Royd, Mountain, Queensbury	1
Robinson, Miss, West Royd, Halifax	1
Robinson, Miss Bina, Hookset, New Hampshire, U.S.A.	1
Robinson, H., 7, Dale Street, Halifax	1
Robinson, H., 8, Raven Bank, Luddenden Foot	1
Robinson, T. A., 18, Abel Street, Pellon Lane, Halifax	1
Robinson, W. D., Banks View, Newcombe Street, Elland	1
Robson, Cyril, Holme House, Mount Tabor	1
Roper, F., North Parade, Halifax	1
Rothery, W., 62, Ripon Street, Halifax	1
Rothery, W., Timber Street, Halifax	1
Rowland, W. Bank House, Keighley	1
Rowley, T., Box 127, Centredale, Rhode Island, U.S.A.	2
Rusby, Mrs. Leonard, Wesley Place, Stradmore Road, Denholme	1
Rushworth, Mrs., 2, Friendly Street, Lee Mount	1
Rushworth, Miss M., 7, Green Hill Terrace, Halifax	1
Rushworth, H., Denfield, Wheatley	1
Rushworth, Jno., 77, Albany Road, Balby, Doncaster	1
Rushworth, J. I., 2, Brighton Street, Halifax	1
Rushworth, T., Roper Green, Wheatley	1
Ryle, Rev. M. F., Wesleyan Minister, Stainland	1
Ryley, J. A., 30, Russell Street, York	1
S, A. S., Sowerby Town	1
Sage, W. T., 123, Boothtown Road, Halifax	1
Sandall, W., Broadley Hall, Ovenden Wood	2
Savile, S., 41, King Cross, Halifax	1
Sawdon, J.R., 17, Commercial Street, Halifax	1
Scarborough, 197, Spring Hall Lane, Halifax	1
Schofield, James, Scotland, Midgley	1
Schofield, John, Scotland, Midgley	1
Schofield, J. V., South View, Sowerby Bridge	1
Schofield, Wm., South View, Sowerby Bridge	1
Schofield, W., 2, Tuel Lane, Sowerby Bridge	2
Scholefield, J., 30, Windsor Park, Fairfield, Buxton	1
Scholefield, R., 6, Water Hill, Friendly	1
Scholey, H. J., 14, Abbey Walk, Halifax	1
Schorfield, C. E., 308, Queen's Road, Halifax	1
Schorfield, John, 10, Tamworth Park, Mitcham Common, Surrey	1
Scott, Emma, Moor Close, Ambler Thorn, Halifax	1
Scott, A., 32, Charlesworth Terrace, Halifax	1
Scott, A., Shroggs Terrace, Halifax	1
Seed, A., 24, Elmfield Terrace, Halifax	1
Senior, A., 33, Spring Gardens, Mill Bank, Triangle	1
Sergeant, A. F., Gibbet Hill House, Halifax	1
Senior, Mrs. Ellen, Cook's Buildings, Sowerby Bridge	1
Seymour, Miss, Cross Royd, Barkisland	1
Seymour, G., 128, Queen's Road, Everton, Liverpool	1
Shackleton, Mrs., Cat i' th' Well Inn, Wainstalls	1
Shackleton, Mrs., Mount Tabor House, Mount Tabor	1
Shackleton, Miss A., Dean House, Luddenden	2

	VOLS.
Shackleton, F., St. Ann's House, Luddenden	2
Shackleton, H., 18, Warner Street, Haslingden	1
Sharp, Edwin, Linden Terrace, Whitehall, Hipperholme	1
Sharp, E., 338, Queen's Road, Halifax	1
Sharp, E., 9, Range Bank, Halifax	1
Sharp, J., 36, Summergate Place, Halifax	1
Sharp, L., Hermon Avenue, Halifax	1
Sharp, M., 63, Thomas Street South, Halifax	1
Sharp T., 4, Mount Terrace, Midgley, Luddenden Foot	1
Sharp, W., 50, Hanson Lane, Halifax	1
Sharp, W., 13, Knight Street, Halifax	1
Shaw, Mrs., 10, Duke Street, Mount Street, Halifax	1
Shaw, Mrs. J. E., 16, Craston Street, Beswick, Manchester	1
Shaw, Mary, 10, Langberries Avenue, Greystone, R.I., U.S.A.	1
Shaw, H., Hoyle Bank, Midgley, Luddenden Foot	1
Shaw, J. E., 44, Queen Street, Morecambe	1
Shaw, John, 4, Windsor Road, Hebden Bridge	1
Shaw, J. S., 6, Bancroft Terrace, Halifax	1
Shaw, S., 13, Upper Brunswick Street, Halifax	1
Shaw, T., 2, Sladdin Street, Boothtown	1
Sheard, Miss Mary, 3, Lumb Terrace, Wainstalls	1
Sheard, F., Carr View, Luddenden	1
Sheard, Herbert, 10, Thrum Hall Lane, Halifax	1
Sheard, S., 3, Calder Avenue, Pye Nest, Halifax	1
Sheard, S., 9, Fairfield Place, Halifax	1
Shepherd, W., Ambler Thorn	1
Shoesmith, W. C., 12, Savile Parade, Halifax	1
Shore, L., 46, Foxhall Road, Blackpool	2
Shulver, E., 12, Margaret Street, Halifax	1
Shuttleworth, Miss, Dyson Lane, Ripponden	2
Shuttleworth, Fred, West Lane, Haworth	2
Siddall, Mrs., 6, Thorn Bank, Mytholmroyd	1
Simpson, J., 117, Great Mersey Street, Liverpool	1
Skelton, Harry, Pellon	1
Smith, Mrs., Banksfields, Mytholmroyd	1
Smith, Mrs., Cragg View, Wadsworth, Hebden Bridge	1
Smith, Mrs., Far Laithe, Midgley	1
Smith, Mrs. B., 6, Siddal Street, Siddal	1
Smith, Mrs., 9, Lower Slack, Wainstalls	2
Smith, Mrs., 10, Rose Mount Terrace, Keighley	3
Smith, Mrs., Salterhebble	1
Smith, Mrs. T. E., 7, Cavendish Street, Keighley	1
Smith, Miss, 14, Cinderhills Lane, Siddal	1
Smith, Miss J., 8, Butts Green, Luddenden Foot	1
Smith, Miss S., Winters, Hebden Bridge	2
Smith, A., 56, Hare Street, Halifax	1
Smith, A., 2, Providence Row, Ovenden	1
Smith, A., Royal Oak Hotel, Haworth	1
Smith, C. W., 36, Devonshire Street, Keighley	1
Smith, F., 84, Hanson Lane, Halifax	1
Smith, F., Junction Inn, Charlestown Road, Halifax	1
Smith, F., Moor Bottom Farm, Wainstalls	1
Smith, F. W., Wycoller, Colne	1
Smith, G. P., Westcroft, Heath Avenue, Halifax	1
Smith, Hy., 9, Jessamine Terrace, Halifax	1
Smith, H., 4, Oak Villas, Charlestown, Hebden Bridge	1
Smith, J., Grove Street, Ovenden	1
Smith, J., 48, Mill Hey, Haworth	1
Smith, J., Upper Reap Hirst, Mount Tabor	1
Smith, J., 2, Upper Slack, Wainstalls	1
Smith, Joseph M., 12, Rose Bank, King Cross	1
Smith, P. H., 9, Hanover Street, Halifax	1
Smith, R. L., 73, High Street, Luddenden	1
Smith, S., Glenwells, Clover Hill, Halifax	1
Smith, S., 1, Sutcliffe's Buildings, Sowerby Bridge	1
Smith, Tom, Junction Inn, Charlestown Road, Halifax	1
Smith, Wm. H., 31, Gibbet Lane, Halifax	1
Smithies, Henry, Longriggin, Mount Tabor	1
Smithies, J., Yew Trees, Illingworth	1
Snowden, Mrs., Wheatley	1
Snowden, Cephas, Hebden Road, Haworth	1
Snowden, Ernest, Montreal, Canada	1
Snowden, S., Calder House, Mytholmroyd	1
Sowerby Bridge Public Library	1
Speight, S., Spring Farm, Warley Edge	1
Spencer, Mrs., Nab End Farm, Boothtown, Halifax	1
Spencer, Mrs., Scar Bottom, Halifax	1
Spencer, Miss, Illingworth	1
Spencer, 3, Dublin Street, King Cross	1
Spencer, C., 83, Pellon Lane, Halifax	1
Spencer, Fred N., 256, Symington Ave., Toronto, Ontario, Canada	1
Spencer, H. B., Heathfield, West Moors, nr. Wimborne, Dorset	1
Spencer, J., Coliseum, N.C. Line, Queensland	2
Spencer, W., 8, Higgin Chamber, Luddenden Foot	1
Spencer, W., Burnley Road, Luddenden Foot	2
Spruce, W. H., 424, Gibbet Street, Halifax	1
Square Church P.S.A., Halifax	110
Standeven, F., Station Road, Luddenden Foot	1
Standeven, T., 16, Egremont Terrace, Sowerby Bridge	1
Stansfield, Mr., Ramsden Wood, Ovenden Wood	2
Stansfield, E., 16, Baines Street, Pellon Lane, Halifax	1
Stead, J. J., Albert Cottage, Heckmondwike	1
Stead, W. H., 34, Cromwell Street, Halifax	1
Steele, E. A., 4, Heathfield Terrace, Halifax	1
Stockman, S. H., 2, Back Archer Street, Halifax	2
Stocks, Miss M., Mount Pleasant Farm, Cragg Vale	2
Stocks, J., 2, Chapel Street, Queensbury	1
Stocks, S., Hazelroyde, Halifax	1
Stokes, Miss K., 101, Hambalt Road, Clapham Park, London, S.W.	1
Stones Wesleyan M. I. S., Ripponden	1
Stopford, J., Pye Nest, Halifax	1
Story, Rev. T. W., M.A., The Rectory, Haworth	1
Stott, Mrs., Bradford	1
Stott, Miss E. A., Meadow View, Kilnhurst, Rotherham	1
Stott, J. W., 23, Providence Place, Luddenden	1
Stott, L., Ash Tree Farm, Mixenden	1
Stott, N., Mill Bank, Triangle	1
Stott, S. H., 69, Redcar Street, Castlereagh Road, Belfast	1
Stow, W., 27, Glen Terrace, Clover Hill, Halifax	2
Stuttard, J., 43, Thomas Street, Halifax	1
Sugden, J., 9, Upper Shaw Hill, Halifax	1
Summerscales, A., 31, Gibbet Street, Halifax	1
Summerskill, J., Warley Town Lane, Halifax	1
Sunderland, Mrs., 28, Broughton Street, Hebden Bridge	1
Sunderland, Mrs., 44, Long Row, Mount Tabor	1
Sunderland, Miss E., Noah's Ark, Cold Edge	1
Sunderland, A., 24, Gladstone Road, Halifax	1
Sunderland, E., Trinity Wesleyan Brotherhood	1
Sunderland, Harold, Dodge Holme Farm, Wheatley	1
Sunderland, J., Aire View, Skipton	1
Sunderland, J. H., Hollas Street, Gt. Grimsby	1
Sunderland, S., Fly Flat, Wainstalls	1
Sunderland, S., 5, South View, Halifax	1
Sunderland, S., 101, Spring Hall Lane, Halifax	1
Sunderland, T., 232, Hanson Lane, Halifax	1
Sunderland, W., 2, Hovingham Terrace, Leeds	1
Sunderland, Wm., 6, St. Alban's Ave., Halifax	1
Sutcliffe, Mrs., 25, Apple House Terrace, Luddenden	1
Sutcliffe, Mrs., Gad's Hill, Halifax	1
Sutcliffe, Mrs., 5, Randolph Street, All Souls' Road, Halifax	1
Sutcliffe, Misses, Old Chambers, Hebden Bridge.	1
Sutcliffe, Miss I., 129, Crown Terrace, Queen's Road, Halifax	1
Sutcliffe, Miss Louie, Mount Tabor, Halifax	1
Sutcliffe, Miss M. H., 4, Ringby Terrace, Boothtown	1
Sutcliffe, Misses M. H. & E., 6, Beckenham Place, Halifax	1
Sutcliffe, C., Upper Mile Cross, Halifax	1
Sutcliffe, Crowther, Gladstone Place, Ovenden	1
Sutcliffe, D., Law House, Hebden Bridge	1
Sutcliffe, D., Springfield Terrace, Midgley	1
Sutcliffe, D., Woodlesford, Pellon	1
Sutcliffe, E. W., 3, Myrtle Avenue, Holderness Road, Hull	1
Sutcliffe, F., 42, Salisbury Place, Akroydon, Halifax	1
Sutcliffe, F., Smith House Road, Lightcliffe	1
Sutcliffe, G., Perseverance Co-operative Society, Milnsbridge	2

VOLS.

Sutcliffe, Halliwell, Troutbeck, Linton-in-Craven, Skipton 2
Sutcliffe, H., 7, Otley Street, Hanson Lane, Halifax 1
Sutcliffe, H., 123, Springhall Lane, Halifax . 2
Sutcliffe, J., Albion House, Luddenden Foot . 1
Sutcliffe, J., New Longley, Norland 1
Sutcliffe, J., 21, Sowerby Street, Sowerby Bridge 2
Sutcliffe, J., 37, Westward Ho, Ovenden . . . 1
Sutcliffe, Joseph, Woodlesford, Pellon . . . 2
Sutcliffe, J. W., 15, Norman Street, Halifax . . 1
Sutcliffe, R., 14, Baines Street, Halifax 1
Sutcliffe, Richard, 15, Heptonstall Road, Hebden Bridge 1
Sutcliffe, T., 42, King Cross Street, Halifax . . 1
Sutcliffe, T., 583, Well Royd Crescent, Warley . 1
Sutcliffe, T., 123, Spring Hall Lane, Halifax . . 1
Sutcliffe. W., 12, Doncaster Street, Salterhebble 1
Sutcliffe, W., Holly Grove, Mount Tabor . . 1
Swaine, Jos., 3024, St. Claire Avenue, Cleveland, Ohio 1
Swaine, J. R., 1, Dunkirk Crescent, Halifax . . 1
Swaine, L., 4, Matlock Street, Lee Mount . . 1
Swift, 27, Clapton Avenue, Halifax 1
Swift, Geo., Cross Keys, King Cross Street, Halifax 1
Swift, G. F., 10, Birks Hall Terrace, Halifax . . 1
Swire, J., King Cross, Halifax 1
Sykes, Mrs., Green Royd, Mount Tabor . . . 1
Sykes, Mrs., 20, Hawthorn Terrace, Halifax . 1
Sykes, Miss, 53, Haugh Shaw Terrace, Halifax . 1
Sykes, B., Bell Hall Post Office, Halifax . . . 2
Sykes, E., Melrose Terrace, Elland 1
Sykes, J., 210, Rochdale Road, Greetland . . 1
Sykes, J., 39, Stretchgate Lane, Pellon . . . 1
Sykes, T., 5, William Street, West Vale . . . 2
Sykes, W., 131, Belle Vue Road, Leeds . . . 1

Tattersall, Mrs., Wainstalls House, Wainstalls . 1
Tattersall, D., Upper Reap Hirst, Mount Tabor 1
Tattersall, L., 4, Roydlands Terrace, Hipperholme 1
Tattersall, R., 4, Woodhead Terrace, Pellon . . 1
Tattersall, R., 3, Daisy Mount, Friendly . . . 1
Taylor, Mrs., 160, West End, Halifax 1
Taylor, Mrs. A., Rake Bank, Wheatley . . . 1
Taylor, Miss A., Guest House, Newlands, Keswick 1
Taylor, Arthur, New Grange Farm, Bradshaw . 1
Taylor, W., 20, South Darley Street, Halifax . 1
Taylor, W., 9, Leamington Avenue, Halifax . . 1
Teal, J. E., 29, Stoney Royd Terrace, Halifax . 1
Tempest, Mrs., Rough Nook, Haworth . . . 1
Tempest, J., 3, Little Street, Haworth . . . 1
Tetlaw, H., 25, Hanover Street, Halifax . . . 1
The Royd, Stainland 2
Thomas, Emily, Goose Clough Farm, Mixenden . 1
Thomas, A., Friendly, Sowerby Bridge . . . 1
Thomas, A. E., Middlesborough 1
Thomas, F., Stannary Hall, Halifax 1
Thomas, F. J., Green Edge, Wainstalls . . . 1
Thomas, H., Booth, Luddenden 1
Thomas, R., South View, Mount Tabor . . . 2
Thomas, W., Lane Top, Wadsworth 1
Thomas, W. H., 1, Clover Hill Terrace, Halifax . 1
Thomson, Mrs. Alexander, 19, Albert Terrace, King Cross 1
Thomson, A., 9, Albert Road, Halifax . . . 1
Thompson, A. Ernest, 8, All Souls' Terrace, Halifax 1
Thornsby, G., Upper Exley, Halifax 1
Thornton, Miss, Lower Pond, Warley 1
Thornton, H. H., 13, Summerville Terrace, Stanningley, Leeds 1
Thorp, Mrs. W., 6, Providence Place, Luddenden 1
Thorpe, Wallace Street, Hopwood Lane, Halifax 1
Thorpe, H., 3, Battinson Road, Halifax . . . 1
Thorpe, J., 2, Wallace Street, Halifax . . . 1
Thorpe, R., South View, Sowerby Bridge . . 1
Thurley, J. W. M., 58, High Street, Luddenden . 1
Thurley, W., Willow Mount, Sowerby Bridge . 1
Thwaite, J., 4, Blackwood Grove, Halifax . . 1
Tidswell, Miss, 4a, Haugh Shaw Road, Halifax . 1
Tidswell, F. E., 63, Northgate, Halifax . . . 1
Tidswell, Fred L., 5, Prince Street, Frances Street, Halifax 1

VOLS.

Timewell, S., 13, Hawthorn Terrace, Halifax . 1
Tindall, Leonard, 22, Lumb Brook, Northowram 1
Tolton, S. P., Ludhill Cottage, Southowram . . 1
Topham, H., 23, Spring Hall Place, Halifax . . 1
Topliss, Mrs. J., c/o Miss Dennett, 80, Bishopthorpe Road, York 1
Tordoff, Lewis, 11, St. Alban's Avenue, Halifax 1
Tordoff, S., 22, Glen Terrace, Halifax . . . 1
Town, Jas., 43, New Crown Street, Halifax . . 1
Town, Walter, 10, Greenroyd, Mount Tabor . 1
Townend, N. S., 18, Birks Hall Terrace, Halifax . 1
Townsend, W., Hadassah Street, Siddal . . . 1
Tozer, A., 10, Walnut Street, Halifax . . . 1
Trigg, W. B., Grove House, Haley Hill, Halifax . 1
Turner, Mrs. S., Lower Harper Road, Norland . 1
Turner, Miss M., Lower High Field, Mount Tabor 1
Turner, 3, Daisy Street, Halifax 1
Turner, D., 82, Edward Street, Sowerby Bridge . 1
Turner, J. Horsfall, Idle 1
Turner, J. H., Shelf, Bradford 1
Turner, J. H., 24, Thackray Street, Halifax . . 1
Turner, R., 297, Gibbet Street, Halifax . . . 2
Turner, W., 27, Mount Pellon, Halifax . . . 1
Turner, W. H., 46, Charlesworth Terrace, Halifax 2

Umpleby, Arthur, 5, West View, Boothtown . . 1
Uttley, Miss Alice, Far Broad Fold, Midgley . . 1
Uttley, E. 11, Keighley Road, Ovenden . . . 1

Varley, C. H., 6, All Souls' Terrace, Halifax . 1
Varley, F., 30, Stoodley Terrace, Halifax. . . 1
Varley, G. H., 49, Essex Street, Halifax . . . 1
Varley, J. E., 29, Hewitt Street, Hoole, Chester 1

Waddington, Miss A. M., 43, Heath Avenue, Providence, R.I., U.S.A. 1
Waddington, A., 29, Boston Street, Sowerby Bridge 1
Waddington, B. P., 19, Westbourne Street, Westwood, Oldham 1
Waddington, J., 2, Moor Bottom, Wainstalls . 1
Waddington, J., Tuel Lane, Sowerby Bridge . 1
Waddington, J. W., New Road, Mytholmroyd . 1
Waddington, T., 20, Gibson Street, Halifax . . 1
Wade, Mrs., 27, Milton Terrace, Halifax . . . 1
Wade, B., Cotefield House, Allerton, Bradford . 1
Wade C., Rhodes Street, Halifax 1
Wade, E., 27, Milton Terrace, Halifax . . . 4
Wade, F., High Lees, Moor End, Mount Tabor . 2
Wade, F., Market Street, Auckland 1
Wade, H. W., 25, Rhondda Place, West End, Halifax 1
Wade, John, 11, Hopwood Lane, Halifax . . 1
Wadsworth, Miss, 14, Jessamine Terrace, King Cross 1
Wadsworth, Miss C., Belmont, Sowerby Bridge 1
Wadsworth, A., Green Lane, West Vale . . . 1
Wadsworth, C., Woodcrest, Dudwell, Halifax . 1
Wadsworth, G. E., 15, Holly Grove, Halifax . 1
Wadsworth, G. P., Savile Grange, Halifax . . 1
Wadsworth, J., Glen View, Sowerby 1
Wadsworth, Wm., Farsides Farm, Queensbury 1
Wadsworth, W., North Parade, Halifax . . . 1
Wainwright, H., 8, Elland Lane, Elland . . . 1
Wakefield, A. B., 7, Lane Ends Terrace, Hipperholme 1
Wakefield, E. B., 7, Lane Ends Terrace, Hipperholme 1
Walker, Mrs. W., Grosvenor Place, Luddenden Foot 1
Walker, Miss Frances M., 11, Cavendish Terrace, Halifax 1
Walker, Miss I., Southfield, Loughboro', Leicestershire 1
Walker, D., Grange Terrace, Lightcliffe . . . 1
Walker, Denton, Heathfield House, Halifax . . 1
Walker, G., Bank Top Farm, Cragg Vale . . 3
Walker, T., 11, Carlton Street, Halifax . . . 1
Wall, Miss L., 28, The Crescent, Hipperholme . 1
Wall, Francis, Holme Lea, Oxenhope 1
Waller, A. T., Holywell Cottage, Skipton. . . 1
Walmsley, Mrs. R., 23, Westbury Place, Mile Cross Road, Halifax 1

VOLS.

Walmsley, Miss Mary, 6, Corbey Street, Huddersfield 1
Walmsley, E., 19, Stretchgate Lane, New Pellon 1
Walmsley, J. H., 118, Ovenden Road, Halifax . 1
Walsh, James, Portland Street, Halifax . . . 1
Walsh, J. H., 5, Clover Hill View, Halifax . . 1
Walsh, S., 2, Ivy House, Luddenden 1
Walsh, T., 25, Lister Lane, Halifax 1
Walton, D., Town Gate, Midgley 1
Walton, J., Langdale Street, Elland 1
Walton, J., 1, North Street, Haworth 1
Walton, W., 10, Woodhead Terrace, New Pellon. 1
Ward, Percy, 49, Crossley Hill, Salterhebble. . 1
Washington, G. N., 11a, Bond Street, Halifax . 1
Washington, J. E., 104, Albert View, Pellon . . 1
Waterhouse, P., Lee Monnt. 1
Waterhouse, T., Ellar Car Road, Cullingworth . 1
Waterworth, H., 7, Kingsley Place, Halifax . . 1
Watson, Mrs., Benns Lane, Luddenden . . . 2
Watson, Miss A., John Street, Oakworth . . . 1
Watson, D., 4, Albany Street, Trooper Lane, Halifax 1
Watson, H., 160, West End, Halifax 1
Watson, Harry, Friendly Inn, Stanbury . . . 1
Watson, J., Lumb House, Wainstalls. . . . 1
Watson, R. P., 19, Westgate, Halifax. . . . 1
Weatherhead, D., 55, Devonshire Street, Keighley 2
Webster, Mrs., E. A., 1, Mile Cross Road, Halifax 1
Webster, Mrs. L. M., 75, St. Mary's Grove, Chiswick, London 1
Webster, J., 3, Jammy Green, Holmfield . . . 1
Webster, S., 1, Ladywood Terrace, Halifax . . 1
Webster, O., Bank View, Luddenden Foot . . 1
Webster, Tom Beresford, 5, Winding Road, Halifax 1
Wheelwright, G., 1, Birks Hall, Cragg Vale . . 1
Whitaker, Miss, 161, Park Crescent, Sowerby Bridge 1
Whitaker, A., 31, Horley Green Road, Halifax . 1
Whitaker, A., 13, St. James's Street, Halifax . 1
Whitaker, J., 5, Bridge Terrace, Wainstalls . . 2
Whitaker, Jno., Scawby, Lincs. 1
Whitaker, J., Warley Cemetery, Halifax. . . 1
Whitaker, S., Navigation House, Salterhebble . 1
White, Mrs. Annie, 942, South Paca Street, Baltimore, Md., U.S.A. 2
Whitehead, Mrs., 446, Highroad Well, Halifax . 1
Whitehead, Miss, 3, Dean House, Luddenden . 1
Whitehead, Miss, 17, Eagle Street, Keighley . 1
Whitehead, E., Bailey Hall Bank, Halifax . . 1
Whiteley, Miss, 23, Harrison Road, Halifax . . 1
Whiteley, Miss, Swift Place, Ripponden . . . 1
Whiteley, A., 30, Mill Bank, Triangle 2
Whiteley, D., South View, Halifax 1
Whiteley, Fred, 18, Malton Street, Boothtown . 1
Whiteley, F., 15, Stretchgate Lane, New Pellon . 1
Whiteley, J. H., 20, Richmond Terrace, Elland . 1
Whiteley, L., Burnley Road, Luddenden Foot . 1
Whiteley, T., Stock Cottage, Midgley. . . . 1
Whiteley, Wright, Rishworth 1
Whitham, T., Rye Cottage, Pellon. 1
Whitley, Mrs., 23, Lord Street, Sowerby Bridge . 1
Whitley, E., Forest Row, Ovenden 1
Whitley, The Right Hon. J. H., M.P., Brantwood, Halifax 1
Whittaker, A. L., Kingston Grange, Halifax . . 1
Whittaker, E. G., Conservative Club, Skipton . 1
Whittaker, J., 74, St. Augustine's Terrace, Halifax 1
Whitwam, P. H., Melrose Terrace, Elland . . 1
Whitworth, Mrs. F., 29, Wilson Road, Halifax . 1
Whitworth, T. H., 153, Gladstone Place, Ovenden 1
Widdop, Miss, 20, Charlesworth Grove, Halifax. 1
Widdop, J. H., Church School House, Haworth . 2
Wignall, J., 3, Kingsley Place, Halifax . . . 2
Wilcock, Mrs., Colne 1
Wild, A. V., 25, Holly Grove, Halifax 1
Wild, Major, Pennine View, Stalybridge . . . 1
Wilde, F., Clay House, Ripponden 2
Wilde, W., 25, The Crescent, Greetland . . . 1
Wilkinson, Mrs., 12, Albert Street, Mytholmroyd 1

VOLS.

Wilkinson, Mrs. J., Flush Lodge, Heckmondwike 1
Wilkinson, F., Lower Priestley Ing Farm, Cragg Vale 1
Wilkinson, J., 43, Burnley Road, Luddenden Foot 3
Wilkinson, J. W., 25, Grant Street, Halifax . . 1
Wilkinson, S., Bridge End, Mytholmroyd. . . 1
Wilkinson, S., Surveyor, Sowerby Bridge. . . 1
Wilkinson, Wm,, 37, Union Street South, Halifax 1
Williams, F., 15, Malsis Road, Keighley . . . 1
Williamson, T., 4, Shaw Hill, Halifax 1
Willis, Miss, Letchworth. 2
Willis, H., 21, Aspinall Street, Halifax. . . . 1
Wilson, Mrs., West Bank Terrace, Skipton . . 1
Wilson, Mrs. J., 11, New Barton, Sowerby . . 1
Wilson, Miss, 8, Tuel Street, Sowerby Bridge . 1
Wilson, Alice, Mixenden Green, nr. Halifax . . 1
Wilson, Miss Alice, Will Clough, Cragg Vale, Mytholmroyd 1
Wilson, A., Forest Cottage, Ovenden 1
Wilson, C., 107, Hyde Park Road, Halifax . . 1
Wilson, E., 61, Woodside Place, Boothtown . . 1
Wilson, F., South View House, Skipton . . . 1
Wilson, H., 9, Bank Street, Range Bank, Halifax 1
Wilson, I., Causeway Foot 2
Wilson, James, King Street, Leeds 1
Wilson, J., 84, Parkinson Lane, Halifax . . . 2
Wilson, R., St. Louis, U.S.A. 1
Wilson, T., 12a, Eldroth Road, Halifax . . . 1
Wilson, W., 53, Emscote Grove, Halifax . . . 1
Wolfenden, G., 27, Evelyn Street, Swindon, Wilts. 1
Wolfenden, N., 77, Wadsworth Street, Halifax . 1
Womersley, Mrs. W., Whitegate, Halifax . . . 1
Womersley, Miss, Corby Street, Fartown, Huddersfield 1
Womersley, Park Nook, Southowram 1
Wood, Mrs., 27, Exeter Street, Salterhebble . . 1
Wood, Mrs., 88, Parkinson Lane, Halifax . . . 1
Wood, Mrs. B., 2, Beech Villas, Sowerby Bridge . 1
Wood, Miss, 9, Albert Terrace, King Cross . . 1
Wood, Coun. A., Main Street, Haworth . . . 1
Wood, Albert, Sowerby Bridge 1
Wood, Arthur, 1, Syke Street, Boothtown. . . 1
Wood, A. E., 11, Arnold Street, Sowerby Bridge 1
Wood, A. H., 57, Palmerston Street, Coventry . 1
Wood, B., Manor Drive, Halifax 1
Wood, E., 6, Church Terrace, Sowerby . . . 1
Wood, H., Westcroft Lane, Northowram . . . 1
Wood, J., 36, Green Lane, West Vale . . . 1
Wood, J., 14, Highfield Terrace, Halifax . . . 1
Wood, J., 9, Mill Lane, Halifax 1
Wood, R. S., Richmond House, Greetland . . 1
Wood, T., Ramsden Wood Farm, Ovenden Wood 1
Wood, Wm., 4, School Street, Church Street, Halifax 1
Woodhead, Miss, Claremount, West Bank Avenue, Lytham 2
Woodhead, H., Wellington Street, Queensbury . 1
Woodward, H. K., Boulevards, Halifax . . . 1
Woodward, W., 10, St. Alban's Avenue, Halifax 1
Woolford, Miss G. A., 5, Dowker Street, Halifax 1
Wormald, Mrs., Rock Hill, Stainland 1
Wormald, Miss Mary, 1, Gibb Farm, Pellon . . 1
Wormald, Hanson Lane, Halifax 1
Wormald, J., Luddenden Foot 1
Wormald, John, The South Cottage, Andover . 2
Wormald, L., 13, Hanson Lane, Halifax . . . 1
Wormald, P., 3, Thorn View, Luddenden . . . 1
Worsley, Miss, Unity Street, Hebden Bridge . . 1
Wrigglesworth, A., 35, The Crescent, Greetland . 1
Wright, F., 29, Hollins Bank, Sowerby Bridge . 1
Wright, F., 33, Wainhouse Road, Halifax. . . 1
Wright, W., Westville, Oxenhope 1
Wright, W. H., 164, Boothtown Road, Halifax . 1

York, W., Princess Street, Halifax 1

Zion Congregational Young Men's Society, Ripponden 1